JULIAN LADERMAN

USEFUL PROBABILITY FOR BRIDGE PLAYERS

MASTER POINT PRESS • TORONTO

Master Point Press
214 Merton St. Suite 205
Toronto, Ontario, Canada
M4S 1A6   (647)956-4933

Email: info@masterpointpress.com
Websites: www.masterpointpress.com
              www.teachbridge.com
              www.bridgeblogging.com
              www.ebooksbridge.com

Library and Archives Canada Cataloguing in Publication

Title: Useful probability for bridge players / Julian Laderman.
Names: Laderman, Julian, author.
Identifiers: Canadiana (print) 2020027225X | Canadiana (ebook) 20200272292 | ISBN 9781771400596
   (softcover) | ISBN 9781771405539 (PDF) | ISBN 9781554947003 (HTML) | ISBN 9781771408998 (Kindle)
Subjects: LCSH: Contract bridge. | LCSH: Probabilities.
Classification: LCC GV1282.3 .L326 2020 | DDC 795.41/5—dc23

Editor   Ray Lee
Copy editor/Interior format   Sally Sparrow
Cover design   Olena S. Sullivan/New Mediatrix

1 2 3 4 5 6 7   22 21 20
PRINTED IN CANADA

DEDICATION

To Antoinette, my great partner in life

ACKNOWLEDGEMENTS

I appreciate the help that I have received while writing this book.

Ivan Petrovic provided me with valuable ideas on which topics to include and offered his opinions on how they should be presented. His proofreading was also extremely useful.

Several other friends and bridge partners also proofread versions of this book: Mich Araten, Farley Mawyer, Amalia Ottemberg, Sandy Prosnitz, and Art Seelenfreund. Cliff Nebel provided me with copies of several old journal articles.

I want to thank Antoinette Blum for her patience and support. I particularly appreciate her willingness to proofread the book since she does not play bridge nor has she ever taken a probability course. Her reading experience must have been painful. Even more so since I refer to her at times in the book.

I want to thank Ray and Linda Lee for their input, editing, and suggested modifications. I also want to thank Sally Sparrow for her copyediting and layout of the book.

Contents

Pages with Important Reference Tables

Preface

In 2009, Master Point Press published my book *A Bridge to Inspired Declarer Play*. The original manuscript contained a thirty-five-page Appendix on the probability of bridge. Master Point Press correctly objected to some of the harder mathematics, since they thought it would discourage many readers from ever getting to some of the useful material that appeared towards the end of the Appendix. After some discussion, we agreed on a Solomonic solution: I would cut the Appendix into two. The first part would contain the more useful techniques and the second the more difficult underlying mathematics. The titles of the two appendices are Appendix 1: Everything You Ever Wanted to Know about Probability and Appendix 2: Much More Than You Ever Wanted to Know about Probability.

The appendices in that 2009 book were the basis for *The New York Times* (Phillip Alder) quote on the back cover of this book. They have been greatly expanded, with their titles carried over for nostalgic purposes, to Part II and Part III of this book.

The rest of this Preface consists of my apologies.

Apology 1: I am assuming readers have virtually no prior knowledge of mathematics – just some arithmetic with fractions. I fear some readers may be insulted. While reading this book, if you feel demeaned, please do not hesitate to roll your eyes.

Apology 2: I am assuming readers have played at least a thousand hands of bridge (roughly forty afternoons) but I rarely assume any specific bridge knowledge beyond that playing experience. Therefore, at times, some readers may feel insulted. Again, please feel free to roll your eyes.

Apology 3: I often steal material (I prefer 'borrow') from my earlier books and articles. Here, as already mentioned, the greatest victim of this theft is *A Bridge to Inspired Declarer Play*. About 15% of the book you are holding is taken from it. My other books were not ignored – approximately 5% of this book was stolen from

Bumblepuppy Days: The Evolution from Whist to Bridge, as well as 3% in total from my other three books.

So, if you have previously read those books, and find that some material looks familiar, you are correct.

Apology 4: The gender problem of using the pronoun 'he' or 'she' is troublesome for writers. I certainly do not like switching between them. Since the bridge world has more women than male participants, I want to inspire the male minority so I will use 'he' rather than 'she'. Besides, this saves me from typing an additional letter. If you are offended, I apologize.

Apology 5: I suffer from the UDBH syndrome. If you are not familiar with the ailment, it stands for Uncontrollably Describing Bridge History. The most troubling symptom is that it forces me to include at least a smidgen of bridge history whenever I write or give a talk about bridge. This was partially provoked by writing a book on bridge history in 2014, but I now realize that I have shown symptoms for more than three decades. If these inclusions trouble you, please remember that I cannot control myself.

I hope you will enjoy this book, find it informative, and not see any need for me to apologize for anything else.

Julian Laderman

PART 1

The only thing we can really be certain of is that from birth to death we are completely bound by the ever-present and wholly inclusive laws of probability that govern every action and event.

Oswald Jacoby

TABLE TALK
AT THE
BRIDGE TABLE

Chapter 1
Who Needs Bridge Probability?

Experience is a Great Teacher

Often at a bridge table an opponent who is aware of my prior professional life comments, 'I hated mathematics. I'm sure glad that playing bridge does not require any knowledge of mathematics.' I immediately look for the nearest Director and estimate the approximate time he needs to cover the distance to my table. This will dictate how lengthy a response I can provide before hearing 'Julian, stop talking! The round has been called.' Sadly, probably only for me, there is never enough time. This book provides me with the opportunity to give a full retort.

Probability is the mathematics of studying how likely an event is to occur. All experienced bridge players have a significant amount of knowledge in this field, whether they realize it or not. Let me demonstrate by asking you four quick questions:

1) Are you more likely to be dealt 14 high-card points (HCP) or 21 HCP?
2) Your partner opens 1♡. Is he more likely to hold five hearts or six hearts?
3) You open the bidding 1♠. Is your partner more likely to have three spades or a void in spades?
4) You open the bidding 1NT. Is your partner more likely to have 6 HCP or 1 HCP?

The first option was the correct answer to each of the four questions. Let's hope you just got a 100% on this probability test. You were using the experience you gained from playing thousands of bridge hands to estimate likelihood. Your performance was likely far better than that of a person equipped with a Ph.D. in mathematics who has never played bridge. Be proud!

One way to measure the likelihood of an event occurring is to measure its relative frequency. This is obtained by simply recording how often an event occurs in a large number of trials.

$$\text{Relative frequency} = \frac{\text{number of times event occurs}}{\text{number of trials}}$$

Suppose a baseball player has had 423 official times at bat and has 132 hits. His batting average is obtained by dividing 132 by 423. The resulting value of 0.312 (or 31.2%) is very impressive and his agent will certainly use it when negotiating the player's next contract. The baseball world ignores the decimal point; the batting average is 312.

Even though you have not kept track of bridge hands* that you have played over the years, you were able to use your experience to answer the above questions. Of course, it would have been much more difficult to estimate the actual likelihood of each of the events rather than to compare the two.

For example, suppose you wish to know the likelihood of being dealt a hand where the longest suit has five or more cards. If you kept track of your next 1000 hands, and recorded how many had at least one suit with five or more cards, you would obtain an extremely accurate estimate of the true value. Please don't carry out this experiment – it would be foolish, since it is very easy to calculate the likelihood of the event. I won't leave you hanging: it is 65%.

In a very early bridge lesson, a beginner is told that the number 26 is special. With a combined 26 high-card points (HCP) a

---

* Bridge vocabulary is a little vague at times. Consider the words 'hand' and 'deal'. A bridge deal consists of all four bridge hands. The word hand can refer either to the thirteen cards a player is dealt or to all four hands. Sometimes the word 'hand' and 'deal' overlap in usage. At the end of a session, we often remind our partners to pick up 'hand records' so that they can be discussed over dinner. It would be more accurate to refer to those sheets as 'deal records'.

partnership has enough good cards that they can probably make a game in notrump or a major. Of course, any bridge player can construct freakish pairs of hands with a combined 30 HCP that cannot make game and pairs with a combined 20 HCP that can. The 26 HCP number is based on the experience of top players; this kind of guideline or maxim allows new players to learn bridge probability more quickly than by relying on their own personal experience. Our bidding systems are based on this and similar maxims. In Chapter 15, we will look at the maxims that relate to bidding and see how bidding systems are designed to communicate the information necessary for a player to employ these maxims.

Bridge players are armed with many probability-based maxims for both bidding and play. I cringe slightly when they are referred to as rules (or even laws) rather than guidelines. We will be looking at many of them throughout the book in order to learn when they are useful and when they may be misleading.

A one-sentence answer to the question posed in the title of this chapter: *You greatly need it, and you already know much more than you think.*

One Can Be Fooled by Experience

After extolling the virtues of intuition generated through experience, I must point out that it often can be quite misleading. Let me add one more question to the earlier four.

Is the next bridge hand you are dealt more likely to be:

♠ A 7 5 4 ♡ K 8 5 ◇ A 8 7 2 ♣ A 6

or ♡ A K Q J 10 9 8 7 6 5 4 3 2 and void in the other suits?

In fact, both are equally likely to be your next hand. It is tempting but wrong to believe that the first hand is more likely to occur. The first hand feels like a common hand whereas the second hand is extremely remarkable. If you were actually dealt the second hand, you would be telling all your friends, even your non-bridge playing friends, 'You won't believe the hand that I was dealt!'

Your intuition can be led astray since all players have been dealt hundreds of hands that are very similar to the first hand. An alternative argument is: since hands with 10 HCP are certainly more likely than 15 HCP hands, a few players (very few) may mistakenly believe that the 10 HCP hand with the thirteen-card heart suit is more likely than its alternative with 15 HCP. But now let's suppose the specific spot cards were replaced by x, so that the comparison is between:

♠ A x x x ♡ K x x ◇ A x x x ♣ A x

and   ♡ A K Q J x x x x x x x x x

Now, the first hand would be more than two million times more likely to be dealt than the second. Really! I am not kidding.[†]

Let's return to the original example with specific spot cards. *Any two hands where all thirteen cards are specified are equally likely to occur.* You will almost certainly live your life without being dealt either of the above specific hands. There are just too many possible bridge hands. There are, would you believe, 635 billion different thirteen-card hands. The United States, Canada, Mexico, and Bermuda have a combined population of 498 million[‡]. This means that if every person (including one-day-old babies) in these countries dealt themselves 1000 hands, and even if miraculously no hand were repeated, it would still be impossible for them to deal out all possible thirteen-card bridge hands. So, if you are ever dealt thirteen hearts, you should expect that a 'friend' set it up as a joke and that an opponent is holding thirteen spades.

When intuition is developed through experience, it is much better at common situations than at rare ones. Extremely excellent hands are not very common. Suppose you were asked whether you are more likely to be dealt a hand with exactly 23 HCP or a hand with more than 23 HCP. You should expect to be dealt a hand with exactly 23 HCP only about once every 900 hands. If you combine

---

† This statement will be justified in Chapter 20. Here, I was just showing off.

‡ You may be surprised that I included the 65,000 residents of Bermuda — I wanted to include all regions that hold ACBL sanctioned events.

all hands in the range from 24 HCP up to 37 HCP (maximum possible), taken together their chance of occurring is still less than the case of exactly 23 HCP. Anything above 23 is in very rarefied air.

A primary goal of this book is to build on your good intuition about bridge probability and point out where you could be fooled by your bad intuition. My hope is that I can modify your bad intuition. The book uses the philosophy that *usefulness* trumps *theory*. This is described in the next section. Similarly, there is a philosophy that *approximation* trumps *exactness*. At the bridge table, approximation is the best that one can hope to achieve. This will be described at the end of this chapter.

Useful Topics and Not So Useful Topics

The book tries to be as gentle as possible with the mathematics. After all, if you cannot understand a topic, or if a result is not compatible with your intuition, the information will not be useful. There are different levels of understanding. It is one thing to understand what you read in a book, and another thing to be able to comfortably apply the knowledge a year from now. The latter requires a much deeper understanding. A procedure that goes against a person's intuition has a very short mental shelf life.

The main goal most players will have in reading this book is to improve their decision-making at the table. Decisions fall into two broad categories. Some are made while actually playing bridge, and others are made between sessions. For example, when forming a new partnership, dozens of decisions about bidding conventions and signaling must be resolved while filling out a convention card. Deciding what system and which conventions to play may be influenced by how frequently certain types of hands occur.

Let's first consider decisions that are made during the bidding or play. These are situations where a knowledge of probability can help you to make the right choice between alternative bids, or between alternative lines of play, or between alternative ways to play a suit combination. The calculations that can be done are obviously very limited – one cannot use a calculating device, and even difficult bridge decisions must be made in a minute or two at most. Not an environment conducive for doing mathematics.

Between sessions you can take all the time you wish; you can even employ the great computational power hidden in your Smartphone. Even though it is clearly too late to change results from your last session, you may be able to learn something that can be applied in similar situations in the future. During a session, it is usually wise for partnerships not to modify the bidding systems, conventions, and signaling methods they are playing. Between sessions, they can discuss changes at their leisure.

When you are driving a car over a bridge, you need only know how to drive and be able to see the road. It is unnecessary to know the engineering and mathematics that enable the bridge to stand. You very reasonably take it for granted. The mathematics of playing bridge is very different. The decision-making issues considered in this book have a probabilistic basis. I agree that fully understanding the details as to how certain mathematical values can be computed, or at least approximated, is not directly useful. However, this knowledge puts you in a better position to trust the results (useful stuff) and thereby use them correctly. It also gives you the courage not to abandon a correct principle just because it leads to a poor outcome on a particular hand. So even though these sections of the book are not directly useful, they may indirectly be very useful.

Questions related to how likely a particular type of hand is to occur are only moderately useful. We will examine such questions even though they are sometimes merely 'intellectual curiosities' rather than helpful decision tools. For example, the problem in the previous section about the probability that the longest suit dealt has five or more cards is not directly useful. For any hand, as soon as you look at your cards, you will know with complete certainty whether or not you actually have a five-card suit. But as already stated, knowing the likelihood of certain types of hands can be useful when designing bidding systems as well as when deciding which conventions to adopt.

Throughout this book, chapters will be given a *usefulness number*, between 1 and 10. Each chapter will start with a description of what is useful in the chapter and what is not so useful, and that description will indicate the reason behind the number. You may choose just to read the useful results and skip the sections where the underlying mathematics is developed. Typically, general mathematics books first present the underlying mathematics and then show how it can be used to derive important results. I will often first present the results, and then you can decide whether you care to see how they were obtained. Sometimes the complete explanation might not come for a dozen chapters, but in practically all cases, it will appear, I promise! By the end of the book you will feel comfortable that I did not just make up the number 635 billion for the number of possible hands.

Sadly, I have to accept the reality that the first half of any of my books is read more than the second half. I realize that I should not take it personally since it is true of all books, and particularly books involving mathematics. This is part of the rationale for presenting results before getting weighed down in the supporting mathematics. That is the key to the distinction between Part II and Part III. Especially in Chapters 19 to 21, you will learn how certain results and values are obtained (I hope you will still care).

Even the chapter on the history of probability is not totally useless. Games are not 'just' games, and gambling was the early motivation for the development of probability theory. Mathematicians and gamblers have had a wonderful parasitic relationship for four centuries.

Approximating, Assuming, and even Pretending

In a mathematics course, accuracy is paramount. I was not impressed by my students when they would tell me that they used estimation to obtain a reasonable answer. However, for bridge players, exactness is overrated.

During the play of a hand, approximation is an essential tool for all probability-related decisions. It is the only way around the constraints of time and not having computing devices. After considering the information learned from the prior bidding and play, you base your decisions either on approximate values that you have memorized, or intuition gained from experience, or a few probability-related bridge maxims.

A well-known bridge maxim is 'With an odd number of cards missing, expect them to split as evenly as possible. With an even number of cards missing, expect them to split unevenly'. Another favorite is 'Eight ever, nine never'. These maxims are themselves very crude approximations that summarize and simplify the actual probabilities. When we look at these maxims, I will air my objections and provide alternatives that result in superior approximate values.

This chapter started off with a probability quiz. You were asked which of two possibilities was more likely. The answers did not require any computation. This type of comparison often occurs when making bridge decisions. A player wishes to know which option is more likely to be successful. It is not important whether Option 1 will be successful 90% of the time and Option 2 only 70% of the time or whether Option 1 will be successful 40% of the time and Option 2 only 25% of the time. With either scenario, Option 1 should be selected.

In this book, I have tried to minimize the inclusion of the tables of numerical entries. However, I did have to include tables for suit splits, shape of hands, high-card points, and joint partnership holdings. The values in these tables are essential. At the start of this book, after the Contents page, I provide page references to six important tables. When a table is introduced, I try to provide an explanation of values that would go against a bridge player's intuition and I try to modify that intuition. I did not compute all the values myself since they have appeared in many other whist and bridge books. However, when using values from tables it is important to always employ some approximation technique, such as your intuition from experience. Ask yourself if the value you find in a table is consistent with your expectation for that value. If so, great; if not, ask yourself whether your intuition is wrong or is the value wrong?

Thankfully, an incorrect value in a table is often significantly different from the correct value. The greater the error, the easier that error is to spot. Suppose table values involve percentages that should logically add up to 100%. Due to rounding of values it is reasonable for the values to add up to some value in the range of 97% to 103%. At times, I have cheated when rounding in this book in order to force the values to add up to 100%. But should you ever encounter a table of this sort that adds up to something like 87% or 114%, you know something is wrong!

There are many ways the values in a table can fail the 'smell test'. Suppose you look at a table for the total HCP of a partnership. It contains an entry for the probability that the North-South partnership is dealt 23 HCP and East-West is dealt 17 HCP. However, it indicates a different value for the probability that North-South are dealt 17 HCP and East-West are dealt 23. Even though you don't know the actual value of either, you know both events should have the same probability of occurring. If they differ, one or both of the entries must be an error. Sometimes you can be certain of a pattern in a table. One would expect the entry for the probability that North-South are dealt 28 HCP to be less than that for 27 HCP. Likewise, holding a combined 27 HCP is less likely than 26. If the values are not decreasing when North-South hold more than 20 HCP, something is wrong.

Since one of my major goals is to make you more comfortable using the results, at times I will resort to less accurate techniques that enable me to justify approximate results. Often I am rounding off values. Sometimes I am slightly shading the truth in order to obtain values and methods that are easier for bridge players to either remember or understand.

There are three general assumptions that are necessary to analyze bridge probability:

1) Assume that the cards, whether they are dealt by hand or generated by a computer, achieve randomness. In Chapter 6, we will see that dealt cards often don't totally achieve that goal. In Chapter 22, we will see a method to test computer-generated hands.
2) Assume players always adhere to standard bridge rules. If a player does not follow suit, you are certain he has no cards in the suit. We are assuming no carelessness or cheating.

3) Assume players are always trying to win. They will play to the best of their ability. This is actually implied by Assumption 2.

Many other specific bridge bidding assumptions are necessary. Consider problems such as: My partner is the dealer, what is the probability that he will open the bidding 2♠? The answer involves assumptions about what type of hand would be appropriate for a 2♠ bid. What is your point range for that bid? Could it be done on a five-card spade suit? Could it be done when holding a four-card heart suit? One must make many assumptions.

In summary, questions such as computing the probability of being dealt a hand with exactly seven hearts can be answered with exactness. No assumptions are necessary since it does not involve anything a player does. But questions related to the bidding or play of a hand require assumptions about player decisions.

At times, the power of assuming and approximating will border on pretending. My goal is to display the mathematics. At times, the arithmetic is easier with questionable assumptions. You don't have to live with my bridge assumptions since you can form your own assumptions and apply similar mathematics.

Sometimes, after explaining when a mathematical principle should not be used, I will go ahead and use it anyway. I am not being stubborn. I will make it clear when I am doing this and why it is useful for me to pretend that what I am doing is acceptable. In Appendix 6, I will summarize my pretending.

Throughout this book I will be assuming that readers have never taken a course that even touched on the topic of probability. My goal is to write a book that is appropriate for bridge players regardless of their background in mathematics, even a Ph.D. in mathematics. I am further doubling down by trying to write a book for all levels of bridge ability.

I certainly feel safe assuming that all readers are bridge players. Who else would read this book?

Chapter 2

Asking the Right Question

Is this chapter useful? Why?
Usefulness number: 8. Most questions asked about bridge probability are not properly constructed. Likewise, the significance of a numerical result is often not properly interpreted. One must be aware of these potential problems in order to avoid any confusion. This chapter will describe common misunderstandings when forming questions and understanding the answers.

Questions are Often Not Properly Asked

Often, bridge players ask me questions in the form 'Does X really work?' (where X is some rule or maxim). A typical question is 'Does Restricted Choice really work?' However, the word 'work' in the world of probability means something different from its common usage. We say a car 'works' if we can turn a key or press a button and the engine starts. Rules of bridge probability only indicate the likelihood of success for different decisions. The line of play that is most likely to be successful is the correct play 'in theory', but it may not be the winning play on a particular hand. Without knowledge of the underlying mathematics, you may be tempted to ignore a maxim which is accurate and useful but just failed in a particular case.

Often, bridge books refer to the correct play, when based on probability, as the *percentage play*. In Chapter 9, you will see that the percentage play is linked to a certain goal (e.g. how many tricks are needed). At times, with the same cards, if the goal is changed, the percentage play will change.

After a session, I am often asked, 'Is the hand record correct that 4♡ can be made?' or I hear, 'The hand record says I should have made 4♡.' I quickly point out that the computer analyzes the boards as double-dummy problems. This means the computer knows where all fifty-two cards are located. It will never lose a finesse to a singleton king. The computer has no use for bridge probabilities. These bridge analyzers are playing a game of perfect information. It is equivalent to all players laying their cards face-up on the table, a game more like chess than bridge. Taking the optimum play based on probability is usually the best a non-cheating human can do.

Knowing the mathematical basis for a maxim should save you from being misled. We will see that at times some maxims should be ignored. When using a maxim that correctly indicates a percentage play, it is useful to know whether that percentage play is far better than another option or only slightly better. The maxim will probably not differentiate.

Several years ago, I gave a talk on bridge probability at the American Bridge Teachers' Association Convention. My goal was to make the teachers more comfortable answering probability-related questions from students. Early in the talk, I told them that one particular answer is correct for more than 90% of questions generated by bridge players. They were surprised and eager to hear the 'magic answer'. The answer is (drumroll please): 'I cannot answer your question because it is not well-posed.' Of course, if the student had a follow-up question, the teacher would have been on his own. Let me give you an example. Consider the question, 'I had a six-five hand with six spades and five hearts. How likely is that?' In order to give the correct answer, we need to know whether they mean specifically six spades and five hearts or just any hand with a six-card suit and also a five-card suit. The latter interpretation has a likelihood twelve times greater than the specific suit interpretation.

Consider the question, What is the probability of my partner opening the bidding X?, where X is any specific bid. Before answering, I have to ask him if his partner is the dealer. It is easiest to answer if that is indeed the proper interpretation of the question. Otherwise, it is necessary to consider the likelihood of some number of passes before your partner has the opportunity to bid. After all, your partner may have the perfect hand to open 1♥, but if another player opens the bidding, he can no longer make an opening bid.

One is often asked a question regarding suit length, such as the likelihood of holding a five-card suit. Does that mean 'exactly a five-card suit' or a 'five-or-more-card suit'? Sometimes it can be inferred from the context. A very old whist/bridge joke that goes back to the 1890s is based on this confusion. A player tells his partner to lead fourth-best from a four-card suit. (Both this advice and the 'rule of eleven' were already well known by whist players in the 1890s.) When that normally obedient partner is strongly criticized for not leading fourth-best on a hand, his defense is, 'I did not have a four-card suit, it was a five-card suit.'

Most probability questions fall into the classification of *word problems*. These require interpretation. In the previous chapter, when I indicated that exactness was overrated, I was referring to calculations. When posing questions, the importance of exactness cannot be overstated.

Throughout the book, readers will sometimes see in large letters 'Common Question Alert', indicating that the upcoming text contains a question that has been posed to me by many bridge players over the past half century. Let's look at a common question.

Common Question Alert

The 1♢ Opening Bid Question

One of the most common bridge probability questions is, 'What is the probability that my partner will open 1♢ with only three diamonds?' I respond, 'Assuming that your partner is the dealer, it is slightly less than half of 1%'. The questioner always looks comforted that it is expected to occur less than once every 200 hands. I quickly point out to players who ask this question that they are likely not asking the question they wish to ask. They wish to ask, 'Suppose my partner opened 1♢. What is the probability that he has only three diamonds?'

These two interpretations are very different. The first answer is a very low probability since partner is unlikely to open 1◊ at all. Partner is more likely to pass or make one of a half-dozen common opening bids. It is further restricted by the three-card diamond suit requirement.

For the second interpretation, one starts with the information that partner has in fact opened 1◊. Now the question relates to supporting partner's diamond suit. Bridge players have been troubled that even though a diamond opening bid usually indicates a four- or five-card suit, there is a small possibility that it is being made on a three-card suit. In standard bidding, that will only happen when the bidder has exactly four cards in each major and exactly two clubs, with a hand outside the ranges for 1NT, 2NT or 2♣.

A recent ACBL ruling made opening 1NT with a high singleton honor in some suit more acceptable. This results in some marginal hands that would have been opened 1◊ now being opened 1NT, thereby slightly altering the answer to the 1◊ question.

My answer to this question with the second interpretation still surprises bridge players. I ask them 'Have you looked at your own hand?' They tend to look confused by this since they feel that they are only asking about what their partner holds. So, I continue, 'If you have not looked, the answer is approximately 5%. But looking makes a big difference. Suppose in your own hand you find ten cards in the diamond suit. Since your partner opened 1◊ you can be 100% certain that he holds exactly three diamonds. If you hold nine diamonds the probability is still very high. But if you hold no diamonds, your partner is very, very unlikely to have only three diamonds. Clearly the answer varies based on the number of diamonds dealt to the partner of the 1◊ opener.'

You may think that part of the answer is silly since you have never been dealt a ten-card suit. A common technique of mathematicians is to carry a situation to the extreme. Studying what happens at end-points can reveal a great deal of information. In the previous chapter, we considered a hand with a thirteen-card heart suit. Throughout the book, we will often be able to learn from similar extreme situations. Don't dismiss them simply because the premise seems ridiculous.

The diamond suit is an example of an interesting principle. The more you have of something, the less you should expect your partner to hold, be it HCP or suit length. Consider this example. You are dealt a hand with 21 HCP. Pleased, you are already dreaming of opening 2NT. Suddenly you see your partner pull out a 1NT card. Aren't you quite shocked? Normally you would not be surprised by your partner opening 1NT, but with your 21 points you certainly are. Happy and excited, but shocked. You had anticipated everyone passing before your opportunity to bid, unless maybe a preemptive bid appeared. Your intuition did not expect your partner's bid since it violates this principle:

The more you have of something, the fewer of them you should expect your partner to hold (or for that matter, the opponents).

Suppose you are in fourth seat and three passes precede your turn to bid. Are you shocked? If you have 2 HCP, the answer is yes, but if you have 21 HCP, certainly not. Holding only 2 HCP, you will be searching your hand or the floor for missing aces.

Early in Chapter 1, I posed the very simple-looking question: 'You open the bidding 1♠. Is your partner more likely to have three spades or a void in spades?' Later I stated that the correct answer was three. Seems obvious. But what if I told you that the spade bidder is admiring eleven spades in his hand? Now I am certain you wish to change your answer, as it is impossible for partner to hold three spades. Even if the spade bidder has only ten spades, partner is almost ten times more likely to hold a void than the other three spades.

You might feel that one would never open 1♠ with eleven spades. But if you open 1♠, and keep bidding like a lunatic, you may very well end up being doubled in 4♠. Very likely an excellent contract. You are the only player aware of your freakish hand. Have some fun with it. Everyone will be surprised (and probably not all pleased) when your hand is eventually revealed.

Throughout the book, you will not only encounter Common Question Alerts but also several Tricky Confusing Issue Alerts.

I will describe a situation where players can easily be confused by my text. In effect, I will be describing a reader's reasonable thoughts, thoughts that are wrong, but may seem right.

Answers are Often Not Properly Interpreted

We have seen that problems, particularly probability questions, are often not posed clearly. But even if the problem is well-posed and the mathematics yields the correct result, the meaning of that result must be understood. What does the value represent? How can it be useful?

With the 1◇ question, does the answer indicate the chance of opening 1◇ with a three-card diamond suit (less than 0.5%), or given that 1◇ was opened, was it bid with a three-card diamond suit (approximately 5%)? The second answer is approximately ten times larger than the first. The values with both interpretations will be computed in Chapter 20. I have seen bridge players obtain the first value, but mistakenly believe that it represents the answer to the second interpretation.

It is possible for the statement of a result to be accurate but very misleading. Consider the comparison of the two specific hands in Chapter 1. We have stated that all 635 billion hands are equally likely. This means that it is correct that no bridge hand exists that is more likely to be dealt than the thirteen-heart hand.

Sometimes an interpreter's biases or wishes interfere with drawing the proper interpretation. An example of misinterpreting a probability result occurred in the movie *Dumb and Dumber*. Jim Carrey (the dumb one, not the dumber one) is enamored of a woman he has just met. He openly tells her his feelings and asks her what the chances are that she could ever feel the same way about him. Her sweet but harsh reply was that his chances are 'one out of a million'. His face lights up and he shouts, 'So you're telling me there is a chance!'

It is helpful if a number has a value that is relatable. Very large numbers and very small numbers are not relatable. Back in the Preface, when I wrote that I assumed that all readers had played a thousand hands of bridge, I included in parenthesis 'forty afternoons' – a much more tangible measuring unit. My goal was to make a thousand hands relatable. In Chapter 1, we encountered the enormous number, 635 billion. It is far too large to be relatable, but the comparison to every man, woman and child in all countries that hold ACBL-sanctioned events dealing 1000 thirteen-card hands is somewhat helpful.

Solving mathematical problems often involves using the ability to generalize techniques. That is, if you know how to do Problem A, can Problem B be solved with the identical method? This is as true when solving non-mathematical bridge problems as when doing mathematics. In my book, *A Bridge to Inspired Declarer Play*, I tried to develop this with an unusual set of exercises. After demonstrating a particular technique with a specific deal, I asked readers to create their own slightly modified deal which demonstrated the identical principle.

Using mathematics as a useful tool requires appreciating its three parts: problem definition, mathematical solution, and finally interpretation of the result. Students often state that they are not good at numbers but have excellent verbal skills. Well, that is certainly useful for applying mathematics to problems.

Chapter 3
Coincidences and the Unexpected

Is this Chapter Useful? Why?

Usefulness number: 6. This chapter contains several well-known examples that are not directly relevant to bridge but will help you develop probability intuition when dealing with unlikely events. That being said, I confess that a major reason that I included these examples is for their 'entertainment' value.

Common Question Alert

Last night, I was dealt a hand with a nine-card suit. What is the likelihood of that? This is just a representative question from a large family of questions. These questions all relate to picking up a hand that is very unusual. In Chapter 1, I pointed out that human intuition is not good at estimating the probability of events that are very unlikely to occur. After all, how useful can relative frequency be if an event can occur, but has never been witnessed by a player? Sometimes questions involve an event that is not very unlikely, but coincidentally occurred several times. For example, what is the probability of being dealt three straight hands with a void?

Don't worry! I will not leave you hanging in regard to the nine-card suit. If I assume the player is referring to the next hand that the player picks up, the probability would be 0.037%. This means it will occur roughly once every 2700 hands. I am answering for exactly nine cards, not nine or more. If the questioner is asking about the probability of it being dealt to him during his next 24-board session of bridge, it would be approximately 24 times greater (0.00037 x 24 = 0.0089 or 0.89%)[§]. The questioner may be asking about the probability of it occurring within a year. If he plays one hundred hands per week (four sessions), it would be expected to occur. It might even occur more than once. If it were not to occur in the year, it would be slightly surprising.

---

§ This answer is a slight lie, which I will explain in Chapter 7.

The probability of a void on your next hand is slightly more than 5%. But to have it on each of your next three hands is only 0.013%. So, a void on each of your next three hands is less likely than your next hand containing a nine-card suit.

The Lights Go Out During Duplicate

Suppose during a ten-table evening session, there is a power failure. The room does not have back-up lighting and nobody even has a Smartphone with a flashlight. Forty players plus the director are sitting in a totally dark room. The Director has a problem that is not covered in the ACBL rulebook. Suppose the Director has already encountered this problem at the club on several occasions. Based on that experience he estimates that the electricity will probably return in no more than fifteen minutes. So the game will be able to continue, possibly shortened by a round. But until the power returns, the Director has the problem of crowd control in a room full of restive bridge players. They came to play – but cannot. The Director should consider employing the following distraction.

The Birthday Problem

Introduce the famous Birthday Problem to the abrasive mob. It involves asking the players in the dark room, one at a time, to shout out their birthdays – not the year, just the date. Very likely two players will find that they were born on the same day of the year. They will be surprised by the coincidence (particularly since they have known each other for twenty years). From that day forward, they will both remember each other's birthday.

There is more than an 89% chance that at least two of the forty players share the same birthday. If the game had had fifteen tables, there would have been a 99.4% chance that two players would have the same birthday. The cutoff point for 50% is twenty-three people, so don't try this with fewer than six tables. Even with six tables you barely have better than a 50% chance of success. I often did this on the first day of my probability classes, but I only tried it when I had at least twenty-eight students in the room. It never disappointed me! I would not want to look foolish on the first day of class. I had fourteen more weeks for that.

This problem made it to the *Tonight* show in 1980. Johnny Carson had heard of the problem but was confused by it. He asked thirty people in his audience to stand up and then he shouted out an arbitrary day of the year. None were born on that date. You can view that episode on YouTube, as well as the two other episodes after he received letters from mathematicians. Carson's initial mistake and the eventual corrections got to the crux of the Birthday Problem. It is unlikely that someone in the sample group will match a particular day. But the birthday problem does not hinge on being born on a particular day. For instance, for the original ten-table problem, a match could occur on any of those forty birthdays of the players. The full mathematics is provided in Appendix 5.

This is an excellent example that demonstrates the distinction between matching a specific event and simply having a match. On page 14, I presented an example to demonstrate that if the entire population of the United States, Canada, Mexico, and Bermuda dealt out 1000 hands, it would be impossible to produce all possible bridge hands. I even included the statement 'assuming that, miraculously, no hand was repeated'. Actually, the principle of the Birthday Problem virtually guarantees that if 498 billion hands were dealt out, a very large number of hands would be repeated.

The Hat Check Problem

Let's return to our ten-table bridge game without electricity, but I will now change the scenario. The electricity will probably be out for hours, and the Director feels that everyone should leave the totally dark club. But it is the winter and everyone needs a coat to go home. Finding one's own coat is clearly impossible. The Director instructs all players to put on the first coat they can find, wear it home, and bring it back to next week's game. Everyone randomly takes home a coat. After next week's game, the proper owner of each coat can take possession. Fortunately, all forty players are women who weigh between 115 and 140 pounds. Quite incredible! This enables each of the women to fit into every coat. So, each player randomly chooses a coat and heads home. Suppose a woman ended up with her own coat. What a coincidence! Not really. There was a 63% chance that at least one woman would randomly end up with her own coat. So, no great surprise. Suppose instead of ten tables there were fifteen tables. There still would be a 63% chance that a woman would take home her own coat. Suppose it was a three-section event with forty-five tables. There still would be the same 63% chance that at least one of the 180 women came home with her own coat.

The 63% for each case is a surprise. One would expect that the chance of a woman bringing home her own coat would shrink as the number of players increases. It certainly does. The lesson is that for each woman, the chance of bringing home her own coat decreases, but 180 women each have an opportunity to bring home their own coat. With ten tables, there were only forty opportunities.

This particular problem is usually referred to as the Hat Check Problem. Normally stated, the hat checks got lost. When just six or more hats are involved and the hats are dispersed randomly to individuals, there is a 63% chance that at least one individual will end up with the proper hat. Another narration involves a large group of drunken friends at a lodge meeting who randomly select house keys, and the probability of at least one ending up with the keys to his home. Some lewder versions involve the probability of husbands climbing into bed with their own wives. The probability is the same 63% that at least one husband will, but most will not.

The Hat Check Problem was first studied by the French mathematician Pierre Rémond de Montmort in his 1708 book on probability (*Essay d'Analyse sur les Jeux de Hazard*). It was for playing a matching game with cards called Treize. You can create your own matching game with two shuffled decks of cards. If you simultaneously turn over one card from each pack until you go through all fifty-two cards in each deck, the probability is 63% that at least once the exposed cards in each deck will be the same.

The premise of losing electricity and randomly bringing home a coat is hardly necessary. At the end of a session, bridge players are sufficiently mentally distracted that they often carelessly grab the wrong coat. It demonstrates how wonderful our game is that it can be such a powerful distraction. Several times, I personally have found that a similar but incorrect coat remained at the end of a session. Within a week or two my coat would reappear on the coat rack (except once). I probably have experienced this problem more than most players. Often at the end of a game, I have sought out some polite person to describe some feature of bridge history that was slightly relevant to a hand during the session. At some point, he would have heard enough from me and would run out of the club and, in his haste, grab any coat he could find. Since there were only a few coats left, I often became the victim.

Suppose you own a bridge club. You have a mixed pairs weekly game with ten tables. You are a little troubled that there are twenty fixed partnerships. All players are extremely loyal to their regular partner and play solely with that player. You would like to encourage player mingling. You decide to have a game where partnerships are randomly determined. When you run this mixed pairs event, you hear a player emphatically announce that he was randomly assigned to his regular partner. What a coincidence! Not really. Mathematically this is identical to the Hat Check Problem. Independent of the size of the game (assuming at least three tables), at least one player will get his regular partner 63% of the time.

In the last chapter, I quickly mentioned generalizing results. I want to return to that with this excellent example. I have often told mathematics majors that skill in mathematics is the ability to generalize and discriminate. The ability to generalize is the ability to solve a problem by appreciating that it is equivalent to a problem that, on the surface, seems very different, but is really the same, such as the hat check and random partnership problems. The ability to discriminate is the ability to appreciate the subtle difference between two similar-looking problems, and then getting around the difference. The ability to generalize and discriminate is as important for high school students learning mathematics as it is for mathematicians doing research.

Since I just made a few comments about math ability, I will add some thoughts about reading mathematics. In just a half dozen words it can be summarized, 'Read slowly. Do not give up.' When a mathematician reads an advanced eight-page article in mathematics, after a first reading, typically the researcher will understand clearly the first page, have a muddled understanding of the second, and be clueless about the last six pages. After a few hours or days, if they reread the article, they will have a clear understanding of the first two pages, a muddled understanding of the third, and be clueless about the last five pages. After several more readings, they will eventually understand the entire article. I like to relate it to waves coming in as the tide is rising.

A common scenario in sitcoms is to have a teenager struggling with some mathematics homework. When a parent offers help, the student quickly reads aloud a long word problem. The parent runs off. This is irritating for me to watch. The parent should respond. 'Read very slowly. Write down facts and numbers from the problem. Then see what the problem really is without all of the words.'

What Do these Problems Reveal?

In summary, for the particular players who share the same birthday or the player who wore home his own coat, a coincidence occurred. But, rather paradoxically, we see that coincidences are *expected* to occur. I remember when I was playing against two national champions and I alerted an unusual convention that my partner and I were playing. They had never heard of it, and remarked that it was useful but would very rarely come up. I agreed. Of course, on the second board of the two-board round, the same convention came up. As best I remember from more than thirty years, both our results were very good. I don't remember any other hands where that convention ever occurred, and I stopped playing it decades ago.

I recall a car trip from NYC to Atlantic City (1991) for a national event. My partner and I spent most of the three-hour drive discussing how to play a particular convention. We could not agree on how it should be played but could only agree that we wasted a lot of time discussing it since it probably would not occur during our week at the event. You guessed it. First board, it came up!

A common coincidence (seems like the ultimate oxymoron) is for both members of a partnership to forget that they are playing some convention. While later mentally replaying the hand and complimenting each other on their precise bidding, they both realize the ugly truth. Who says two wrongs cannot make a right?

Monkey at a Typewriter

If a monkey were to sit at a typewriter and randomly hit keys, given sufficient time any specific word would be typed. If we simply ignore the fact that monkeys don't live forever, within a few thousand centuries the word will appear. The length of the wait depends on the length of the word and how hard the monkey is willing to work. Actually, if this monkey does not quit in boredom, he will eventually type any combination of words, even any work of Shakespeare. When I informed my wife (a non-mathematician) that a monkey could type any of the works of Shakespeare, she told me that this was the dumbest thing that I had ever said. I was taken aback because I had already said so many dumb things in our decades together! It particularly hurt when I asked her if she would concede that a monkey could type any of my bridge books: that, she was willing to accept.

So, there is mathematics behind the old proverb, 'All good things come to those who wait.' Unfortunately, physics tells us the sun will not last long enough to enable the required wait.

A common tale in probability courses is about a mathematician who would always pack a bomb when traveling by plane. His thinking was that there is an extremely small probability that one bomb would be on the plane, and virtually zero probability that two bombs would be on the flight. I would not recommend that you repeat this joke to a TSA agent, as you probably will miss your flight.

I acknowledge that this chapter is only marginally relevant to bridge. Would it have been any better if I had modified it so that the monkey was dealing out bridge hands rather than typing Shakespeare? Given unlimited time, the monkey would eventually deal out all 635 billion different bridge hands. Don't worry, the remaining twenty chapters are much more practical for bridge players. Joggers perform stretching exercises before going out for a jog. I view this chapter as a collection of mental exercises before starting to study bridge probability.

P.S. If you want to know more about these problems, check out descriptions on the Internet and YouTube. You will find a cute chimpanzee at a typewriter.

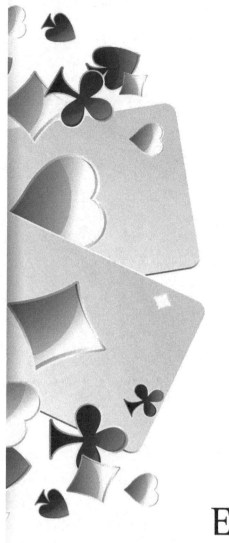

PART 2

Were it not for the somewhat obvious fact that bridge is played by human – sometimes all-too human – beings, the game would be mostly one of odds and percentages.

Charles Goren

EVERYTHING YOU EVER WANTED TO KNOW ABOUT PROBABILITY

Chapter 4
Likelihood of Suit Splits

Is this chapter useful? Why?
Usefulness number: 10. This is the most directly useful chapter in the book. So, I placed it early. The material will aid you when deciding between alternative ways of playing a hand as declarer. Of course, you must be able to interpret the results properly.

Think in Terms of Suit Splits

New bridge players are often introduced to a bad habit. They are taught that when you play a suit, after one round is played and everyone follows, four cards have been played in the suit; after two rounds are played and everyone follows, eight cards have been played in the suit. There is nothing incorrect about this statement but, instead, one should learn to think about how the suit can split. For instance, suppose between your hand and dummy you have eight cards in a suit. This leaves the two defenders with five cards and they will split 3-2, 4-1 or 5-0. Now, if both defenders follow for two rounds of that suit, there is only one card remaining in this suit. Thinking in terms of suit splits is much less mentally taxing and is an essential skill for counting a hand.

With five missing cards, it is common to think of only the three possible splits 3-2, 4-1, and 5-0. However, it is important to realize that this is just a compact representation for the actual six possible splits: West 3–East 2, West 2–East 3, West 4 – East 1, West 1–East 4, West 5–East 0, and West 0–East 5.

It is not only necessary to think of how a suit may split but also the likelihood of each possibility. Here are the most useful suit split tables, shown in their compact form.

Two cards held by the defense		Three cards held by the defense	
1-1	52%	2-1	78%
2-0	48%	3-0	22%

Four cards held by the defense		Five cards held by the defense	
2-2	40%	3-2	68%
3-1	50%	4-1	28%
4-0	10%	5-0	4%

Six cards held by the defense		Seven cards held by the defense	
3-3	36%	4-3	62%
4-2	48%	5-2	31%
5-1	15%	6-1	7%
6-0	1%	7-0	< 1%

Many of these values have been rounded off. I also took some liberties. For example, for the 2-2 split the actual value is 40.7% but I chose to use 40%. I did this in order to have the percentages in each table add up to exactly 100%. These approximate values are useful at the bridge table while the more exact values with four significant digits are useful for greater accuracy when one is able to use a computing device. In Appendix 1 you will find the same tables, but with four decimal digits.

In these six tables, the ordering going down the left column is from the most even split possible to the least even split possible. Some books order the entries from highest percentage to the lowest, based on the values in the right column. Even though it contains the identical information, I find that representation less useful.

I would recommend that you commit to memory the first two lines of each of these six split tables. This will provide you with a great amount of useful information about suit splits when playing bridge. Only these twelve values need to be memorized. If you are upset over my suggestion, later in this chapter I indicate that memorizing just six of these values is almost as good as knowing the full twelve. Occasionally, during a post-mortem, I will mention the likelihood of a particular suit split, and someone will say, 'You know that because you are a mathematician.' They are surprised when I tell them that I had memorized the value. I am sure they lose some respect for me. Not wanting to allow that to happen, I immediately assure them that I could indeed figure out the value on my own but it would require several minutes and a calculating device. Not doable in the middle of a hand.

I hope these tables provide readers with values that have an appropriate balance: *accurate enough to be very useful but simple enough to be memorized.*

Tricky Confusing Issue Alert

Consider the table that is appropriate for four cards held by the defense. You may be troubled that an even split of 2-2 is less likely than 3-1. Since each defender is equally likely to receive each of the four cards, shouldn't an even split of 2-2 be the most likely?

Yes, it should, and it is! Remember that the above tables use the compact form to represent the various splits. Below you will find a table for four cards held by the defense which displays all five possible splits, with West's number of cards followed by East's:

West-East splits for four cards held by the defense	
West 4 – East 0	5%
West 3 – East 1	25%
West 2 – East 2	40%
West 1 – East 3	25%
West 0 – East 4	5%

In this table we see that among the five splits, West 2–East 2 is indeed the most likely. However, there is only one way to have a 2-2 split, but there are two ways to have a 3-1 split (West 3-East 1 and West 1–East 3). Since the probability of each of those splits is

25%, together they have a 50% probability. So, when combined they are the most likely split.

Not to beat a dead horse – but to beat a dead horse – the same principle can be demonstrated with coin flips. If a coin is flipped ten times, the most likely result is five heads and five tails. It is obviously more likely than either six heads and four tails or four heads and six tails. But it is not more likely if we compare it to six of one face and four of the other face, where they are combined.

The main advantage of the full suit split tables over the compact form is to give you a better understanding of what the values in the tables actually represent. However, for memorizing table values it is best to use the compact form. Thanks to the obvious symmetry, one can just divide some of the entries by two to obtain the corresponding entries in the full table.

The suit split examples are usually presented for cards held by the defense in a suit. It is actually more general than that. Suppose you are declarer and neither your hand nor dummy have any kings. How are the four kings split? It is the same problem as four cards missing in a suit. This is a good example of generalizing a mathematical result.

A Very Famous Maxim (actually a twofer)

The information in these six tables is roughly approximated by one of the most well-known maxims (actually two maxims) in the world of bridge.

> *With an odd number of cards outstanding, assume they will break as evenly as possible. With an even number outstanding, assume they will break unevenly.*

The part of this maxim that refers to an odd number of cards is certainly justified by the tables. The part about an even number of cards is problematic, and with two cards held by the defense the maxim is wrong. The appropriate table indicates that they are slightly more likely to split evenly. With four or six cards, the maxim is only true when the suit split is represented in compact form, not the full form.

Earlier in this chapter, I recommended memorizing twelve values, the first two lines of the six tables. For the truly lazy, I can simplify my advice. Since this maxim works well when there are three, five, or seven cards outstanding, you can choose to use the maxim rather than memorize the six values that appear in those three tables. Now we are down to memorizing just the six values that appear in the first two lines of the three tables where an even number of cards are outstanding.

Common Question Alert

I am often asked: 'Since a 3-1 split is more likely than a 2-2 split, why have I been told to play for the drop when the defenders hold the queen and three low spot cards?' A very quick short answer is to point out that there are two possible ways a 3-1 split can occur: each has a probability less than that of a 2-2 split, and declarer cannot finesse both defenders. This often quickly pleases the inquirer, or at least seems to. It is the best I can do in one long sentence when the round is being called. A longer answer that provides more understanding will be given in Chapter 6.

Tricky Confusing Issue Alert

Suppose the defenders hold four cards in a suit and declarer plays the ace with both defenders following. Now declarer is missing just two cards in the suit. It is tempting to believe that it is now correct for declarer to use probabilities from the table for two cards held by the defense. No, that table is not appropriate. That table would falsely lead the declarer to believe that the two remaining cards held by the defense are more likely to split evenly (1-1) than unevenly (2-0). I will provide an explanation for this in Chapter 6 after I have presented the necessary tools.

Information Can Destroy the Table Entries

These tables are most useful when comparing alternative lines of play *prior to playing any tricks*. The percentages are in flux during the play of the hand, as more information becomes available. The auction, too, affects the probabilities. Surprisingly, even if the opponents never bid, and merely say 'pass' throughout, the table may lose some accuracy. For example, suppose the opponents are willing to sell out to you at a low level while holding approximately 20 high-card points: the chance of their having voids or singletons is less than you would otherwise expect. Why didn't they find a way to come into the bidding?

In the last table, the symmetry yielded identical values for West 3–East 1 and West 1–East 3. Mathematically, this is logical. But West makes the opening lead. If this suit is a side suit in a trump contract, since players enjoy leading singletons, inferences may be drawn from whether or not the suit was led. If this suit is the trump suit, inferences may still be drawn since players tend to avoid leading a singleton trump. Bridge thinking trumps probability!

The six suit split tables are based on not having any information either about that suit or about how any other suits are split.

When declarer plays a suit, the defenders' played cards provide information in three major ways.

1) By a defender not following suit. In this case everything about the suit is revealed.

2) By playing a higher card (usually honor) than the defender would wish to play. Much is revealed since it probably indicates the lack of a lower card.

3) By following with a spot card, when you know from experience that a particular defender always plays his lowest spot card. If you are playing against such a defender while you are missing the 6, 4, 3, and 2, and on the first round that defender plays a 6, then you can be certain of a 3-1 split. I think defensive signaling is useful even if both the signaler and his partner have no knowledge of what their signals mean. It generates the playing of random spot cards, rather than a defender always

playing his cheapest. Throughout the book, we will assume that a defender with several insignificant spot cards will play them randomly.

Suppose declarer and dummy were dealt a total of seven spades, and when declarer plays two rounds of spades, East shows out on the second round. Obviously, there is nothing more to learn about that suit. Declarer knows that West was dealt five spades and East one spade. But this alters all other suits. Suppose declarer is missing four cards in hearts. In light of the 5-1 spade split, and lacking any other information, the heart suit probabilities are:

West-East splits for four cards held by the defense	
West 4 – East 0	2%
West 3 – East 1	14%
West 2 – East 2	38%
West 1 – East 3	36%
West 0 – East 4	10%

The known 5-1 spade split certainly dramatically altered this table from the one on page 39. The probability of a West 2–East 2 split did not change much, but now West 3–East 1 is much less likely than West 1–East 3, and West 4–East 0 is much less likely than West 0–East 4. This lack of symmetry obviously would prevent representing these values in the compact table form.

Suppose instead that East had shown out on the first round of spades. Now, instead of West having four more spades than East, West would have been dealt six more spades than East. The above figures for the four hearts held by the defense would become 1%, 9%, 34%, 41%, and 15% respectively. Not surprisingly, even further from the original table with splits for four cards. It is the difference between the defenders' spade holdings that is important to declarer. Suppose you are declarer after East opened a weak two-bid. Don't just remember that East has a long suit, but observe how many cards you are missing in that suit. If missing eight, East probably has four more than West, but if missing ten, East probably has only two more than West.

Back to the situation where we are missing six spades. Let's suppose that East and West both follow with a spade for three rounds. Now each defender was dealt three spades. The five values in the table for the heart split would then be 4%, 25%, 42%, 25%, 4%. The symmetry is no surprise. When compared to the table on page 39, this table has a slightly increased chance of a 2-2 split and a decreased chance of the two possible 4-0 splits. I confess that a very slight difference was accentuated by my somewhat reckless rounding.

Suppose it is known that each defender was dealt exactly three spades and four diamonds. Now the five values in the table for the four hearts held by the defense would be continuing this pattern. The chance of a 2-2 split will increase and both 4-0 splits will decrease.

Suppose it is known that West was dealt five spades and East one. Suppose it is also known that West was dealt two diamonds and East six. As in the previous example, both defenders were dealt seven cards in spades and diamond combined, so we would have the identical values for the heart splits. The fact that spades and diamonds each broke so unevenly does not in any way indicate that hearts will not break evenly. The spade and diamond splits cancel each other out. Actually, if neither defender entered into the bidding with their long suit, there is an additional reason to believe that hearts will break evenly.

Chapter 21 explains how to calculate the correct percentages for the other three suits. The technique for obtaining these values is not difficult but they cannot be computed in the middle of a hand. So the technique is useless to you while playing a hand, but may be invaluable during the post-mortem when you want to convince your partner that you made the proper decision. Does this all mean that dozens of tables have to be memorized? Certainly not! Just be aware of how information about one suit can alter the probabilities for possible splits in another suit. In short, don't just use table values without asking, 'With all the information obtained, how appropriate are the values for this particular hand?'

A historical note about the term 'post-mortem'. In the 1890s, whist clubs would set up a table where an expert would answer questions about recently played hands. That table was called the 'coroner's table.'

The table values from this chapter will be used later on for assessing the likelihood of success with various lines of play. Don't worry that I am going to ask you to memorize other suit splits. That is not necessary. Whist was played without a dummy. So, when playing whist, any unseen card could be located in any of three hands. But when playing bridge, after the dummy appears, any unseen card can only be in two places. Therefore, only these tables for suit splits are important. I promise, no additional memorizing.

Chapter 5

The Hideous Hog's View of Probability

Is this chapter useful? Why?

Usefulness Number: 9. This chapter has no direct usefulness for bridge decision-making, but it does provide the basics of computing probabilities as well as an explanation of what is meant by the values that are obtained. It is so fundamental that it really deserves a 10. I just don't want to look like an easy grader so I only gave it a 9.

Introduction to Probability

The *probability* of an event is a numerical value that indicates how likely it is that the particular event will actually occur.

An essential tool in obtaining probabilities is to use the following formula:

$$P(\text{event}) = \frac{\text{Number of outcomes in which event occurs}}{\text{Number of possible outcomes}}$$

This formula can only be applied when all possible outcomes are equally likely to occur. We will see many situations where this condition is not satisfied, and bridge players can easily be misled by trying to apply the formula.

Since the denominator (bottom number) cannot possibly be smaller than the numerator (top number), the fraction can never be greater than 1. And since neither of them can ever be negative, this fraction can never be negative. In summary, the only possible values for P(event) are numbers greater than or equal to 0 and less than or equal to 1.

For bridge probability purposes, a probability of 1 means that you can be certain that the event will occur, and a probability of 0 means that you are certain that the event will not occur.

Picking a card from a shuffled bridge deck[¶]

The probability that it will be an ace is:

$$P(ace) = \frac{4}{52} = \frac{1}{13}$$

The probability that it will be a heart is:

$$P(heart) = \frac{13}{52} = \frac{1}{4}$$

The probability that it is a red ace is:

$$P(red\ ace) = \frac{2}{52} = \frac{1}{26}$$

The probability that it is a black card is:

$$P(black\ card) = \frac{26}{52} = \frac{1}{2}$$

The probability that it is a honor card (honor cards include the 10) is:

$$P(honor\ card) = \frac{20}{52} = \frac{5}{13}$$

¶ Throughout the book, we'll assume the shuffling is sufficient to achieve randomness – not an easy objective to achieve. Assuming randomness is easier than generating randomness. More on this in the next chapter.

The probability that it is either a heart or a black card is:

$$P(\text{heart or black card}) = \frac{39}{52} = \frac{3}{4}$$

The probability that it is either a heart or an honor card is:

$$P(\text{heart or honor card}) = \frac{28}{52} = \frac{7}{13}$$

The number 28 is the sum of the 13 hearts and the 15 cards that are honors in the other three suits.

Of course, this is a very different approach for obtaining probability than the relative frequency approach used in Chapter 1. In that chapter, we were using relative frequency to estimate the actual probabilities. Now, in the present chapter, we are no longer conducting trials, using observations or learning from experience.

In Chapter 1, I mentioned that when you pick up your next thirteen-card hand, there are 635 billion equally likely possibilities. Actually, I ignored more than 13 million hands – the actual number is 635,013,559,600. In this context, ignoring 13 million is no big deal, and be prepared, I will do it again. However, let's use the actual number now to calculate some more probabilities.

$$P(\text{hand consisting of thirteen hearts}) = \frac{1}{635,013,559,600}$$

$$P(\text{hand consisting of thirteen cards in one suit}) = \frac{4}{635,013,559,600}$$

$$P(\text{hand with any specific thirteen cards}) = \frac{1}{635,013,559,600}$$

$$P(\text{hand containing 37 HCP}) = \frac{4}{635,013,559,600}$$

Since 37 HCP requires all four aces, four kings, four queens, and any one of the four jacks, there are four ways to generate a 37 HCP hand.

At times the simplest way to obtain the probability of some event occurring is by figuring out the probability of it *not* occurring and subtracting that value from 1.

P(hand containing fewer than 37 HCP) =

$$1 - \frac{4}{635{,}013{,}559{,}600} = \frac{635{,}013{,}559{,}596}{635{,}013{,}559{,}600}$$

The probability that you will be the declarer on the next deal is

P(declarer) = 1/4

Of course, this is only correct if we assume that all four players are equally likely to be the declarer. If any of the players are very timid or aggressive bidders this figure would be off.

How often would you expect to be the declarer in a 24-board session?

1/4 x 24 = 6

How often would you expect to be the declarer if you played 300 deals?

1/4 x 300 = 75

If you could keep a record of several hundred deals (one week of bridge for those living the good life) with your favorite partner, you might be able to demonstrate that he is a hand hog.

Fractions Should Not Be Avoided

The examples that have appeared in this chapter used fractions to represent the probability of an event. Since the advent of small calculators forty years ago, fractions have somewhat fallen out of fashion, and decimal representation of values is preferred by society. That is a shame, since expressing a probability in the form of a fraction is often very revealing.

It would only be a good mathematical approximation to write:

P(red ace) = 0.03846154

whereas expressing it as 2/52 indicates the exact value. Even more important, 2/52 reveals how the value was obtained. I often prefer a fraction to be left in its non-reduced form, as I think 2/52 is more informative than 1/26. Another advantage of not reducing the fraction is that it might simplify future arithmetic with that fraction.

An excellent example of how one can be misled by calculations that suppress dealing with fractions is the IQ Score. It is fine to say that a person has a high intelligence level but it is problematic to say that a person has a high IQ. The letters IQ are a shorthand for Intelligence Quotient. This quotient (fraction) is obtained by dividing a person's mental age by their chronological age. To 'clean up' this fraction, the quotient is multiplied by 100. So, if an eight-year old takes an IQ test and performs at the level of a twelve-year old, the child's IQ score is 12/8 multiplied by 100, which is 150. Most ACBL members are around the age of seventy so I assume that if you are a typical reader, you are around that age. If you have an eight-year old grandchild with an IQ of 150, you can proudly brag about your descendant. However, beware − for a seventy-year-old, an IQ of 150 would indicate the mental capacity of the average 105-year-old person, whereas an IQ of 50 would indicate the mental capacity of the average thirty-five-year-old. I recently heard a man in his seventies boasting of his high IQ and attempting to insult other seventy-year-old enemies by stating that they have a low IQ. Is he being humble? Did he wish to compliment his enemies? I doubt it. This is an example of trying to 'work around' a fraction, and losing sight of what the fraction represents. Actually, through its incorrect usage in the past several decades the meaning of IQ has been altered. Language can evolve in strange ways.

This example not only demonstrates that avoiding fractions can generate a loss of meaning, but also the importance of correctly interpreting values that appear in a result. Chapter 2 had a section about drawing the correct conclusions from numerical values. A small but very famous 1954 book by Darrell Huff has the title *How to Lie with Statistics*. It gives many examples of how one can be misled by numerical values and graphs.

Percentages and Odds

When I am writing stand-alone bridge columns, I typically use percentages to indicate the likelihood of events. I don't want to assume that readers have any experience with probability. Bridge players are most comfortable when values are presented using percentages such as those in the suit split tables in Chapter 4.

In spite of being a neurotic checker of anything I write, I want to prepare you for a mistake that may exist someplace in this book. If you ever read that the probability of an event is a number like 32, you know something is wrong. We saw that a probability can never be greater than 1. Clearly, I either left off a percentage symbol or a decimal point. Either 32% or 0.32 would be fine — take your pick. Fortunately, leaving off a percent symbol produces such a blatant error that you will not be fooled, except perhaps with extremely small values.

Gamblers find it more convenient to think in terms of odds rather than either probabilities or percentages. The odds are useful for indicating the payoff for a bet of any size. For example, if P(event) = 3/5 when using probabilities, the chance of it occurring expressed as a percentage is 60%, and the odds of that event occurring are 3 to 2. In a fair game (one which favors neither you nor your opponent), if you believe the probability that E will occur is 3/5 and you place a bet that E will occur, it is reasonable to risk three dollars for a payoff of two. Likewise, you could risk 30 dollars for a payoff of 20, and risk 60 for a payoff of 40. You can see how useful odds are for gamblers. Throughout this book, I will usually refer to probabilities rather than odds, but on rare occasions, odds will be used. In general, if the P(event) = a/b, the odds for event occurring are a to (b-a). If the odds are c to d, the corresponding probability of the event is c/(c + d).

Be forewarned that gambler's betting lines often reverse the meaning of odds. For example, when a horse is listed at 20 to 1, it does not mean that the horse is extremely likely to win but quite the opposite — it is extremely likely to lose. This method is used to show the payout on a two-dollar bet. Actually, the horse has odds, as we have defined them, of 1 to 20.

I will usually represent likelihood as a fraction or decimal number rather than odds, since doing arithmetic with odds is very awkward. It normally requires converting the odds to probability. Many bridge books on this topic seem to avoid the word 'probability', at least in their titles; it seems to have a more intimidating ring than 'odds'. If you glance at the bibliography on page 271, you will see that only two use 'probability' in their title (although some place it in their subtitle).

Vacant Places

A common bridge situation is when declarer needs to figure out which defender holds some particular card. It's quite rare to be able to do this with complete certainty. Usually, the best that declarer can hope for is to obtain the probability of a defender being dealt a specific card. Of course, obtaining the probability for one defender results in knowing the probability for the other one too.

Suppose declarer wishes to know which defender holds the ace of hearts. Assume that declarer magically knows that West has two spades and East has six spades, but nothing else. This means West has eleven cards that are not spades and East has seven cards that are not spades. So, the odds that West holds the heart ace are 11 to 7. The odds that East holds it are 7 to 11.

P(West holds heart ace) = 11/18 and
P(East holds heart ace) = 7/18

Obviously, these two values must add up to 1.

This idea is usually called 'vacant places' or, occasionally, 'empty places'. The vacant places concept will surface throughout the book. It is one of the rare topics where odds are more intuitive than probability. It is easy and simple to use, but can be tricky, as you will see in the next section.

Suppose an astute declarer is certain that West was originally dealt three spades and East two. The five cards held by the defense consist of the queen and four low spot cards. Based on these certain facts and no other information, P(West holds the queen) = 3/5, P(East holds the queen) = 2/5, so equivalently, the odds that West holds the queen are 3 to 2.

Now declarer plays the ace, and both defenders follow with low spot cards. This leaves West with two cards in the suit and East with only one card. Has the probability that West holds the queen increased to 2/3? No, no, no! Declarer has not obtained any information from the defenders following suit with small spot cards. That was totally predictable. Each defender was known to hold at least one spot card and each would choose to play a spot card rather than the queen. The probability that West holds the queen has not changed: it is still 3/5. If a defender was having a real off day, and decided simply to choose a card randomly when following suit, that would be a different situation. Avoid such a partner! We will look at this sort of random card playing in Appendix 4; it's not important to a bridge player.

One should observe, however, that from a particular card perspective, there *has* been a probability change. Before the ace was played, each of the five cards held by the defense had a 20% chance of being the queen. After the ace was played, the one remaining card held by East has increased to a 40% chance, while each of the two cards held by West has increased to 30%. Notice that the total is 100%.

The Law of Large Numbers (The Law of Averages)

In a probability course for mathematics majors, the Law of Large Numbers is always introduced at some stage. A simple but often confusing version of this has found general use under the name Law of Averages. In the first draft of this book, I incorrectly wrote that the Law of Averages is never mentioned in mathematics textbooks. Actually, when I checked I realized that many books do include a few lines stating that the Law of Averages does not exist.

Let me describe with a few examples what is implied by the Law of Large Numbers. Consider an experiment where one draws 1000 cards from a deck. Between each card being drawn, that card is replaced in the deck and the fifty-two-card deck is reshuffled. This is certainly a lot of work. Don't try this at home! Suppose the event we are looking for is drawing a heart. Since the P(heart) is 1/4, after the 1000 cards are drawn, you would expect about 250 hearts will have been drawn. You should not expect exactly 250. The probability of that particular result is only about 3%. But the probability of being within a ten-point range either way, i.e. between 240 and 260, is approximately 55%. When performing this experiment there are 1001 possible results − any result from drawing 0 hearts to 1000 hearts. But there is more than a 50% chance of seeing one of the 21 results between 240 and 260. Expressed as a percentage, more than 50% of the time, the percentage of hearts after 1000 draws will be between 24% and 26%.

Suppose the above experiment were modified to 10,000 draws instead of just 1000. There would then be a 98% chance that hearts would be drawn between 24% and 26% of the time. We can see that probability theory is very accurate at predicting what will be the result after a large number of trials. On any individual trial, probability theory is far less impressive: it is not capable of predicting the outcome.

Now let's repeat the original experiment of 1000 draws but suppose that the first 20 cards drawn include not a single heart. This is strange. What does it mean? Very little! The probability of the twenty-first card being a heart is still 1/4. The deck has no ability to know that it is producing too few hearts. The deck has no desire to catch up. Cards have absolutely no memory. The next 980 cards each have a probability of 1/4 of being a heart. So, one should expect that after all one thousand cards are dealt, the number of hearts dealt will be about 980 x 1/4 = 245. The probability of obtaining between 235 and 255 hearts (within 10 of that value) is slightly more than 50%. Notice that it is close to the original expectation for the 1000 draws. A useful alternative line of reasoning can be used. In the first 20 cards drawn, we observed no hearts instead of the expected five hearts, so it is not surprising that after the 980 additional draws we should still anticipate five fewer hearts.

Gamblers often watch the results of a roulette wheel. If a wheel has come up black more often than expected in the last one hundred spins, they feel it is wise to bet on red. This is sometimes called the *Balancing Principle*. But the roulette wheel does not know that it should catch up. It has no memory and no desire to compensate for prior results. Each spin is independent of the previous spin. Other gamblers do the opposite – they figure that there might be a mechanical malfunction in the wheel. With older, less scrutinized roulette wheels, this made some sense.

After a bridge player has completed the first ten boards of a session without receiving a single hand with 8 or more HCP, he might anticipate excellent hands in the remainder of the session. He certainly deserves them. But there is no basis for believing that there will be a balancing or compensating element. His cards should improve, but only to the extent of being dealt average quality hands. However, that unlucky card day will be swamped by the hands played in a lifetime.

This type of error is particularly popular with baseball commentators. They often mistakenly state that an excellent batter who has not had a hit in his last twenty-five opportunities is 'due for a hit'. Actually, it is quite the opposite. He is in a slump. He is wondering whether he will be removed from the starting lineup or, worse yet, sent down to the minor leagues. This distraction and the natural lack of confidence will only result in keeping the batter in his slump. His opportunities to bat are not independent events. His mental state from prior failures can take its toll. He remembers the past failures that can alter the likelihood of a future success. By contrast, the physical playing cards have no memory. Playing cards never think: 'I just provided Julian with a hand holding only 2 HCP, let me compensate and give him a great hand. He is a nice guy.' Likewise, the mental state of a player will not have any bearing on what cards he is dealt, only what he does with them. His next hand is independent of the present hand.

In summary, think of the Law of Large Numbers (Law of Averages) as eventually producing what is expected, *not by balancing, but by swamping.*

The Hideous Hog's Disdain for Probability

The Hideous Hog is a fictional bridge player created by the wonderful imagination of Victor Mollo (1909-1987). The Hog achieved worldwide fame when *Bridge in the Menagerie* appeared in 1965, but at that time the character was already alive and well thanks to magazine articles by Mollo. I am happy to report that he has had the good fortune of most fictional characters: he is still alive and has not aged a single day in the last half century.

He has never hidden his disdain for using probability at the bridge table. Two of the Hog's most famous quotes are:

'When I take 50-50 chances, I expect them to come off at least four times out of five.'[**]

'Odds and percentages ... they take the place of thinking, which is why they are so popular.'[††]

The Hog's dismissal of probability is rather understandable. An excellent player has a lot of evidence to aid decision-making. We saw in the last chapter how greatly the table for 2-2 splits was altered by the knowledge of a 5-1 split in another suit.

Excellent declarers can gather information in many ways: the opponents' bidding (and as we saw, even their passes), the opponents' defensive approach and opening lead. They are capable of making that information useful by drawing all positive and negative inferences. Probably they get most from negative inferences; they ask themselves, why didn't an opponent do such and such?

Card sense, whatever it is, can be extremely useful for decision-making. I would recommend that readers never ask a very good

---

[**] "The Hog in Charge", Victor Mollo, p.6. From *Destiny at Bay*, 1987, Batsford.
[††] "Bidding with the Odds," Victor Mollo, p.189. From *Masters and Monsters*, 1979, Methuen.

player, 'What is card sense?' You will probably hear, 'If you have to ask, you will never understand the answer.' So, I finally stopped asking! My best guess at a definition would be the ability to make negative inferences. I do strongly feel that the skill that separates a great player from a good player is the ability to recognize all the negative inferences that are floating around on every hand.

Therefore, great players can at times know exactly what cards are in each defender's hand. This converts standard bridge into double-dummy bridge. Once bridge becomes a game of perfect information, probability is useless. It adds nothing. Indeed, when there is any information about the location of the defender's cards, probability is less important.

Many great players have dismissed probability at the bridge table and have gone so far as to boast to me how little mathematics they know. On the surface they sound humble. But actually, they are boasting that their bridge level is so outstanding, they have no use for probability. Obviously, they agree with the Hideous Hog. Of course, I am sure they have never considered how much probability they learned simply through playing bridge.

This disdain for probability is far from new. Way back in 1743, a satirical play, *The Humours of Whist...*, was written. It includes a character with the name Sir Calculation — a player who can appreciate the nuances of whist probability but is an awful player. I will say more about the satire in Chapter 23, so I hope you make it that far.

I Have a Bone to Pick with the Hideous Hog (Not One of His)

The Hideous Hog is an extremely arrogant player who insults everyone who has the misfortune of being at the same table. A frequent partner, the Rueful Rabbit, has been overheard stating, 'One gets used to abuse. It's waiting for it that is so trying.'‡‡ Normally, I would not attack a living person or animal (even fictional). If you don't have something nice to say, why say anything? Too hurtful.

---

‡‡ "Kibitzers take Arms," Victor Mollo, p. 99. From *Bridge in the Menagerie*, 2013 Master Point Press.

Throughout this book, I make an exception for the Hog by complimenting his great bridge ability but attacking his arrogance. I am sure he would be flattered on both accounts.

But what about the Hog's thoughts on probability? I can understand them. The Hog is an outstanding player; his experience and ability reduce the importance of probability for his decision-making. But very few players ever play at the level of the Hog. A typical player cannot draw all the inferences that the Hog is capable of using when making decisions. There is certainly some truth that 'Odds and percentages ... they take the place of thinking' but for a beginner, that may not be such a bad thing. If the Hog were not so arrogant, he might appreciate that new players are very busy thinking about many important issues while playing a hand. Toward the end of a session, when I realize that I am playing against a totally new duplicate player, I ask, 'Have you enjoyed yourself'? I have learned to anticipate hearing 'I enjoyed it but I am totally exhausted.'

We have seen how probabilities change as more information becomes known (for example, a 5-1 split in one suit changes the inferences about other suits). Obtaining that information and using it properly depends on the bridge ability of the player. Most bridge techniques are more useful for the advanced player than the beginner. However, using probability at the bridge table may be more helpful for the beginner than the advanced player. As beginners improve, they will appreciate all the bridge information floating around and modify how much and when they wish to use probability when making decisions.

Chapter 6
Equally Likely Outcomes

Is this chapter useful? Why?
Usefulness number: 10. No, several sections are not directly related to bridge, but I consider the second section on notrump ranges and the third section on almost equally likely outcomes as *must-reads*. The principles introduced in these sections will resurface throughout the book. While you are at it, you might as well read the whole chapter. The chapter is really focused on situations where outcomes are not actually equally likely but are often mistaken for being so, both at the bridge table and in con games.

Dealing Random Hands

Prior to computer-generated hands, duplicate players shuffled the cards and dealt them out before the first round. Social bridge players still have to perform that chore on every hand. Mathematicians who studied this process have concluded that well over two dozen shuffles are required to achieve the desired goal of hands being random. Let us consider the world of whist and bridge. These and other trick-taking games often result in four cards all in the same suit being stacked together in the fifty-two-card pile. So, after a hand is finished, it is common for the deck of cards to be composed of many groups of four cards in the same suit. A sloppy shuffler of the cards for the next hand might not adequately disturb the location of those four cards from the same suit. When they are eventually dealt out, each player receives one of those four cards. Since the four cards are all from the same suit, this leads to balanced hands occurring too often and unbalanced hands too rarely.

Who enjoys shuffling? This reminds me of the following story from 1887. A lady fond of gaming was confessing her weakness and receiving the reproval of her priest. Among other arguments against gaming, he spoke of the great waste of time; to which the lady eagerly replied, 'Ah! That is just what vexes me – so much time lost in shuffling the cards!'[§§]

She clearly was born one hundred years too early. Our computer-generated hands are randomly dealt. This means that not only are all possible hands equally likely, but in addition there is no pattern where anything can be inferred about an upcoming hand from the prior hand or from any group of prior hands. If you doubt the claim that computer-generated hands are random, Chapter 22 will provide you with a method to test them.

In Chapter 2, I indicated that there are more than 635 billion different specific thirteen-card hands. I tried to make that enormous number relatable and intuitive but understandably, I am sure I failed. It is interesting that both of the below statements are true, since they seem to contradict each other.

You'd better play your present hand well because you will never be dealt it again.

Whatever your present hand is, it is as likely to be your next bridge hand as any of the other 635 billion hands.

I feel a need to justify the first statement. Bridge players just don't play enough bridge. I seriously doubt that anyone has ever played even one million hands. If a player were to play forty hands a day every day of the year for sixty years, it would only be 40 x 365 x 60 = 876,000.

A typical serious bridge player might play four sessions a week for fifty weeks a year. That would be 4 x 25 x 50 = 5000. After twenty years at this pace, he would have played 100,000 hands. A miniscule number, when compared with the total number of possible hands. It violates one's intuition that corresponding to every single hand that this serious player has played, there are more than six million hands that he has not played. You don't believe me! I understand. But in my defense, six million multiplied by 100,000 is only 600 billion.

---

§§ Quoted in Rudolf H. Rheinhardt, *Whist Stories and Card-Table Talk with a Bibliography of Whist* (Chicago: A.C. McClurg & Co., 1887), p. 301.

Not to belabor the point, even though I must confess that I am belaboring the point, suppose all 170,000 ACBL members were at the end of their playing career of 100,000 hands. Suppose duplicate bridge had not been invented[¶¶], and instead, every deal were dealt out independently, so each deal would produce four new hands. In addition, suppose no specific hand was ever dealt twice – a ridiculous premise in light of the Birthday Problem, but it makes the point even stronger. All ACBL members together would have played a total of only seventeen billion hands (170,000 x 100,000). Therefore, I can strengthen my above statement 'You'd better play your present hand well since you will never be dealt it again' to indicate that probably no ACBL member has played your thirteen-card hand in the past nor will play it in the future. You almost certainly will be playing it for the first time it was ever played and for the last time it will ever be played. I find that hard to believe! Certainly, it is not intuitive.

As large a number as 635 billion actually is, it is a very tiny number when compared to the number of possible deals of all fifty-two cards. There are actually 53,644,737,765,488,792,839,23 7,440,000 equally likely deals. I am not going to attempt to make that number relatable. I'm still in shock over learning that no one else will probably ever play my thirteen-card hand.

Now let's explore another idea, that of independence. Suppose a set of hand records (really 'deal records') displays thirty-six deals. If you consider just one player's hands, say South, on those thirty-six deals, the thirty-six hands are random. But all 36 x 4 = 144 hands on the sheet are not random since they clearly are not independent. Suppose on Deal 15, South has the spade ace. Obviously, East, North and West cannot also have the spade ace on Deal 15. So, the four hands that form any deal are not four independent hands. Let's see how this lack of independence affects an important aspect of bidding.

¶¶ Actually, duplicate bridge was not invented, rather adapted from duplicate whist. Our famous movements, named after their inventors Howell and Mitchell, were both created in the 1890s for whist players. Howell died in 1907 and Mitchell in 1914, so neither could have played contract bridge.

Notrump Bid Ranges

Suppose a partnership opens 1NT with 15-17 HCP and the partnership never upgrades a great 14 HCP hand or downgrades a bad 18 HCP hand. If you also assume they don't miscount their points, there are only three possibilities. Those possibilities are not equally likely to occur. The probability of that bid being made on 15 HCP is 44%, 16 HCP is 33%, and 17 HCP is 23%. Note that the chance of holding a 15 HCP hand is practically twice the probability of a 17 HCP hand.

Even though the 635 billion hands are equally likely, once a condition is placed, then usually events are not equally likely. More of those 635 billion hands hold 15 HCP than 17 HCP. Generalizing, since the average hand has about 10 HCP, hands close to 10 HCP are more likely than hands that have far fewer or many more than 10 HCP.

Your intuition may be aided by considering the extreme situations. If you have 25 HCP and your partner opens 1NT, the probability is 100% that your partner has 15. If you have 0 HCP and your partner opens 1NT, the average points of the three other players is 13 1/3, so your partner is almost as likely to have 17 as 15. If you have 26 HCP and your partner opens 1NT, you would be recounting your points for five minutes before deciding that it is your partner who cannot count.

This effect is even more pronounced when bids indicate a higher range. Suppose your partner opens 2♣ and after your 2◇, your partner bids 2NT showing a 22-24 HCP range. The probability of 22 HCP is 55%, 23 HCP is 30%, and 24 HCP is 15%. We will return to this in several chapters.

Not Quite Equally Likely, But Close Enough

Suppose the defense holds ♡Q432. These cards can be split in sixteen ways between West and East. All are listed in the table following:

Line	West	East
1	Q 4 3 2	—
2	Q 4 3	2
3	Q 4 2	3
4	Q 3 2	4
5	4 3 2	Q
6	Q 4	3 2
7	Q 3	4 2
8	Q 2	4 3
9	4 3	Q 2
10	4 2	Q 3
11	3 2	Q 4
12	Q	4 3 2
13	4	Q 3 2
14	3	Q 4 2
15	2	Q 4 3
16	—	Q 4 3 2

This list contains the sixteen possibilities. These sixteen outcomes are not actually equally likely to occur, but each of them has a probability close to 1/16. For bridge purposes, one can pretend that the probability of each outcome is indeed 1/16. Of course, I am assuming that no relevant bridge information is available that would alter the value for some of the sixteen outcomes.

With an example, let me first justify why these outcomes are not equally likely. Suppose twenty-six cards from the fifty-two-card deck are being dealt out to the two defenders. Suppose they contain the four heart cards indicated above. Suppose thirteen cards are dealt out face-up one at a time to West and the remaining thirteen cards are given to East. Suppose the first three cards are all hearts: the ♡Q, the ♡3 and the ♡2. The remaining twenty-three cards only contain one card in the heart suit, the ♡4. Who is more likely to receive the ♡4, West or East? Correct answer: East. East will be receiving thirteen cards while West will only be receiving ten additional cards. In summary, since West is known to hold three specific cards, he only has ten opportunities to receive the undealt heart card. Stated another way, West has only ten vacant spots where the ♡4 could land, whereas East has thirteen. This reasoning is just an alternative view of the Vacant Places Principle, which we encountered on page 53. Likewise, with similar reasoning, one can justify that each specific 2-2 split is slightly more likely than each specific 3-1 split.

For simplicity, let's pretend that each of the sixteen cases has a probability of 1/16 even though we realize that each of the six cases where the suit splits 2-2 is slightly more likely than 1/16, and each of the two splits with a void is less likely than 1/16.

We can use these sixteen outcomes to get a crude estimate of the various suit splits with four missing cards. Since in six cases the suit split is 2-2, in eight cases 3-1, and in two cases 4-0, we can form the following table.

2-2	6/16 = 0.375
3-1	8/16 = 0.5
4-0	2/16 = 0.125

These results, assuming 1/16 for each, are of course less accurate than the table that appeared on page 38 for four missing cards. The differences, however, are never greater than 3%: 40% to 37.5%, 50% to 50%, 10% to 12.5%. In Chapter 21, we will look at techniques to obtain accurate values rather than approximations. For our purposes, we will often be very content using as the value for the probability of each: 1/16 = 0.0625[***].

Since there are only sixteen cases when four cards are missing in a suit, it is possible to list all the possibilities. Even before making a complete list, it is easy to see why there are sixteen possibilities. Since each of the four cards will be located in one of two

---

[***] For the curious, each of the six 2-2 splits is actually 0.0678, each of the eight 3-1 splits is 0.0622 and both of the two 4-0 splits are each 0.0479. Only in the case for the 4-0 split is the difference rather significant. These values are obtained in Appendix 1.

hands, the total number of possible outcomes is 2 x 2 x 2 x 2 = 16. If the defense holds five cards, there are thirty-two possibilities – much more difficult to list. But on a brighter note, if the defense holds only three cards, there are only eight possibilities. In several chapters, we will resort to listing all possible outcomes for guidance in deciding how a suit should be played.

Let's now modify this example by removing the queen from the cards held by the defense and replacing it by the six. So now the defense only holds the ♡6432. This suit is much less interesting. Declarer does not face the classic decision of finding the missing queen. But if we write out the sixteen possibilities, we can gain some probability insights by comparing this holding to ♡Q432.

Line	West	East
1	6 4 3 2	—
2	6 4 3	2
3	6 4 2	3
4	6 3 2	4
5	4 3 2	6
6	6 4	3 2
7	6 3	4 2
8	6 2	4 3
9	4 3	6 2
10	4 2	6 3
11	3 2	6 4
12	6	4 3 2
13	4	6 3 2
14	3	6 4 2
15	2	6 4 3
16	—	6 4 3 2

We are now in a position to provide an answer to the Tricky Confusing Issue Alert on page 41. It dealt with the question: if the defenders hold four cards and declarer plays the ace and both defenders follow, can declarer now use the table for two cards held by the defense? My answer was 'No'. Now we are in a position to analyze the situation. Suppose declarer leads his ace, and both defenders follow. We have learned that line 1 and line 16 are no longer possible. In the fourteen remaining lines, six lines correspond to the original even 2-2 split, while eight lines correspond to the original uneven 3-1 split. Even though each of the six original 2-2 splits is slightly more likely than each of the eight 3-1 splits, since eight outcomes are larger than six, the original 3-1 split is still more likely than the original 2-2 split. So, using the table for two cards held by the defense would be wrong.

Tricky Confusing Issue Alert

In the last paragraph I indicated that when the ace was played, both defenders followed. What if I am more specific and indicate that West played the ♡6 and East played the ♡2? Now only four of the sixteen lines are possible for the original holding: Lines 2, 6, 7, and 12. Two lines correspond to an even split of the four cards, and two lines correspond to an uneven split. It seems to contradict the last paragraph. It certainly seems that after the ♡6 and ♡2 appear, an even split is more likely. Not so. Let's look deeper into line 2 where West had ♡643 and East held the singleton ♡2. From that holding West can play any of the three cards. All three are low spot cards of little value, but equal value. Assume West selects one randomly while East, with the singleton, must play the ♡2. So, with the holding on Line 2, West will play the ♡6 and East the ♡2 only one-third of the time. Compare this to Line 6, where West will select the ♡6 one-half of the time and East will select the ♡2 one-half of the time. Therefore, only one-fourth of the time will West play the ♡6 and East the ♡2. So, in summary, the two uneven splits are slightly less likely to be dealt than the even splits, but defenders with the uneven splits are more likely to produce the ♡6 from West and the ♡2 from East than when holding the even splits. Overall, the two uneven splits are slightly more likely than the two even splits. Please don't be troubled if you were confused by this explanation. In the future, I will usually avoid this type of argument; I will just indicate that they followed suit with some low spot card. I will have to tackle it head-on in Chapter 11 on Restricted Choice.

Now we can look at a prior example, where the defense holds the queen. Seems like the same situation. When declarer leads the ace, if both defenders follow on the first round, the probability of the original 3-1 split is greater than 2-2. As before, there are eight possible holdings to six possible holdings. But suppose on that trick, a defender plays the queen. Assume the defender will virtually never choose to play the queen unless it is a singleton and he is forced to play it. Even if the defender holds queen-doubleton and realizes that the declarer will see the queen on the second round before declarer has to decide between finessing or playing for the drop, why play the queen? As a defender, you know declarer will not go wrong but why not let declarer learn this for himself? When a queen is unnecessarily played by a defender holding queen-doubleton, it is probably because the defender holding queen-doubleton did not see that he held the spot card. Therefore, when the queen appears, declarer should assume that it is a singleton, and can be virtually certain that the suit was originally 3-1. So, when the queen is played by a defender, declarer should assume that the probability of a 3-1 split is 100%. This information is rarely useful since the appearance of the queen is likely to have solved all of declarer's problems, at least in this suit. Possibly knowing of the 3-1 split will still be useful for other decisions on the hand.

Suppose, with the defense holding ♡Q432, both defenders follow suit with a spot card. Look back at page 64. Now for the list of outcomes: we can eliminate line 5 and line 12 because they involved the singleton queen. There remain twelve possible outcomes. Six lines involve different original 2-2 splits and six involve 3-1 splits where the queen is not a singleton. So now the 2-2 split has become slightly more likely than 3-1.

I just want to make an additional comment about the holding we recently considered, where West held ♡643 and East had just the singleton ♡2. When we observed the specific card played, we concluded that if West picked a spot card at random, each of the three spot cards would be played one-third of the time. By comparison, in the more recent example where West held ♡Q43, each specific spot card would be played one-half of the time.

Let's consider the sixteen possibilities when the defenders hold ♡KQ32.

Line	West	East
1	K Q 3 2	—
2	K Q 3	2
3	K Q 2	3
4	K 3 2	Q
5	Q 3 2	K
6	K Q	3 2
7	K 3	Q 2
8	K 2	Q 3
9	Q 3	K 2
10	Q 2	K 3
11	3 2	K Q
12	K	Q 3 2
13	Q	K 3 2
14	3	K Q 2
15	2	K Q 3
16	—	K Q 3 2

Declarer starts by leading the ace. (I don't want to imply that laying down the ace is the way in which this suit should be played. It rarely is. But obviously, on the lead of the ace, neither defender would have any motive to play an honor.) Now suppose one of the defenders plays either the king or queen. It is virtually certain that the cards are split as indicated on one of the six lines: 4, 5, 6, 11, 12, or 13. So the probability that an honor will appear on that trick is 6/16. It is possible that a great defender will play the king from king doubleton in order to enable his partner to get on lead with the queen. But few players would be that confident that their partner holds the queen and make such an excellent play. If you are such a player, I am very flattered that you are reading my book.

If we assume an honor would be played from only those six lines, we now can see that the probability is approximately 2/3 that a defender holds a singleton honor and 1/3 that a defender holds the king-queen doubleton.

Suppose declarer were to lay down the ace and the two spot cards appeared. Now only eight of the above sixteen cases would be possible. In four of the eight, the suit is splitting 2-2 and in four, it is splitting 3-1. So now it is slightly more likely that the suit will split evenly.

Common Question Alert

When the defense is dealt five cards, what is the probability of either defender holding doubleton queen-jack?

Usually this question is provoked by a hand containing a suit such as,

A K 3 2   10 6 5 4

I indicated that it would be hard to list all thirty-two possibilities but there is no need to list them. It is sufficient to merely know that there are thirty-two possibilities. The event can happen in two ways since either defender could have been dealt that doubleton: the answer is 2/32 = 0.0625. If the question was about specifically East holding doubleton queen-jack, the answer would obviously be 1/32.

Comparing Tables in Chapter 4 to Listing All Cases

Listing all cases is certainly more visual and intuitive. This makes it easy to understand. You don't have to trust the percentage values that appeared in those six tables in Chapter 4.

Unfortunately, listing all cases becomes unwieldy when there are five or more cards held by the defense. At the bridge table, even when the defense holds four cards, considering the sixteen cases can be difficult. If you follow my advice of memorizing a dozen values from the Chapter 4 tables, you will find those tables easiest to apply in the middle of a bridge hand.

A major advantage of listing all the cases is that it enables declarer to adjust to the information gained by observing which cards the defenders play. In the last example, where the defense held ♡KQ32, we saw that if an honor appeared on the first round, the probability of an even split decreased to about 1/3, whereas if two spot cards appeared, the probability was slightly greater than 1/2.

Remember that the tables in Chapter 4 only reflect the probability before any cards are played in the suit. As a result of the bridge requirement to follow suit, much can be learned when a defender plays a card that he would not choose to play. In the example with the defense holding ♡6432, none of the cards would be painful to play. With the example with ♡Q432, the queen would be painful to play. So, the play of the queen supplies the declarer with information. Likewise, with the defenders holding the queen, if the queen does not appear, obviously, declarer can rule out the cases where a defender holds a singleton queen. You may wish to compare this example with the example on page 54, where declarer knew with certainty how many cards each defender held in the suit.

In the example with ♡KQ32, the defense holds two cards that a defender would not wish to play when the ace is led. Declarer will gain information if one of those honors has to be played. Likewise, if both defenders follow suit without playing an honor, information is also obtained.

Listing all the possibilities, as we have done in this chapter, may seem crude and not 'mathematically elegant'. It is common for mathematicians to 'play around' with problems. If they intuitively feel a relationship or result is correct, they set out to prove their belief. Students get to see the clean proof without the grunge work and trial and error process.

In summary, we have three alternative sets of values for the probabilities of suit splits. Seems strange! But they can be useful in different ways. Listing all possible outcomes and pretending they are equally likely is the most intuitive way to obtain the probabilities. The values in Chapter 4 are easy to memorize and useful while playing a bridge hand. The values in Appendix 1 are the most accurate but require a calculating device, so they are only useful for analysis when you are away from the bridge table.

The Monty Hall Problem and its Bridge Relevance

Common Problem Alert

The Monty Hall Problem reached a surprising degree of fame in its heyday almost thirty years ago. I was not only asked about this problem by bridge players, but also by mathematicians who had never played bridge and even by curious non-mathematicians who had never played bridge. This problem was first described by Steve Selvin in *The American Statistician* (1975). It had nothing to do with bridge. Phil Martin deserves credit for formulating the problem in an article for *Bridge Today* (May/June 1989). The problem appeared in Ms. Savant's column in *Parade* magazine, several *New York Times* articles, and lives on in several applied mathematics textbooks. It actually made the front page of the *New York Times* on July 21, 1991. Usually their front-page space is too valuable to include an article relevant to either mathematics or bridge, let alone relevant to both!

The problem relates to a very popular television program in the 70s, *Let's Make a Deal*, of which Monty Hall was the host. Here is a generic version of the problem. A contestant has to choose one of the three doors (label them A, B, C) on stage. Behind one door is a new car, behind each of the other two is a goat. The three doors are equally likely to have the car. After the contestant chooses a door (say door A), which remains closed, Monty Hall selects either door B or C. The door Monty Hall chose is opened, and a live goat is seen eating grass or performing some other activity appropriate for a goat. The contestant is now asked whether he wishes to stick with his original choice or switch to the other unopened door.

This problem is not well-posed the way I stated it. The issue is what Monty Hall knew and when he knew it. One scenario is that he was tipped off by either his producer or a goat as to which doors held a goat behind them. A second scenario is that he picked the door at random. For either scenario, when the contestant selected door A, the probability was 1/3 that he picked the door with the car. The probability is 2/3 that the car was behind either door B or C. Monty did not want to show the big prize since the game would immediately end without any excitement. He wanted to open a door behind which was a goat.

Under the first scenario, if the car was behind B, Monty Hall would open C. Likewise, if the car was behind C, he would open B. The probability was 2/3 that the car was behind whichever of the two doors, B and C, was still unopened. The contestant should therefore switch.

Under the second scenario, the probability would be 1/3 that the car was revealed and the game would immediately end. If, by chance, Monty picked a door with a hidden goat, the game would continue and the two remaining unopened doors each had a probability of 1/2 of containing the car: no gain or loss by switching.

Regular watchers realized that Monty Hall would never expose the big prize. Usually, articles and books imply that Monty Hall was aware of the location of the prize but when the problem is retold orally that information tends to be left out. Most written descriptions seem to enjoy pointing out that mathematics professors are often tricked by this problem. From my many discussions with that crowd, I must defend them. They do not find it mathematically challenging but rather they get it wrong because they have not watched a sufficient number of episodes of *Let's Make a Deal*. They are faced with a problem that was not well-posed and fail to ask the right questions. I still remember an astute mathematician telling me that the problem was not well-posed unless he knew where the contestant lived. When I asked why he needed that information, he correctly pointed out that if the contestant lived on an island without any roads, he would want to win a goat rather than a car! Actually, when this problem was first posed, the new car was a gas guzzling 1975 Lincoln Continental. Almost fifty years later only a classic car collector with an excellent mechanic would wish to own such a car (not that a dead goat is any better).

The relevance of this problem to bridge is not immediately obvious. But the crux of the Monty Hall problem is appreciating what if anything was learned from Monty Hall opening a door.

That was the distinction between the two scenarios. From declarer's perspective, let us now consider what can be learned from the card led by the opening leader. Suppose declarer would like to know which defender holds some specific card (say, the ♡K). Let's consider the scenario where the leader studies his cards, summons up all of his bridge knowledge and then makes what he believes (or at least hopes) to be an intelligent lead. Let's consider an alternative scenario where the opening leader never looks at his cards. He merely randomly picks one of the thirteen unseen cards that have just been dealt to him, possibly while lamenting, 'I have not made a good opening lead in twenty years so I might as well choose the lead this way.' The Hideous Hog had such a high level of disrespect for his partner's ability that he was known to suggest, 'Just lead the third card from the left.' Suppose that lead is not the ♡K. With this random selection, the probability the leader has the king is 12/25 while the probability that the leader's partner has the king is 13/25. However, under the realistic bridge scenario, applying the vacant spaces principle is incorrect. For example, if the ♡A is led and you are informed that they always lead the ace from ace-king, the opening leader is very likely to have the king.

In summary, just like the Monty Hall Problem, a bridge player must realize that most information received when cards are played is not random and it would be incorrect to treat it as random.

I am not a big fan of the Monty Hall Problem, but I include it because it appears in so many books. I am troubled that Monty Hall did not always offer the option to switch doors. Possibly he wanted to save money and only offered the switch option when he knew a contestant picked a winning door. In that case, the contestant should not switch, but just ask for the car keys.

Terence Reese's 1958 book, *The Expert Game* (published in the USA under the name *Master Play*), demonstrates the same principle with the following example. Five coins are involved. Four are placed with their head up while one has its tail up. They are randomly placed into two piles. One pile has three coins while the other has the remaining two. Obviously, the probability is 3/5 that the coin that is tail up resides in the pile with three coins. Suppose the pile of three coins is examined and two coins that are heads up are removed. What has changed?

From the perspective of the stacks, nothing was learned. There is still a 3/5 probability that the tail up coin is in the original stack of three. But that one remaining coin now has the much greater probability of 3/5 of being tail up. This example is very similar to the example with cards on page 54.

Con Games in the Non-bridge World

Many con games are based on the player falsely believing that all possible chance outcomes are equally likely. Actually, I must confess that my first real job required me to be involved in the running of a con game. In the mid-1960s I was an innocent seventeen-year-old pumping gas at a station affiliated with a major national brand. I will not give their name for fear of legal consequences but it began with an 'S' and ended with an 'O'. Every time they came in for gas, customers received an envelope with a piece of a jigsaw puzzle. As best I can recall, it required approximately twenty pieces to complete. There was a substantial monetary reward for completing it. Of course, as a teenager any monetary reward seemed substantial, but I am sure it was in the thousands.

Initially the gas customers would usually receive a needed piece of the puzzle since they needed most of them. Of course, as their puzzles filled up with pieces, they were not surprised to receive pieces that they already possessed. Eventually customers would need just one piece and began dreaming of newfound wealth. They felt close; their intuition was telling them that they had a 1 in 20 chance of winning next time they filled up. But they would always be disappointed when their 5% chance did not pan out. Some would show me the puzzle and tell me what piece they needed. Of course, I had no knowledge of which piece I was giving them, but still some anger was directed at me. Some would offer to split the prize with me if I gave them their missing piece. Some offered to split the prize with any customer who had that piece. Some purchased only a small amount of gas each time so that they could frequently return for a new piece. This made my job as a gas-pumper harder – less downtime to sit and read. After a while, it was clear to me that every customer was looking for the same exact piece! I assume some had actually been manufactured but I never saw one. Certainly, customers did not have their anticipated 5% chance for that piece. Of course, customers were never told that they were equally likely to get each of the 20 pieces, but it is quite natural that they falsely assumed it.

I recall chatting with a WW2 veteran who told me how he won money rolling dice during the war. The game he ran would let players roll a pair of dice. If the player rolled a sum of 2, 3, 4, 5, 10, 11, or 12, the player would win. If the sum was 6, 7, 8, or 9, the house would win. This game was appealing since the house could only win on four numbers, but a player could win on seven numbers. The problem is that those eleven outcomes are not equally likely. It is true that if one die is rolled, the six possible outcomes are equally likely. If two dice are rolled there are 36 equally likely possible outcomes. If you are not comfortable with that statement, it might help to imagine one die being blue and the other red. If the blue die is 5 and the red die is 3, we can represent it as (5,3). If you list all possibilities, there are thirty-six. But there is only one way that their sum is 12 – both the blue and red dice are 6. Meanwhile the sum of 8 can occur five ways; (2,6), (3,5), (4,4), (5,3), and (6,2). Therefore, the *sums* of a pair of dice are not equally likely. For the above game, the probability of the house winning is 20/36.

Sometimes a device that does not produce equally likely outcomes can be used to generate equally likely outcomes. Imagine a coin that when flipped comes up heads 70% of the time. Two players would like to use it to generate a game of chance where each player has an equal chance of winning. No problem! Flip it twice. If it comes up heads-tails in that order, player A wins. If it's tails-heads in that order, Player B wins. If it's heads twice or tails twice, there is no winner and the coin must be flipped two more times. It is interesting to note that the 70% value was unimportant, the procedure works for any coin except one that is either always heads or always tails. Of course, if it comes up heads 99% of the time, it will require a very patient flipper since the game will often be very long.

Fifty years ago, the Vietnam War was raging. For the sake of fairness or possibly merely for an appearance of fairness, a draft lottery was conducted on December 1, 1969. The prize was a low draft number which translated into quick consideration for the draft. This first lottery was televised. All looked very official. The 366 possible dates of birth were each put into a separate little capsule and each was pulled out of a large bin. The later one's date of birth was picked, the less likely it was that the draft board would be sending an invitation. The January capsules were put in the bin first, then February, and so on through the twelve months. These capsules were barely mixed — if mixed at all. Not surprisingly, when capsules containing dates were pulled out of the bin a disproportionate number of individuals born in the months of December and November found themselves unfortunate 'winners'. Those capsules were placed last in the bin. With all the scrutiny, the 366 dates merely appeared equally likely to be selected. But no real harm was actually done since no social class or ethnic group was hurt by this poorly thought-out lottery. The mechanics of this lottery can be seen on YouTube. The January 4, 1970 *New York Times* article "Statisticans Charge Draft Lottery was Not Random" gives a complete explanation.

Chapter 7
Combining Bridge Probabilities

Is this chapter useful? Why?

Usefulness number: 9. The likelihood of success in a contract may hinge on two events both occurring, or instead, at least one of the two events occurring. For that matter, it could be three events all occurring or at least one of three events occurring. How can declarer determine his best chance? This chapter starts by describing when and how to do arithmetic with bridge probabilities in order to answer this type of question.

Adding Probabilities

When two events cannot both occur at the same time, they are called *mutually exclusive events*. In order to obtain the probability of either of those events occurring one can simply add together the probabilities of the two individual events.

Suppose we are again drawing one card from a shuffled deck, what are the chances of drawing either a heart or a black card?

In order to obtain the probability of either a heart or a black card, their respective probabilities can be added since they are mutually exclusive events. There are no cards that are both a heart and black.

Since we found that $P(\text{heart}) = \dfrac{1}{4}$ and $P(\text{black card}) = \dfrac{1}{2}$

then $P(\text{heart or black card}) = P(\text{heart}) + P(\text{black card})$

$$= \dfrac{1}{4} + \dfrac{1}{2} = \dfrac{3}{4}$$

This result is the same as value obtained on page 49 when we considered that thirty-nine of the fifty-two cards are either a heart or black.

We are again drawing one card. What is the chance of drawing either a heart or an honor?

In order to obtain the probability of drawing either a heart or an honor card, we cannot simply add their respective probabilities. These are *not* mutually exclusive events. There are five heart honor cards. These five cards would be counted twice. We must subtract the probability of getting any of those five cards.

Since we found that $P(\text{heart}) = \dfrac{1}{4}$, $P(\text{honor card}) = \dfrac{5}{13}$

and $P(\text{heart honor card}) = \dfrac{5}{52}$

then $P(\text{heart or honor card}) = \dfrac{1}{4} + \dfrac{5}{13} - \dfrac{5}{52} = \dfrac{13}{52} + \dfrac{20}{52} - \dfrac{5}{52} = \dfrac{28}{52} = \dfrac{7}{13}$

This result is the same value as obtained on page 49 when we considered that twenty-eight of the fifty-two cards are either a heart or an honor.

Many bridge books and players prefer an alternative way of obtaining the probability of either of two events when the events are not mutually exclusive. They would add the probability of a heart to the probability of an honor card that is not a heart.

$P(\text{heart}) + P(\text{non-heart honor card}) = 13/52 + 15/52 = 28/52$

Same answer.

One can take the two events in the opposite order.

$P(\text{honor}) + P(\text{non-honor heart}) = 20/52 + 8/52 = 28/52$

Still the same answer.

Throughout the book we will often be dealing with mutually exclusive events, so we will be able to just add their respective probabilities. But before simply adding, it is always necessary to consider whether or not two events are mutually exclusive.

The next few examples are concerned with suit splits. The tables that appear in Chapter 4 on the likelihood of the various suit splits will be used. Assume declarer has not learned anything about the hand that would make these tables inappropriate to use. The suit split values are from the compact table representations unless otherwise indicated.

Suppose declarer is in an eight-card trump fit and he chooses a line of play that will succeed whenever the trump suit splits 3-2 or 4-1. What is the probability of success?

P(3-2 split) = 0.68 from a table in Chapter 4.

P(4-1 split) = 0.28 from a table in Chapter 4.

Since a suit cannot split both ways, these are mutually exclusive events.

Therefore, P(success) = 0.68 + 0.28 = 0.96.

An alternative method is

P(success) = 1 − P(5-0 split) = 1 − 0.04 = 0.96

This uses the fact that the probability of all cases adds up to one. That is, instead of figuring out the probability that an event will occur, figure out the probability that it will not occur and subtract that value from 1.

Suppose success depends on either the spade suit breaking 3-3 or the heart suit breaking 2-1.

Now it would be incorrect to just add together the chance of each. These two events are *not* mutually exclusive. It is possible for both events to occur simultaneously on a hand. For this example, there is an obvious warning that it would not be correct to simply add 0.36 and 0.78 − the sum would be greater than 1. This is an impossible value for any probability. In the next section we will complete this example.

For approximation purposes, when dealing with events that have an extremely small probability of occurring, we can ignore the fact that they are not mutually exclusive and just add their respective probabilities. This is a form of mathematically pretending – it is not really kosher. I did this on page 28 when I obtained the probability of a nine-card suit in a 24-board session of bridge. I ignored the issue that a player can have more than one nine-card suit in the session. I just indicated that one can merely add together the probability of a nine-card suit on each hand.

Multiplying Probabilities

We can often multiply probabilities to find out the probability of two events both occurring. One must realize that the occurrence of one event may affect the probability that the second event will occur. We previously found that if you chose one card from a deck, P(ace) = 4/52. When two cards are drawn from a deck, it is essential to consider whether the first card is returned and the deck is reshuffled before the second card is drawn. If so, the probability of both being aces is 4/52 x 4/52 = 0.0059.

If you select two cards from the deck without returning the first card, the probability that they are both aces *cannot* be obtained by multiplying 4/52 x 4/52. In order for both cards to be aces, the first card chosen must be an ace, so when the second is chosen, there are only fifty-one cards left and only three of them are aces.

Therefore, P(both aces, without replacement) = 4/52 x 3/51
= 0.0045.

If someone poses a problem that involves drawing two cards, without specifying that the first card is returned to the deck, the second interpretation would most likely be appropriate. Even when two cards are drawn simultaneously, when the cards' suits and ranks are observed, one card will be identified before the other. So, it is equivalent to one card being drawn first and then a second card being drawn.

Consider a bridge hand. Whether you politely wait to be dealt all thirteen cards or impolitely examine each card as it is dealt, the hand will not change.

In Chapter 5, the section 'Law of Large Numbers' described an experiment where cards were drawn and then returned to the deck. In the context of bridge, playing cards are not returned to the deck until the next hand. That important distinction is much more general than just experiments with drawing playing cards. In the fields of probability and statistics, often an experiment is described as either 'with replacement' or 'without replacement'.

It is common to define two events as 'independent events' if the occurrence of one event does not alter the probability of the other event. When we draw two cards with replacement, the probability of the second card being an ace is not altered by whether or not the first card was an ace. If we are drawing without replacement, we have to consider whether or not the first card was an ace. Without replacement, if the first card was an ace, the probability of the second card also being an ace is 3/51. If the first card was not an ace, the probability of the second card being an ace is 4/51.

Independent events are often simply two unrelated events — such as rolling a 3 when rolling a die and drawing a heart from a deck of fifty-two cards. Obviously, the outcome of either does not alter the likelihood of the other. So, the probability of both occurring is 1/6 x 1/4 = 1/24.

You are declarer (South) and your dummy (North) has just hit the table. Ignore the opening lead. You are missing the ♠K. What is the probability that West has the king?

There are twenty-six missing cards held by the defenders, and West has thirteen of them. The king can be any of those twenty-six cards.

P(West was dealt spade king) = 13/26 = 1/2

It is tempting to believe that this value changes if you observe the opening lead since West only has twelve missing cards. Actually, this reasoning, which seems logical, is incorrect because the opening lead is not chosen at random (remember the Monty Hall Problem, page 72). Suppose the defense never bids, and holds no spade honors except the king. The ♠K would virtually never be led. Therefore, when the ♠K is not led, you have not learned anything. Well, maybe something, but not that much.

What is the probability that West was dealt both the ♠K and the ♡K?

P(West has spade and heart kings) = 13/26 x 12/25 = 0.24

This example shows another application of the Vacant Place Principle that was introduced in Chapter 5. The 12/25 results from that principle. If West holds the ♠K, he has only 12 vacant places out of the remaining 25 to hold the ♡K.

At the bridge table, declarer should simplify this calculation by treating this as 1/2 x 1/2 = 1/4.

If you have to finesse West for both kings your chance of being successful both times is approximately 1/4.

Declarer has an eight-card trump fit. The only honor that the defense holds in that suit is the queen. What is the probability of either defender holding queen doubleton?

This can only happen when the suit splits 3-2. P(3-2 split) = 0.68 from a table in Chapter 4. In addition to this split occurring, the queen must be in the two-card suit rather than the three-card suit. P(queen in the two card suit) = 2/5. It must be in two of the five vacant places in the suit.

P(3-2 split with queen doubleton) = 0.68 x 2/5 = 0.27

Same as last question except with specifically West holding queen doubleton.

P(3-2 split with West holding queen doubleton)
= 0.68 x 2/5 x 1/2 = 0.135

Declarer has an eight-card trump fit. What is the probability of either defender holding queen-jack doubleton?

P(3-2 split with queen-jack doubleton) = 0.68 x 2/5 x 1/4 = 0.068

The queen can be in either of the two places in the two-card suit and then the jack must be in the one empty location in the two-card suit. On page 70, we had crudely estimated this value by considering all thirty-two possible splits for the five cards. With that method we obtained 0.0625. That value was less accurate but easier to obtain.

What is the probability that spades split 3-3 and hearts split 2-1?

P(spades 3-3 and hearts 2-1) = P(spades 3-3) x P(hearts 2-1)
= 0.36 x 0.78 = 0.28

I admit that the splits of the two suits are not really independent. But the two balanced splits are 'close enough' to being independent, so please pretend that they are independent. I am even willing to assume independent events for the following two events.

What is the probability that spades do not split 3-3 but hearts split 2-1?

P(spades not 3-3 but hearts 2-1)
= P(spades not 3-3) x P(hearts 2-1) = 0.64 x 0.78 = 0.50

Remember the example, at the end of the last section, where the declarer will be successful if either the spade suit splits 3-3 or hearts 2-1? Now we have the tools to complete it. These two events are not mutually exclusive so:

P(spades 3-3 or hearts 2-1)
= P(spades 3-3) + P(spades not 3-3 but hearts 2-1)
= 0.36 + (0.64 x 0.78) = 0.86

In a suit, declarer (South) has the singleton 4 while dummy holds AKJ532. What is the probability of taking six tricks?

The only line of play that can succeed is to finesse against the queen. This will only succeed when both the suit splits 3-3 and West holds the queen.

P(3-3 split) = 0.36 from a table in Chapter 4.
P(West holds the queen) = 3/6 = 1/2.
Therefore, P(3-3 split with West holding the queen)
= 0.36 x 1/2 = 0.18

Likelihood of Contract Success

In the last section we were looking at the arithmetic of combining different events. It is easy to reframe those questions into questions pertaining to the likelihood of a particular line of play resulting in declarer being successful.

Suppose declarer needs two finesses both to be successful to make his contract. Those two finesses may be in the same suit, such as AQ10 opposite xxx, or in two different suits. Declarer may be finessing through the same defender twice or each defender once. Of course, the example with AQ10 involves finessing the same defender twice. If declarer has no other information about the lie of the cards, the probability of both finesses succeeding is approximately $1/2$ x $1/2$ = $1/4$. It should be clear why I used the word approximately. In the last section, we saw the example of West being dealt both the ♠K and the ♡K. If a defender holds one of those honors, the vacant places principle indicates that the chances that he also holds the other honor drop slightly. For practical purposes at the bridge table, using the approximation of $1/4$ is fine. (In similar cases, I will usually drop the word 'approximate'.) If declarer had to take two finesses against different defenders, the chance of success would have been slightly better than $1/4$.

In order to prevail in a contract declarer needs three finesses all to succeed.

P(three successful finesses) = $1/2$ x $1/2$ x $1/2$ = $1/8$

In order to make a contract declarer needs at least one out of two finesses to succeed.

These two finesses are not mutually exclusive events since both finesses may win.

P(at least one out of two finesses succeed)
= P(first wins) + P(first loses but second wins)
= $1/2$ + ($1/2$ x $1/2$) = $3/4$

In order to make a contract, declarer needs both a finesse to succeed and a suit to split 3-2. It may be the same suit or two different suits.

P(finesse and 3-2 split) = 1/2 x 0.68 = 0.34

In order to make a contract declarer will need either a finesse to succeed or a suit to split 3-2. It may be the same suit or two different suits.

P(finesse or 3-2 split) = 1/2 + (1/2 x 0.68) = 0.84

These two events are not mutually exclusive. Again we add the chances of the finesse succeeding (1/2) and the finesse losing but the suit splitting 3-2 (0.34).

The last two examples are similar. As expected, when you need either of two events to occur your probability of success is much greater than if you need both events to occur.

In order to make a contract, declarer will need at least one out of three finesses to succeed.

These three events are not mutually exclusive. The prior technique for two events that are not mutually exclusive cannot be extended to three events in an intuitive fashion.

The following alternative approach is easier:

P(all three finesses fail) = 1/2 x 1/2 x 1/2 = 1/8

Since if they don't all fail, at least one must succeed, then,

P(at least one of the three finesses succeeds) = 1 − 1/8 = 7/8

In order to make a contract, declarer will need at least two out of the three finesses to succeed.

P(at least two of the three finesses succeed) = 1/2. This event will occur whenever you win the majority of the finesses. One is equally likely to win the majority as to lose the majority.

Suppose you are playing two days in a Regional pairs event. You magically know that your four sessions will involve two sessions where you score exactly 60% and two sessions where you have exactly 50%. You hope the two 60% sessions occur on the same day, guaranteeing you to finish very high in the overalls for that day. You could even win with a great deal of luck. What is the probability of having the two big sessions on the same day?

Break it into two cases. Assume a 60% game on first day, first session. The probability that the second session that day is also 60% is only 1/3. Now assume a 50% game on first day, first session. Now you would need the second session on that first day to also be 50% (probability 1/3), so that the second day will have the two 60% sessions.

Since it is as equally likely on the first day for the first session to be 60% as it is to be 50%:

P(two 60% games same day) = P(two 60% first day) + P(two 60% second day) = 1/2 x 1/3 + 1/2 x 1/3 = 1/6 + 1/6 = 1/3

An alternative approach would be to list all possibilities. The six equally likely order of results are:

60% 60% 50% 50%
60% 50% 60% 50%
60% 50% 50% 60%
50% 60% 60% 50%
50% 60% 50% 60%
50% 50% 60% 60%

The first and the sixth lines would achieve the goal. Of course, we are assuming the results are independent, and this is really not the case when dealing with human performance. After a big first session, some players will concentrate more and are more likely to have a big second session, while others will feel pressure to produce and are less likely to have a big second session.

Using and Abusing the Tables

Don't forget the Hideous Hog's disdain for probability. The values provided by the tables and computed probability values are only accurate when declarer lacks any useful information about how any of the other suits are splitting. This usually is not the case, since any bidding by the defense or the opening lead often reveals at least a smidgen of information. As already mentioned, if the defense only passed throughout the auction with approximately half the points, all of the suits are probably breaking more evenly than indicated by the tables.

Presently, the tables in Chapter 4 only help declarer learn how likely he is to get a specific split rather than guiding him on how to play a suit. In Chapters 8 and 9 we'll explore how to use probability to decide how to play a suit and calculate the chance of success of a line of play. Chapter 10 contains full deal examples where the winning line results from not being distracted by probabilities. That chapter is dedicated to the Hideous Hog.

Chapter 8

Deciding How to Play a Suit

Is this chapter useful? Why?

Usefulness number: 10. While playing a bridge hand, one must often choose between alternative ways of playing a particular suit. At the point when a decision has to be made, it is obviously essential to consider all the information known about the entire hand.

Suit Combinations

The ACBL Official Encyclopedia 7th ed. has fifty pages under the entry 'Suit Combinations'. It describes the best line (often lines) of play for 656 different suit combinations. Certainly the longest entry in the Encyclopedia, but I fear it is greatly ignored by bridge players. I find it very clear and logically organized, but one does have to become familiar with how to use it. And it is not necessary to purchase the latest edition — the Suit Combination entry is a carryover from the original edition of the ACBL Encyclopedia published in 1964 with the same 656 suit combinations.

Common Question Alert

What is the chance of taking four tricks in this suit by playing the three top winners rather than finessing?

Dummy

A 10 4 2

■━━━━━━━■

Declarer

K Q 3

The suit in this example provokes many questions. Usually, the player asking the question states that he knows that there is only a 36% chance that a suit splits 3-3, and that finessing against the jack has a 50% chance of success, but he is not comfortable with the seemingly obvious conclusion from these facts.

If three top cards are played, there are three ways declarer will take four tricks.
1) When the suit splits 3-3.
2) When it splits 4-2 with a doubleton jack.
3) When it splits 5-1 with a singleton jack.

No two of these three possibilities can occur at the same time so the probability of each can be obtained separately and then those three values can be added together.
1) P(3-3 split) = 0.36 using the appropriate table.
2) P(4-2 split, doubleton jack) = P(4-2 split) x P(doubleton jack) = 0.48 x 2/6 = 0.16 The jack can be in any of six locations, but only two of six locations are in the doubleton.
3) P(5-1 split, singleton jack) = P(5-1 split) x P(singleton jack) = 0.15 x 1/6 = 0.02 The jack can be in any of six locations, but only one of them is in the singleton.

P(taking four tricks by playing three top) = 0.36 + 0.16 + 0.02 = 0.54

Tricky Confusing Issue Alert

You probably checked out the Encyclopedia (this suit appears as suit combination number 30) and found out that when playing the three top cards the success rate for four tricks is 61%, not 54%. Is the Encyclopedia wrong? Am I wrong? Very troubling! Don't worry. The Encyclopedia is correct and even more importantly for me, I am also correct. We actually are solving two different problems. I approached it literally, that is, always playing the three top winners, but the Encyclopedia approached it like a bridge player. Declarer's intent was to play for the drop and not finesse. Of course, if declarer has a marked finesse, he will take it. He is no fool. There is approximately an 8% chance that East will show out on the first or second round, and then we can finesse. Since we already counted the particular holding of West having five spot cards and East a singleton jack and we don't want to count it twice, there is a net increase of 7%. Therefore, the chance of taking four tricks is 0.54 + 0.07 = 0.61.

Now let's consider how to play this suit in real life. There is a choice between playing for the jack to drop and finessing the ten. Declarer should obviously first cash the king and queen. If either opponent shows out the decision will disappear. Either you have a marked finesse (if East shows out) or you will learn that you are limited to only three tricks in this suit (if West shows out). Similarly, if the jack drops, you have four tricks.

After the first two tricks, if both defenders have followed with spot cards, it is clear that our original table for six missing cards is no longer appropriate. The splits of 6-0 or 5-1 are not possible. Likewise, the 4-2 split with a doubleton jack is not possible. All splits that are still possible have become more probable.

On the third round, declarer leads the three. If West shows out or plays the jack, declarer does not face a decision. However, if West plays a spot card, declarer finally does have to choose between playing for the drop or finessing. This will be referred to as the *point of decision*. There are only two possibilities: either West started with Jxxx and East with xx or West with xxx and East with Jxx. Prior to playing any cards in this suit, the chance of the first holding was 0.16 and the second holding was 0.18. Since they add up to 0.34, 66% of the time declarer will not have to face this decision. Well, what if declarer does actually face this decision?

The mathematician in my head would say that since the second holding is slightly more likely than the first, you should play for that one. At the point of decision, the probability of the second holding is slightly over 50%. However, the bridge player in my head is shouting 'Ignore the mathematician, he doesn't know much about bridge'. The bridge player makes a good point. The closer a decision actually is, the more a declarer should search for bridge information that will help. Remember that probabilities can only offer advice to declarer. Declarer should try to delay playing on this suit till as late as possible. At that time, he may have a full count of the hand, or at least a partial count. In Chapter 10, declarer faces this very decision with a complete count. The bridge player in my brain should make this decision while the mathematician should sit quietly in the corner.

It is useful for one's intuition to list all possible West–East holdings. For this example, with six cards held by the defense, the list would have 2 x 2 x 2 x 2 x 2 x 2 = 64 items. Too much work to list them. Just above, I used the split West Jxxx –East xx. If I had indicated this split with specific spot cards, there would have been ten entries. Likewise, the split, West xxx–East Jxx would also have involved ten of the 64 entries if specific cards were indicated. But remember the 64 options are almost equally likely, but not exactly equally likely. The second group of ten options is slightly more likely than the first group. Earlier, I gave the values 16% and 18%. Actually, more accurate values, computed from a table in Appendix 1, yield the even closer values – 16.15% to 17.76%.

It is important to consider similar suits that should be played in the same way and also suits that look very similar but that declarer should play in a different way.

For the following examples, assume that the other suits provide all necessary entries.

What is the chance of taking four tricks in this suit by playing the three top winners rather than finessing?

Dummy

A K Q 10

Declarer

4 3 2

This suit is identical to the previous example. The mathematical analysis is still correct.

What is the chance of taking four tricks in this suit by playing the three top winners rather than finessing?

Dummy

A 4 3 2

Declarer

K Q 10

The probability of either the suit splitting 3-3 or dropping the jack is still 54% as in the previous two examples. The chance during the actual play of taking four tricks, however, is slightly poorer than those examples. With this holding, declarer will have to decide whether he wants to finesse or not on the second round. Declarer can cash the king, enter dummy and lead low toward the Q10. Since the point of decision is on the second round rather than the third, he will only have a marked finesse if West shows out on the first round. Declarer can still try to gain information from other suits but is limited by the earlier point of decision. The probability of taking four tricks only increases by 1% to 55%. With the point of decision on the second round, the chance of success was reduced.

What is the chance of winning four tricks in this suit by playing the three top winners rather than finessing?

Dummy

A K 3 2

Declarer

Q 10 4

This is identical to the last example where the point of decision was on the second round.

What is the chance of taking four tricks in this suit by playing the three top winners rather than finessing?

Dummy

A K Q 10

Declarer

3 2

Having only six cards in the suit substantially reduces declarer's prospects of dropping the jack.

P(4-3 split, jack third) = P(4-3 split) × P(jack third) = 0.62 × 3/7 = 0.27

P(5-2 split, jack doubleton) = P(5-2 split) × P(jack doubleton)
= 0.31 × 2/7 = 0.09

P(6-1 split, jack singleton) = P(6-1 split) × P(jack singleton)
= 0.07 × 1/7 = 0.01

These three potential opportunities to drop the jack only total 0.37. The chance that East shows out on the first round is less than 1%. Therefore, declarer should clearly finesse on the second round unless some strong bridge information indicates otherwise.

What is the chance of taking five tricks in this suit by playing the two top winners rather than finessing?

Dummy

A J 9 5

Declarer

K 10 8 7 6

There are two ways to take five tricks without finessing: if the suit splits 2-2 or if it splits 3-1 with a singleton queen. Since these two events are mutually exclusive, their probabilities can be obtained separately, and the two values can be added.

P(2-2 split) = 0.40

P(3-1 split, singleton queen) = P(3-1 split) x P(singleton queen)
= 0.50 x 1/4 = 0.125

P(taking five tricks by playing the ace and king) = 0.40 + 0.125
= 0.525

Now let's consider the actual play. Suppose you start with the ace. If East shows out on the first round, you will unfortunately learn that you must lose to the queen. If West shows out, you have a marked finesse for the queen and will take five tricks. Obviously, declarer should consider the expected length of both defenders in this suit. If declarer has any reason to expect East to be longer than West, the ace should be cashed first, but if there is any reason to suspect West to be longer, cash the king first. It would be nice to delay playing this suit to get a partial or full count on the hand. Unfortunately, nine-card suits, particularly in a major, tend to be trump suits so declarer will probably choose to make the decision in this suit early in the hand.

Suppose both defenders play a low card on the first round. After winning that trick with the ace, you lead a card from dummy; suppose East follows with a low card. Now you face the point of decision. There are only two possibilities: West started with Qx and East xx, or West started with x and East Qxx. The mathematician in my brain would say that the first possibility is slightly more likely than the second. You have seen every card in this suit except the queen. East has already played a card on this trick but West has not. Therefore, West is slightly more likely to hold the queen, since at the point of decision West has one more card in his hand than East.

Of course, the bridge player in my brain would say 'Hold on a minute. The probability of success for either line of play is extremely close. Is there any information from the defender's bids, opening lead or play that would indicate how the other suits are breaking?' If there is some good reason to believe that West is longer than East in other suits, declarer has no advantage in playing for the drop on the second round. If your inferences are correct, you should take the finesse.

I mentioned earlier that a nine-card fit tends to be the chosen trump suit. Sometimes the bidding would encourage a trump lead – for example, if declarer has shown a two-suited hand. Now, if the opening lead is not a trump, there is some slight evidence that the leader holds the queen.

The chance of success if declarer lacks any useful information and sets out to play for the drop is 57.5%. When the ace was played on the first round, declarer gained the 5% chance of West showing out, thereby enabling declarer to have a marked finesse. Of course, if East shows out, the situation is hopeless. Declarer will be annoyed with not having played the king on the first round.

One may wish to look at all possible West-East holdings. On page 64, this exact suit is studied, and the sixteen possibilities are listed. That list includes all distributions when using specific spot cards. The point of decision takes place half way through the second round. At that point, when East follows with a spot card, there are only the following six remaining possibilities:

West	East
Q 4	3 2
Q 3	4 2
Q 2	4 3
4	Q 3 2
3	Q 4 2
2	Q 4 3

With the first three possibilities, declarer should play for the drop. With the last three, one should finesse the queen. It looks like a 3-3 tie. *Almost.* Remember those 16 possibilities are not exactly equally likely. The last three are slightly less likely than the first three.

A well-known maxim to guide declarers is 'eight ever, nine never'. In the first chapter, I mentioned its catchy name but provided no description. It implies that missing the queen, declarer should finesse with an eight-card fit, but play for the drop with a nine-card fit. Since this example involves a nine-card fit the maxim says to play for the drop. We have seen, however, that declarer faces a very close decision. There is only a slight advantage and if declarer can draw some inference, he may realize that it is better to finesse. Therefore, the word *never* in the maxim is clearly not correct. *Never* should really be replaced by 'probably not, but a close decision'. Unfortunately, 'eight ever, nine probably not, but a close decision' does not have the nice memorable ring of 'eight ever, nine never'.

Suppose the jack and king are switched in the previous example.

Dummy
A K 9 5

Declarer
J 10 8 7 6

Now there are only two options: playing for the drop or finessing West. Declarer can no longer finesse East. Assuming there is no information prior to playing this suit and that South has an outside entry, declarer should play a top honor to see whether the queen drops, or either defender shows out. The mathematics behind whether declarer should finesse or not is identical to the last example: it slightly favors not finessing. Remember *eight ever, nine probably not, but a close decision.*

It goes against one's intuition to accept that two options are just as good as three options. Suppose you are buying a new car. With extensive research, three models seem equally desirable. As you approach your decision date, you learn that one of the models is no longer available. This does not mean that you will be less happy with your final purchase, only that the decision may be a little simpler.

The standard maxim correctly indicates that the percentage play is to finesse with an eight-card suit. For some suit combinations declarer should finesse on the first round, for others on the second.

How should declarer play this suit to take six tricks?

Dummy

A K J 10 5 4

Declarer

3 2

Declarer should finesse on the first round so that a winning finesse can be repeated. This play is necessary when West holds Qxxx. The probability of that holding is 0.28 x 4/5 x 1/2 = 0.11 (0.28 from table, 4/5 from queen in four-card suit, 1/2 from West rather than East holding Qxxx). Unfortunately, finessing on the first round will result in unnecessarily losing a trick when East holds queen single-ton. Quite embarrassing, particularly to a declarer who is new to the game. The probability of that holding, however, is only 0.28 x 1/5 x 1/2 = 0.03.

How should declarer play this suit to take five tricks?

Dummy

A K J 10 5

Declarer

4 3 2

Declarer should first play a top card, in case East has a singleton queen. Declarer's three-card suit gives him the luxury of still being able to finesse twice, on the second and third rounds. So why not try to drop the singleton and receive the adulation of your partner and opponents?

Chapter 9

Percentage Plays

Is this chapter useful? Why?

Usefulness number: 9. This chapter provides additional important information on how to play suits. Questions involving percentage plays are often not well-posed; it usually is necessary to specify a goal. We will see that, at times, a declarer should make a point of avoiding the percentage play.

Setting a Goal

Until this chapter, I have avoided using the expression *percentage play*. It is often used loosely to mean the best play based on probability. But one must also consider the goal of declarer. It is tempting to feel that declarer's goal is simple —taking as many tricks as possible. Not always[†††]! In all examples, assume that you have all the entries that you could possibly wish for.

Let's suppose you and your partner are the club's great overbidders, and you have got to a small slam in notrump. When dummy appears, you realize that no one else will go to slam. The good news is that you will make the contract if you can take five tricks in this rather ordinary-looking diamond suit.

Dummy

A Q 7 5 3 2

▭

Declarer

8 6 4

[†††] A recent book by Gitelman and Rubens, *Playing Suit Contracts* (see Bibliography), contains sixty-six exercises on the correct play for different suit combinations. In this book, a goal of taking a specified number of tricks is included for every exercise.

Here you want to know the percentage play (the line with the maximum chance) to take five or more tricks. If you needed to take six tricks in this suit, you would want to know the percentage play to take six tricks. Consider the following two options: 1) on the first trick of this suit play small to the ace and later play small to the queen 2) on the first trick, play small to the queen. Let's list all sixteen possibilities.

Holdings		Tricks won	
West	**East**	**1st trick play to the ace**	**1st trick play to the queen**
K J 10 9	—	4	4
K J 10	9	5	5
K J 9	10	5	5
K 10 9	J	5	5
J 10 9	K	5	4
K J	10 9	5	6
K 10	J 9	5	6
K 9	J 10	5	6
J 10	K 9	5	5
J 9	K 10	5	5
10 9	K J	5	5
K	J 10 9	5	5*
J	K 10 9	4	4
10	K J 9	4	4
9	K J 10	4	4
—	K J 10 9	3	3

There are sixteen lines in the table, as expected. Each of the four cards can be in either West's hand or East's. For readability, extra space was provided before the 6th line and the 12th line. They are natural break points since, in the first five lines, West has more cards in the suit than East; in the middle six lines both defenders have the same; in the last five lines, East has more cards in the suit than West. This line spacing makes numbering all lines less important. The asterisk on line 12 indicates an anomaly. Declarer had every intention of playing the queen on the first trick, but upon seeing West reluctantly play the king, declarer will naturally play the ace. Declarer can also simply play a spot card – either way he will take five tricks.

Similar to previous examples, the sixteen possibilities are not equally likely to occur but they are *almost* equally likely. In twelve of the cases, the number of tricks won by the two lines of play is identical. In eleven cases, declarer takes five or more tricks by playing to the ace. In only ten cases, declarer takes five or more tricks by playing to the queen. So, if the goal is to take five or more tricks, the percentage play is to play to the ace on the first round. The probability of success is $11/16 = 0.6875$. Finessing on the first round only has a probability $10/16 = 0.625$ of success. For more accuracy, we can use the tables in Chapter 4. Finessing on the first round will take five or more tricks whenever the suit either splits 2-2 (40% chance) or 3-1 with king being onside (50% x 1/2 = 25% chance). This totals 65%. If declarer does not finesse on the first round, a singleton king in the East hand may be dropped, with a slight increase of 50% x 1/8 = 0.0625. Now the total yields the approximation of 71.25%. The Encyclopedia (suit combination #403) indicates 72% because it is using even more accurate values, which appear in the tables of our Appendix 1.

You may be tempted to combine some cases – for example, Lines 2 through 4 are identical from a bridge point of view. But if you combine the three situations into one line, the table will convey less information about likelihood.

If we change the goal to taking all six tricks, we clearly must finesse on the first round. On three of the 16 lines, declarer will take six tricks. So, the chance of success is $3/16 = 0.1875$, or, using the table, 40% x 1/2 = 20%. Quite close! We don't have to concern ourselves with playing up to the ace on the first trick, since it would be impossible to take six tricks by doing that.

If we change the goal to taking as many tricks as possible, the list demonstrates that in three cases declarer gains a trick by finessing on the first round but loses a trick only in one case. So, a slight gain by finessing, but only slight. The Encyclopedia refers to this as the 'Max'.

Let's slightly alter this suit by removing a card from declarer:

Dummy

A Q 7 5 3 2

Declarer

6 4

A player would never set a goal of taking six tricks here unless he was delusional. It cannot be done. A reasonable goal is five tricks. Another reasonable goal is four or more.

With five cards held by the defense, a full listing would involve 2 x 2 x 2 x 2 x 2 = 32 possibilities. With only 16, we were able to list them easily. With 32, it is often desirable to consider just some of the more interesting cases. Surprisingly, in none of the 32 cases does declarer take an extra trick by finessing on the first round. But there is one case where playing to the ace on the first trick gains: when West holds J1098, and East a singleton king. But that play only enables declarer to take four tricks, not five, while playing the queen on the first round results in only three tricks.

Therefore, if the goal is to take five tricks, it is a tie. With either method, declarer will take five tricks when the suit splits 3-2, and the king is onside:

P(3-2 split and king onside) = 0.68 x 1/2 = 0.34

Suppose the goal is to take four or more. If we play the ace first,

P(four or more) = P(3-2 split) or P(4-1 and king onside) or
P(4-1 and singleton king offside) = 0.68 + 0.14 + 0.03 = 0.85.

Many players would automatically play to the queen on the first round, but that would only have a 0.82 chance of taking four or more tricks. So playing the ace on the first round provides the most tricks on the average.

At times, it is more natural to frame the goal in terms of losing no more than a specified number of tricks, rather than in terms of taking them. Sometimes the suit combination may require declarer to face a different problem when choosing between two lines of play. For example, one line gives a chance of escaping with no losers but may result in two losers, whereas the alternative line will always result in one loser – rather like a double or nothing situation on a TV game show. You can either take one loser, or go for none but risk two.

In notrump the goal may be to give up the lead only once, since if you give up the lead twice the defense can grab enough tricks to set the contract. It will be unimportant how many winners you have set up if you end up painfully discarding some of them.

In a suit contract, success may depend on being able to draw trumps with only one loser. Suppose the suit in the following example is the trump suit in a small slam.

Dummy
A 9 8 5 2

▭

Declarer
Q 10 7 6 3

It is possible, and more importantly, easy, to look at the eight possibilities:

West	East
K J 4	—
K J	4
K 4	J
J 4	K
K	J 4
J	K 4
4	K J
—	K J 4

We see that if the ace is played on the first round, declarer will not lose any tricks in this suit whenever either defender holds the singleton king.

For the present discussion, it is useful to view all possibilities. In the next few paragraphs, the values obtained for probabilities come from our familiar tables rather than from these eight almost equally likely outcomes.

P(2-1 split, singleton king) = P(2-1 split) x P(singleton king)
= 0.78 x 1/3 = 0.26

This is the good news. The bad news is that declarer will lose two tricks when West started with all three cards in the suit. That probability is 0.22 x 1/2 = 0.11.

Even though declarer must make the crucial decision on the first round of this suit, the point of decision can be slightly delayed by playing a low card toward the ace. If West plays the king, it is certainly a singleton, so when declarer plays the ace, he loses no tricks in this suit. If West plays the jack, declarer should win the trick with the ace. He will lose one trick, but no more than one in this suit. If West shows out, declarer can win the trick with the ace and play low to the queen, resulting in one loser. Only when West plays the four will declarer face a problem.

Declarer is now at the point of decision. If he goes up with the ace, he will have no losers if East drops a singleton king, but he faces two losers, and an unwanted lesson on safety plays from his partner, if West was dealt all three missing cards. If, however, declarer plays the nine, he can never lose more than one trick. Even though declarer knows that West did not start with the singleton king, the chance that East holds a singleton king has risen from 13% to 26%. Since West played the missing spot card, East can no longer hold all three missing cards, but the chance that West has them has risen from 11% to 22%.

This is a decision that must be made by a bridge player and not a mathematician. Using any form of scoring other than matchpoints, declarer should be guided by the requirements of making the contract. At matchpoints, however, declarer may wish to jeopardize a cold contract for an overtrick. The decision often involves considering what contracts the rest of the field may be playing in, and how successful declarer's play has been up to this point on this hand. For example, did the opening lead give declarer a trick or hurt him? In short, the mathematician should be viewed as a consultant, merely useful for providing a player with information.

This last example was phrased in such a way as to set up a goal in terms of losers rather than winners. Very often a goal can be viewed either way. The suit combinations in Chapter 8 all involved a maximum of one loser, so the goal was always to avoid having that one potential loser, or equivalently, take all the tricks in the suit. So, for all of the examples in that chapter, the best play from the probability point of view is simply the percentage play.

Purposely Avoiding the Percentage Play

Suppose you are playing a team event where you know your team is behind as you approach the end. You only care about winning the match, not the margin of defeat. Your only hope is a big swing board. You are pleased to get to a small slam but realize that it will probably be bid at the other table. The trump suit is the example at the bottom of page 94:

Dummy

A J 9 5

Declarer

K 10 8 7 6

After the three small cards have appeared, you realize that there is a slight advantage to playing for the drop (the percentage play). But the declarer at the other table will face the same problem, and he too will know that there is a slight advantage playing for a drop. But if you are both in slam and both take the percentage play, you will either both be successful or both fail – either way, no swing. If your premise is correct, take the finesse. It is not the percentage play, but it is almost as likely to be successful as the percentage play. This could be the needed swing board if indeed the finesse is successful. Of course, it could also make the walk back to your teammates much longer.

Bridge books and articles often describe a particular grand slam hand played in 1957 by Pedro Cabral that involved this type of play. Both teams reached the seven-level, one in notrump, the other in spades. Declarer and dummy each held a three-card heart suit and all honors except the queen. Prior to playing this suit, it was clear that West held more hearts than East. The declarer of the team losing the match badly purposely played East for the queen, and his dream of generating a big swing board was realized. At that time total scores were usually used in team events, and this particular deal helped bring about the conversion to the modern International Match Point (IMP) scoring, which shrinks the size of a potential huge swing. The actual deal was recently described in *The Bridge World* (December 2018 editorial).

Chapter 10

Examples of Bridge Overriding Probability

Is this chapter useful? Why?

Usefulness number: 9. This chapter contains several examples of full deals that demonstrate situations where declarer can easily go wrong by using the probability tool. At times, figuring out the probability of alternative lines can be a terrible distraction at the bridge table. The Hideous Hog would enjoy the philosophy of this chapter but would roll his eyes at the straightforward examples. The hands are certainly not sophisticated enough for the Hog.

Examples and Where to Find More

My goal in this book is to make readers comfortable with the underlying probability of bridge situations so that it can be helpful to them. With this goal (dream) of making the probability concepts intuitive while producing a relatively short book, I have not provided a great many full deal examples. Many bridge books have been written in which probability is used to analyze many hands. I would recommend the following authors who are particularly good at providing hand examples: Kantar, Reese, Kelsey, Vivaldi, MacKinnon and Rubens (see Bibliography).

The Kantar and Reese books are small books that contain primarily full deal examples related to bridge probability. The other books provide examples, but delve into probability more heavily.

In the previous chapter, I mentioned the recent book by Gitelman and Rubens (see Bibliography). It is very good for individual suits but it does not contain any full deals.

Examples of the Probability Distraction

I have tried to stress that, at the table, it is a mistake to rely on probability to the exclusion of bridge knowledge. Let's look at some examples.

```
                 ♠ A Q 7 5 3 2
                 ♡ 5 3
                 ◇ 9 6
                 ♣ K Q 2
  ♠ J 10 8                        ♠ K 9
  ♡ 8 7 4            N            ♡ A 10 9 6 2
  ◇ 10 7 4 3    W       E         ◇ A 5 2
  ♣ 9 8 3           S             ♣ J 10 5
                 ♠ 6 4
                 ♡ K Q J
                 ◇ K Q J 8
                 ♣ A 7 6 4
```

West	North	East	South
		1♡	1NT
pass	4♡*	pass	4♠
all pass			

West leads the ♡4. In order to make this contract declarer must hold his spade losers to one. The good news is that there are two ways to be successful. The bad news is that when we studied this very suit in the last chapter, we never considered either line of play. From East's opening bid and with North-South holding 27 points, declarer is certain that East holds the spade king. Certainly, then, there's no point in playing to the queen: that would be sending her to certain death. Declarer must hope that East holds the doubleton king. Assuming that situation, declarer can play the ace on the first round. On the second spade trick, declarer can lead the deuce from dummy and enjoy the pleasant sight of East's king landing on the table. Eventually, declarer can use the queen to pick up the remaining trump from West. Declarer needed specifically to find West with three spades and East with two. When considering that East has more hearts than West, it is quite likely that West has more spades than East.

It is tempting to feel that declarer would be pleased to see East's ♠K fall under the ace on the first round. That pleasure would be fleeting since it will still result in declarer losing two spade tricks.

An alternative line of play would be to play low from both hands on the first round of spades. On the second round of spades, declarer plays the ace and hopes to see the king drop so that the queen can pick up the remaining trump.

In summary, the bridge information gained from East's opening bid was the key to this hand. Bridge is a game with many distractions. All declarers realize that the bidding (even passes) must be remembered, but it's easier said than done. Before that information can be used by the declarer, he is also faced with figuring out all that can be learned from the opening lead. And if that isn't enough, within five seconds of seeing the opening lead the dummy appears. The bidding easily becomes old news. But you must retain and use all the information you have.

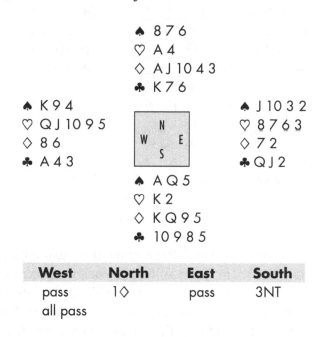

West	North	East	South
pass	1◇	pass	3NT
all pass			

West leads the ♡Q. Declarer has eight top tricks and can make a ninth with either the ♠Q or ♣K. Which finesse do you take? Both of course, with approximately a 75% chance of joy. Why did I include this obvious example? Probability tells you that the two finesses are equal, and can be taken in either order with the same chance of success. However, the two finesses are not equal in a bridge sense.

It is wrong just to take one at random, falling back on the other if it fails. If the spade finesse is taken first and loses, declarer's remaining heart stopper is driven out. If declarer then plays up to the ♣K, West can win with the ♣A and take three heart tricks, setting the contract even though the ♣K could have provided a ninth trick. If the club finesse is taken first, then even when it loses the spade finesse can still be tried. You may go down several tricks when both finesses lose — but that is life.

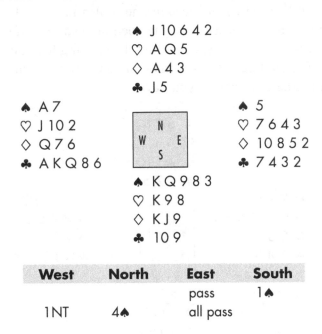

♠ J 10 6 4 2
♡ A Q 5
◇ A 4 3
♣ J 5

♠ A 7
♡ J 10 2
◇ Q 7 6
♣ A K Q 8 6

♠ 5
♡ 7 6 4 3
◇ 10 8 5 2
♣ 7 4 3 2

♠ K Q 9 8 3
♡ K 9 8
◇ K J 9
♣ 10 9

West	North	East	South
		pass	1♠
1NT	4♠	all pass	

West leads the ♣A, and the defense grabs their two club winners and shifts to a heart. The ♠A is still out, so declarer needs to avoid a diamond loser. If there had not been any bidding by the defense, the success of the contract would ride on a standard finesse in diamonds. Declarer would play the ace and then a low diamond to the jack, succeeding whenever East had the queen. *But that cannot possibly be the case!* West's overcall showed 15-18 HCP, so West almost certainly has the ◇Q. After drawing trumps, declarer should lead the ◇J, and let it ride if it is not covered. Feels strange, but you are confident that West holds the queen. If West covers, which he probably will, declarer can win with the ace and then play a diamond from dummy toward the king-nine, taking a finesse against the ◊10 with the ◊9.

This unusual way of playing the diamond suit is called a *backward finesse*. It requires two cards to be placed properly, the ◊Q with West and the ◊10 with East. Without any information about the defenders' holdings, the chance of success is only about 25%. On this hand, the bidding provided declarer with the information that the standard finesse had no chance of success, whereas the backward finesse had better than a 60% chance of success. The 1NT overcall placed most of the honor cards held by the defense in the West hand, so East holds the majority of the missing spot cards.

The defense was helpful by overcalling 1NT rather than 2♣. Many Wests might have chosen that bid, and then declarer would have had less information.

In summary, figuring out where cards are located is more satisfying than merely making quick guesses based on probability. And also, much more rewarding.

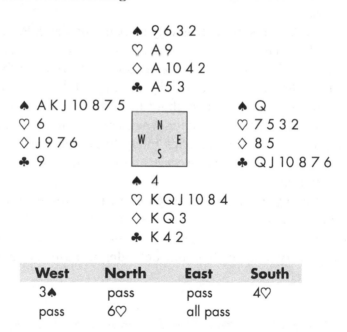

West	North	East	South
3♠	pass	pass	4♡
pass	6♡	all pass	

West starts with two top spades, and declarer ruffs the second round. The crux of this hand is to take four diamond tricks. How should diamonds be played? We know the percentage play, but there is more information to be had here.

When declarer trumped the second round of spades, he noted that East had showed out. This was not a surprise in light of West's bid, but it reaffirmed that West definitely started with seven spades and only six cards that were not spades. This is not good news for declarer. Since East's hand has twelve non-spade cards, it is very likely that it will not be possible for declarer to take four diamond tricks.

When declarer draws trumps, he learns that West started with one heart, so West has five cards in the minors. To aid the impending diamond decision, declarer can now play two rounds of clubs. West follows for only one round, so he must have exactly four diamonds, and on the third round the finesse will be guaranteed to succeed. Since declarer wins four diamond tricks, the slam succeeds. If West had followed for two rounds of clubs, West could have had at most three diamonds, so a finesse would have been pointless.

We studied this suit extensively back in Chapter 8. We saw that usually the decision will disappear before either alternative needs to be chosen. In this example, the decision as to whether to finesse or not has not disappeared. But by getting a full count of West's hand, all has become known about the diamond split, so declarer has total certainty when deciding whether or not to finesse. Declarer played clubs before diamonds solely to gain as much information as possible. The term *discovery play* is often used to describe such situations.

Probability is not needed when one can learn which defender has which cards. Notice that when declarer learns the shape of one defender, he learns the shape of both defenders. So usually it is best to just try to learn about one defender because his partner will have the 'leftovers'.

```
                    ♠ K Q 3
                    ♡ 7 5 3
                    ◇ J 9 6 2
                    ♣ 8 7 6
   ♠ 10 7                          ♠ J 9 2
   ♡ A K Q          ┌─────────┐    ♡ 10 9 6 2
   ◇ K Q 4 3        │   N     │    ◇ 10 8 7 5
   ♣ 9 4 3 2        │ W     E │    ♣ J 10
                    │   S     │
                    └─────────┘
                    ♠ A 8 6 5 4
                    ♡ J 8 4
                    ◇ A
                    ♣ A K Q 5
```

West	North	East	South
	pass	pass	1♠
pass	2♠	pass	4♠
all pass			

After taking three heart winners, West switched to the ◇K. Declarer can now draw trumps, and if spades are split 3-2 and clubs
are split 3-3 the contract succeeds. A theoretically better line is to
play just two rounds of spades, cashing the king and queen. Assuming the desired 3-2 trump split occurs, you then play the three
club winners. If they split 3-3 as hoped, declarer can then draw the
last trump and claim. The advantage of playing only the king and
queen occurs when a defender with four or more clubs also holds
the one remaining defensive trump. The defenders cannot prevent
declarer from ruffing the ♣5, returning to the South hand and finally drawing the last trump.

I realize that this line will not succeed with the above layout. West has four clubs while East is holding the one outstanding
trump card. East will ruff the third club winner. After East's ruff
sets the contract, the ♣5 can be ruffed in dummy. No real loss by
taking this line of play since if East's last trump is drawn before
declarer plays clubs, the ♣5 will be a loser. With this layout of the
cards, either way, down one. Declarer cannot be too surprised by
the result since if one defender is longer than his partner in a side

suit, his partner is more likely to be longer in trumps and therefore to hold the outstanding trump card. In Rubens' book, *Expert Bridge Simplified* (See Bibliography), Chapter 7 is titled 'Short-Shorts.' It studies the probability that a defender who is short in one specific suit will be short in a second specific suit.

An alternative line of play might be more likely to succeed, particularly against poor defenders. Those four clubs in the West hand are not nearly as impressive to West as the ◇Q. If declarer just cashes the five spade winners, West may well discard a club, and one club discard by West is all that declarer needs. This is not the best percentage play, but it may be quite successful at the table.

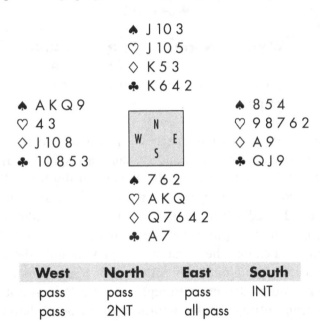

West	North	East	South
pass	pass	pass	INT
pass	2NT	all pass	

After the greedy defense grabs four spade tricks, West shifts to a club. Clearly, declarer must not lose more than one diamond trick. Not an easy goal to achieve – declarer needs a 3-2 split and the ace to be doubleton. If that isn't enough, declarer must make an intelligent guess as to which defender has ace-doubleton. Declarer is fortunate here because he knows that East holds the ◇A. After all, if West had that card along with his powerful spade holding, he would have opened the bidding. Therefore, declarer wins the club trick in dummy, and plays low to the ◊Q. When the queen wins, as expected, he leads toward dummy, and calls for a low card. On the above layout, he will see the ace reluctantly pop out of East's hand.

This play is called an *obligatory finesse*. When knowing the location of the ace, the chance of success is initially 0.68 x 2/5 = 0.27. If declarer has to guess which defender holds the ace, the chance of success is cut in half. But a small chance of success is much better than a zero chance of success.

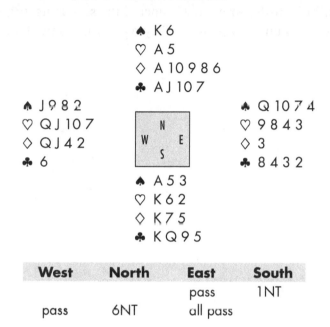

| ♠ K 6 |
| ♡ A 5 |
| ◊ A 10 9 8 6 |
| ♣ A J 10 7 |

♠ J 9 8 2   ♠ Q 10 7 4
♡ Q J 10 7   ♡ 9 8 4 3
◊ Q J 4 2   ◊ 3
♣ 6   ♣ 8 4 3 2

| ♠ A 5 3 |
| ♡ K 6 2 |
| ◊ K 7 5 |
| ♣ K Q 9 5 |

West	**North**	**East**	**South**
		pass	1NT
pass	6NT	all pass	

West leads the ♡Q, and declarer must take four tricks in diamonds. If the suit splits 3-2 or 4-1 with the singleton being an honor, declarer will be successful by just playing the two top honors. Therefore, P(success) = 0.68 + (0.28 x 2/5) = 0.79. Chances look very good, but the declarer can still improve on them. Declarer should decide which defender is more likely to hold four diamonds. If declarer plays four rounds of clubs, he will learn that East has more clubs than West, so West is the more likely defender to hold four diamonds. (Playing the clubs in order to gain information about how to play diamonds is another example of a discovery play.) Therefore, when playing diamonds, declarer should win with the king and then lead low toward dummy. If West follows low, declarer plays low from dummy. Even if this loses to an honor, the ace can pick up the other honor. In effect, once West followed low on the second round, declarer could guarantee that he would not lose more than one trick in the suit by playing a spot card from dummy.

I included this hand because it shows a common error. It is tempting to play the ace on the second round, and on this particular hand that would result in two losers. Usually declarer will not be punished for the wrong play, since if the suit splits 3-2, he will be unscathed. But why gamble? Playing low is a sure thing.

Chapter 11

Restricted Choice and Bayes' Theorem

Is this chapter useful? Why?

Usefulness number: 10. The very high level of usefulness is based on so many bridge players doubting the correctness of the Principle of Restricted Choice. I hope my explanation will remove any doubts — even when following the principle results in losing a trick unnecessarily.

(Most) Common Question Alert

The Principle of Restricted Choice does not work when I use it. Is it mathematically correct? Please convince me!

The answer is 'Yes'. Now I will try to convince you and then speculate why you need to be convinced. The explanation includes three Tricky Confusing Issue Alerts.

The Most Popular Example of Restricted Choice

Let us look at the classical model for Restricted Choice.

Dummy (North)

A 9 5 4

Declarer (South)

K 10 8 7 6

Suppose on the first round, Declarer leads the king, and East plays an honor, either the queen or the jack. When declarer plays a low card toward dummy, West also plays a low card. Now declarer faces a decision very similar to the example on page 94. Restricted Choice informs declarer that it is wise to finesse rather than lay down the ace. Assuming no other information is available, this decision will be the proper one with a probability of almost 2/3. Notice that this is a different choice from the decision on page 95 where the defense held the queen and three small spot cards. Restricted Choice violates the well-known maxim: *eight ever, nine never.* All very troubling.

Suppose on the first round West had been the defender to drop an honor, declarer would have suspected a singleton but would have had no way to take advantage of that information. He would have regretted not having played dummy's ace on the first round, after which he have been able to finesse against East.

Prior to the justification, I want to indicate that we must assume that East, when holding specifically the doubleton queen-jack, will play the jack half of the time and the queen half of the time. Don't be troubled! We will soon see the importance of this assumption and a justification for it.

Consider all sixteen possible holdings for the defense:

Line	West	East
1	Q J 3 2	—
2	Q J 3	2
3	Q J 2	3
4	Q 3 2	J
5	J 3 2	Q
6	Q J	3 2
7	Q 3	J 2
8	Q 2	J 3
9	J 3	Q 2
10	J 2	Q 3
11	3 2	Q J
12	Q	J 3 2
13	J	Q 3 2
14	3	Q J 2
15	2	Q J 3
16	—	Q J 3 2

This list should look very familiar. I'm sure it reminds you of the list on page 64. As with the earlier example, these sixteen outcomes are not equally likely, but they are close enough in likelihood that we can pretend that they are indeed equally likely.

Prior to the point of decision, an honor was played by East and two small cards were played by West, so most of the sixteen possibilities can be eliminated. The only remaining ones are line 4 where East has a singleton jack, line 5 where East has a singleton queen, and line 11 where East has the doubleton queen-jack. In two of these three possibilities, it would be correct to finesse, and in only one is declarer rewarded for playing for the drop. This agrees with the Principle of Restricted Choice.

First Tricky Confusing Issue Alert

A reader may think that the above argument sounds good but still find it disturbing because a specific honor can be observed by declarer. Suppose when the king is played, East plays the jack. Now, one can argue that there are only two possibilities since line 5 with the singleton queen is no longer a possibility.

Remember, though, we are assuming that from the doubleton queen-jack, the queen will be played roughly 50% of the time and the jack will be played roughly 50% of the time. But from the holding of the singleton jack, the jack will always be played. Therefore, when the jack is played by East, it is roughly twice as likely to come from the line 4 split than the line 11 situation. Again, we see that the finesse is the winning play approximately two out of three times.

Second Tricky Confusing Issue Alert

You may feel that the argument for Restricted Choice is dependent on assuming that a defender who holds doubleton queen-jack plays each of those cards with equal frequency. Does that mean that a sharp defender can defeat the Principle of Restricted Choice by always playing the jack when holding the doubleton queen-jack?

That reasoning is sort of correct, but we will see that the defender is very slightly worse off by using this particular technique. Imagine you sit down for the 64-board final of the Spingold Teams Championship. Suppose East brags that he has never been a victim of Restricted Choice when holding the doubleton queen-jack since he always plays the jack. He proves to be a man of his word. On the first 63 boards, you were always declarer and the exact declarer-dummy suit we are analyzing came up on all 63 hands; East held that doubleton on each board, and always played the jack — a miracle that only a book author can create. You are totally convinced that East is a man of his word and will always play the jack when holding the doubleton queen-jack. How is this knowledge useful to a declarer?

Let's consider what declarer has gained from this knowledge by considering the three holdings where an honor would be played. Suppose on Board 64 East plays the queen. Now declarer can be 100% certain that East does not hold the jack (or he would have played the jack). Declarer, of course, will take a winning finesse. But if declarer used Restricted Choice, he would have finessed in any case. So, either way the same play would be chosen. The only difference is that declarer's knowledge made the finesse certain to succeed rather than just likely to be successful. This means that, during the finesse, declarer's blood pressure will be lower. But since the finesse would have been taken either way, there is no gain in the result.

The bridge gain occurs when this predictable East plays the jack. East may indeed have the queen. So there are two possibilities — either queen-jack or singleton jack. Both possibilities are almost equally likely — but not quite. Actually, the situation is equivalent to the earlier example on page 95 where East held the queen and three spot cards. Just like that example, declarer should now play for the drop. The 2-2 split is slightly more likely than a singleton jack. In summary, East successfully interfered with the Principle of Restricted Choice but only when declarer has a slight gain by playing for the drop rather than finessing.

Similarly, if a defender always played the queen from doubleton queen-jack, declarer would know with 100% certainty that if the jack is played, it must be a singleton. Therefore, the queen is in his partner's hand, and the finesse is certain to win. But if the queen is played, declarer has a slight gain by avoiding the finesse and playing for the drop.

In short, if a defender holding the doubleton queen-jack is not known always to play a specific card, declarer should use restricted choice and will have a probability of success of slightly less than 2/3. If a defender is known always to play a specific card from that holding, declarer can do slightly better by finessing when one honor appears, while playing for the drop when the other honor appears. This will result in a success probability slightly better than 2/3. Since declarer's knowledge results in such a slight gain, a defender does not have to play each card 50% of the time – just vary enough not to be predictable.

Third Tricky Confusing Issue Alert

You may feel uncomfortable that this example is so similar to the one on page 94 but the conclusion is so different. Even more troubling is that the defense has two honors instead of one but seems less likely to take a trick.

In that earlier example, there were six possible holdings at the point of decision. In this example, the first-round drop of an honor card provided a great deal of useful information for declarer. After all, East would never willingly play that card. The bridge rules of following suit forced it out of the defender's fingers. Clearly, that defender was restricted in his choice of cards to play.

Don't feel sorry for declarer in the example on page 94. It is true that a more difficult decision was faced at the point of decision, but the declarer will often have the pleasure of seeing the queen appear prior to the point of decision. In that case, no problem.

The Principle of Restricted Choice is certainly not intuitive. This is all the more reason to acknowledge the wise players who first appreciated its importance and wrote about it. Its first appearance was in 1955 in Borel and Chéron's *Théorie mathématique du bridge...* (see Bibliography). This book, originally published in French, has thirty pages on Restricted Choice that include the underlying mathematics of Bayes' Theorem. The first book in English that covered the topic was *The Expert Game* (1958) by Terence Reese (published as *Master Play* in the USA). The presentation was only six pages long; it included several examples but barely touched on the mathematical underpinnings. Reese refers to articles by Alan Truscott in 1954 that studied problems where 'Restricted Choice thinking' was required. Who gets the credit? All of the above and many more. I will provide a more complete answer in my Afterword.

Bayes' Theorem

A more mathematical justification of the Principle of Restricted Choice involves Bayes' Theorem, named after Thomas Bayes, an early eighteenth-century mathematician. Let's look at the type of problem where Bayes' Theorem is helpful and then carry out the mathematics on a typical non-bridge example before moving on to Restricted Choice. In Chapter 17, on bidding decisions, we will see Bayes' Theorem applied to a third example.

Here's a typical example one would find in many probability textbooks. Suppose a manufacturing firm produces bidding boxes. They are produced by either Machine 1 or Machine 2. Machine 1 produces 40% of the boxes while Machine 2 produces 60%. Quality Assurance tells us that 10% of the boxes produced by Machine 1 are defective while only 5% produced by Machine 2 are defective. Suppose a random box is examined before it is shipped out, and it turns out to be defective. What is the probability it was produced by Machine 1?

Bayes' Theorem is useful for problems where the solver is provided with some *result* and then must obtain probabilities as to where an item was originally from. We can refer to that as the *source*. In this example, we can label the 'result' as the defective item, while the potential sources are the different machines.

The probability that a manufactured bidding box was produced by Machine 1 and is defective is 0.40 x 0.10 = 0.04. The probability that a manufactured bidding box was produced by Machine 2 and is defective is 0.60 x 0.05 = 0.03. Since all boxes are produced by either Machine 1 or 2, the probability of a defective box is 0.04 + 0.03 = 0.07.

Given that a bidding box is defective, the probability that it had been produced by Machine 1 is 0.04/0.07 = 4/7 = 0.5714.

Given that a bidding box is defective, the probability that it had been produced by Machine 2 is 0.03/0.07 = 3/7 = 0.4286.

Not surprisingly, these values add up to 1. So, in this case, if one probability is known, the other can easily be obtained by subtracting from 1. If there had been several possible sources (such as four machines that manufactured bidding boxes), the sum of their probabilities would, of course, add up to 1.

Now consider our example of Restricted Choice:

Dummy (North)
A 9 5 4

▭

Declarer (South)
K 10 8 7 6

Declarer leads the king, and East plays the jack. We can use the label 'result' as the jack appearing on the first round. The two potential sources of that result are East having been dealt either a singleton jack or the doubleton queen-jack. At the point of decision, the declarer must determine the probability that it was a singleton jack.

In summary, when a jack is played, what is the probability that it is a singleton?

In order to get a very precise answer, I will use the values found in the Appendix 1 table for four cards held by the defense. The eight possible 3-1 splits have a combined probability of 0.4974. The probability of a singleton jack in the East hand is 0.4974/8 = 0.0622. With a singleton jack, that card is certain to be played (probability is 1). There are six ways for the suit to split 2-2. The probability of doubleton queen-jack in the East hand is 0.4070/6 = 0.0678. We assume that, with this holding, a defender will play the jack 50% of the time. Therefore, the probability that East has been dealt a singleton jack and plays it is 0.0622 x 1 = 0.0622, while the probability that East was dealt the doubleton queen-jack and plays the jack is 0.0678 x 0.5 = 0.0339. Therefore, the probability of East playing the jack is 0.0622 + 0.0339 = 0.0961.

So, the probability that the finesse will be successful is 0.0622/0.0961 = 0.647.

As expected, almost two out of three times the finesse will be the correct decision.

These two examples demonstrate how to use Bayes' Theorem (Bayes' Formula). You probably were expecting a mathematical looking formula. I hid it in Appendix 2.

Bayes' Theorem is a powerful tool. Many situations are appropriate for using it. Several years ago, when I was being questioned as a potential juror, a lawyer pointed out that criminal cases are not mathematics, and that I should not expect to see an absolute proof of guilt. I felt compelled to point out that mathematics often involves reaching uncertain decisions. My free courtroom lesson was an attempt to explain how Bayes' Theorem would enable one to look at evidence and figure out the probability that the crime was committed by the defendant. The judge quickly shut me up, asked me to leave the courtroom and, the worst part, never let me complete my fine lesson. On my way out of the room, I heard the judge say, 'If any prospective jurors understood anything that the dismissed juror has just said, they are dismissed from the case.' None seemed to take that option, so now I really wanted to finish the lesson.

As I don't want to look like a jury dodger and thereby lose your respect, I must point out that I have served as a juror on many trials. I even recall the pain of being sequestered and being forced to call my bridge partner to cancel a game. Often the somewhat mathematical notion of 'reasonable doubt' would come up. It is hard to define reasonable doubt, so it is a common problem. I can recall one juror refusing to find a defendant guilty because of reasonable doubt. Fine, but this juror had a very odd definition. Based on the overwhelming evidence of guilt, the juror felt the defendant was definitely guilty. So obviously it was reasonable to doubt that the defendant could possibly be innocent. Therefore, the juror had reasonable doubt! That juror could not be swayed. My self-esteem as an educator took a temporary nosedive.

Missing the King and Queen

Let's compare two similar holdings:

Dummy (North)
A J 10

Declarer (South)
8 7 6

If declarer finesses twice in this suit, he will lose only one trick about 75% of the time (actually 76%). The only layout where declarer will lose two tricks is when East was dealt both the king and queen. If the first finesse loses, declarer's probability of losing just that one trick drops to below 70%. No longer could West have started with both honors. On the second round, if West does not produce the other missing honor, declarer should remain with the game plan and finesse again. Please note that I have never mentioned Restricted Choice. We did not need it. Taking both finesses was obvious.

Now we can turn our attention to the following suit.

Dummy (North)
A J 10 9 5

Declarer (South)
8 7 6 4

This nine-card suit, with the identical honors, has an element of evil temptation. Suppose on the first round, West plays low and East wins with an honor. Now on the second round, after West plays low, you begin to think. But thinking can be a mistake at the bridge table. The confusing thought results from the fact that only one card in the suit has not been played – the still unseen honor.

It seems that it could equally be held by either defender. Actually, it even seems that East is more likely to hold it since he has played one fewer card in the suit. You start sweating from the mental exertion. Relax! The Principle of Restricted Choice is at your service. West is almost twice as likely to hold that missing honor card. I understand it is embarrassing to lose to both the king and queen when they are doubleton, but it is good bridge!

On page 69, we listed all sixteen possible defense holdings with those four cards. After West follows with a low card on the second round, there are three possibilities. When East holds doubleton king-queen he is as likely to win with the king as the queen. If it is known or observed that East always plays the king from doubleton king-queen, then playing the queen would guarantee that he is not holding the king. Likewise, if East always plays the queen from that doubleton, playing the king would deny the queen. It is the same reasoning used in the earlier example of Restricted Choice, when declarer was missing the queen-jack. The ACBL Encyclopedia is a good source of many additional examples of Restricted Choice.

The Principle of Restricted Choice is correct, even though the second-round finesse will lose about one-third of the time. Please don't blame me. I am only the messenger.

Chapter 12
Game Theory and the Cheater's Dilemma

Is this chapter useful? Why?
Usefulness Number: For non-cheaters, 4. For cheaters, 9. You can see why I hope this chapter is rather useless for you.

The Subject and Terminology of Game Theory

Game Theory is a field of mathematics that covers both competing and cooperating situations. It is much broader than merely studying artificial game situations. Applications include the domains of economics, politics, warfare strategy, psychology and sociology. A short introductory book that shows its breadth of applications is *Game Theory: A Very Short Introduction* (2008) by Ken Binmore.

Since game theory creates a general structure for studying a broad range of applications, it was necessary to develop a universal vocabulary to describe games that involve both competing and cooperating situations. Much of its terminology has carried over to general usage, none more than the distinction between a *zero-sum game* and a *non-zero-sum game*. A game like poker is an excellent example of a zero-sum game. Suppose four players have an evening of poker. If one player wins $10, another wins $20, and one wins $30, clearly the fourth loses $60 since the wins and losses must add up to zero. Recently, many economists and politicians have pointed out that world economics is a non-zero-sum game: there are not just winners and losers as all countries can gain through cooperation. Game theory provides us with a structure for studying the element of a threat, such as a labor union threatening to call a strike or a country threatening to impose tariffs on another country.

In 1934, the American Bridge League (the ACBL did not exist until 1937) started issuing masterpoints. The masterpoint system converted a zero-sum game into a non-zero-sum game. Prior to that date, bridge was a big gambling game, like most card games. There were winners and losers. The losers lost money; the winners lost friends. But with the ingenious masterpoint system there were no actual losers. All that is lost by a bad session of bridge is an opportunity to be a winner. In *Bumblepuppy Days*, I described the masterpoint system as a trophy system rather than a rating system. The bridge world replaced the physical trophies with numerical values. The numerical trophies last even longer and require no dusting. Physical trophies in the standard form of a cup have the best possible shape to maximize their dust-collecting ability. In books and articles, I often refer to masterpoints as 'no-dust trophies.'

Let me describe a very simple game that is typical of many situations where game theory is applicable. When I was a child, we would play ball every afternoon. We would first have to pick the players on each team. Our method of selection involved playing a little contest, one that is often called the *odds and evens finger game*. The two best players would be designated as the captains. This had the desirable result that the two strongest players would be on opposing teams. So, every afternoon a ball game would start with the same two kids, the captains, playing the odds and evens finger game. Simultaneously, the captains of each team would put out either one or two fingers. One captain would win if the result was an even sum, the other, if an odd sum occurred. Therefore, if both captains put out one finger or if both captains put out two fingers, the even captain would win. If one captain put out one finger and the other two fingers, the odd captain would win. Both captains had a 50% chance of success. The winning captain had the first right to choose a teammate; after that, the captains would have alternate picks. The standard method for synchronizing the finger display is for both players to simultaneously say, 'One, two, three.' The fingers are exposed on 'three'. This simple game is almost exclusively played by children. The only time that I ever saw adults playing it was on an episode of *Seinfeld*. Whether Jerry and George are adults is, however, somewhat debatable. (You can see the contest on YouTube by searching for *Seinfeld*, Odds and Evens Finger Game.)

This odds and evens finger game involves outguessing your opponent. Typical of game theory! Your opponent will try to use your previous plays to infer whether you are more likely to put out one finger or two. In the above example, the same two captains would play the finger game every afternoon. It would obviously be foolish always to put out one finger because your opponent would know what you are going to play and could win every time. When the game theorist analyzes a game, it is always assumed that all players will exhibit rational (intelligent) behavior. Therefore, on repeated plays, a player just tries not to telegraph what he is likely to play. The optimal strategy for each player is to equally often put out one finger and two fingers. But the choices must be random, without any pattern. It would be ridiculous for a player to simply alternate between one finger and two fingers. Even though each is being played 50% of the time, your opponent will be able to win every time once the pattern is detected.

Even though the knowledge of game theory has made some mathematicians rich through certain competitive situations, such as auctions of financial instruments, it is useless for the typical casino gambling game. Roulette and craps are games that can easily be totally analyzed simply by using probability theory. We will glance at them in the next chapter. These casino games may seem more complicated than the odds and evens finger game, but they are actually much simpler. The odds and evens game is a two-person game where the players are trying to outguess each other. The casino games really have only one player competing against a machine that plays in a predefined fashion. Even in blackjack where human dealers seem to be playing, they are required to play in a predetermined way. Otherwise, they might choose to play very poorly when their friends and family are in the casino. These games involve no outguessing of an opponent.

Some serious games are really the equivalent of our finger game. In baseball, the batter and the pitcher are each trying to outguess the other. It is a tremendous advantage for a batter to know the type of pitch the pitcher will throw him. All teams keep records of past matchups between each batter and each pitcher. Consider soccer when a penalty kick is taken. The penalty taker and the goalkeeper are trying to outguess each other. The goalkeeper must decide whether to dive left or right at the time the ball is kicked. Often, he looks foolish by diving to protect one side of the goal as the ball flies in at the other end. He actually was just outguessed. In virtually all professional sports there are examples where two players or two teams study the past decisions of their opponents in order to outguess them on future decisions.

Let's get back to bridge. In the last chapter, on the justification for the Principle of Restricted Choice, we saw that it would be a mistake for a defender holding doubleton queen-jack to always play the jack or for that matter to always play the queen. It would provide too much information to declarer. We saw it was necessary to vary which card the defender plays. In game theory terminology, this is called a *mixed strategy*. A game where a player always selects the same option is called a *pure strategy*. We have seen that a defender does better when playing a mixed strategy than either pure strategy. But what is the best mixed strategy? That would be called the *optimum strategy*. For some games, it might be best to choose one option 80% of the time and the other 20%. Playing the finger game, it would be best to play each choice 50% of the time. Of course, no pattern must be detectable, for example simply alternating the choice.

Tricky Confusing Issue Alert

Consider the Restricted Choice example on page 117. The reader may be troubled that this decision does not come up often enough for even a sharp declarer to recognize the pattern of a defender's plays. That is a good point. Game theory is most interesting and useful when analyzing games that involve repeated plays. In the last chapter, I gave a very artificial example where Restricted Choice came up repeatedly; in addition, the defender was foolish enough to announce what choice he would always make.

Throughout my more than half-century of playing bridge, when holding the doubleton queen-jack, I do not know how often

I played the queen and how often I played the jack. I know I vary my choices but, if I favor one over the other, I really don't know. And besides, if I always played the same honor, I would not be foolish enough to reveal it to potential bridge opponents who may be reading this book.

I am sure some defenders always play the jack or always play the queen. I certainly could not name any. I asked several players and the consensus is that the queen is played more often than the jack; maybe the queen is played roughly 60% or 70% of the time by defenders. Players like to feel deceptive. I have no real basis for that estimate – but that never stops me from making an estimate.

We saw that the declarer only has a very slight gain even when he knows a defender is totally predictable. As long as the defender is not totally predictable, the declarer should use Restricted Choice. Therefore, a defender does not have to play each honor 50% of the time. Why do books and articles on Restricted Choice indicate that the defender should play each card 50% of the time? It is not really necessary but the argument for Restricted Choice is easier to understand with 50-50 than 60-40.

Even though bridge is played by four people, for game theory purposes it would be classified as a two-person game since it is played by two fixed partnerships. Just one hundred years ago, one of the most famous bridge writers, Robert Foster, was endorsing converting bridge to a four-person game called Pirate Bridge. After an opening bid, any of the three players could accept the bid, thereby becoming dummy and forming a partnership for the hand. If no one accepted the bid, it was voided. If the bid was accepted, the other two players had the right to overcall. That also had to be accepted. The dummy might not be seated opposite declarer, so often a partnership could play two cards one after the other. Strange! Card games like this, where a partnership is formed during a hand, are in a family of games called 'alliance games'. When Foster's book appeared in 1917, many players saw Pirate Bridge as the next step in the evolution of bridge. Actually, some versions of three-handed bridge were an alliance game. Sometimes a player purposely obtained a poor score on a hand because it would be strategically wise to inflict damage on that player's temporary partner. This is why some forms of three-handed bridge were called 'cutthroat bridge'.

The study of games where coalitions are formed is very extensive. If either Pirate Bridge or cutthroat bridge had become popular, they would have been much more interesting for game theorists to analyze than our relatively bland form of bridge.

I have used game theory as a useful tool to rationalize some of my worst bridge plays. We have seen that a fundamental principle is to be unpredictable. Based on my writing several bridge books, many excellent players assume that I am a fine player and that my plays are therefore somewhat predictable. My regular sprinkling of boneheaded plays makes me unpredictable. At least, I try to convince my partners of that.

The Cheater's Dilemma

Consider the following scenario. Both members of a partnership are extremely rude to all opponents and the club's director. Although they have previously been barred for several months from play, when they return, they are as bad as ever. Still worse, there is a general suspicion the partnership is cheating using finger movements (this is a club pair, so they are not playing behind screens). However, no one has been able to decipher their code, so there is no clear evidence of their cheating.

Officials of the bridge league interrogate each of them separately, so that each is unaware as to whether or not their partner will confess to cheating. The Disciplinary Committee first tells each player that, for the partnership's rudeness at the table, he will be barred from any sanctioned bridge events for a period of two years. But, if one of the pair confesses to cheating and explains their finger signals, and his partner does not confess, the confessor's ban for rudeness will be reduced to one year (no additional ban for cheating) while the non-confessor will be banned for ten years. Furthermore, if both confess, they will each be banned for five years.

On an individual basis, the rational action for each player is to confess because of a shorter ban. Let's name the two players Player

A and Player B. Suppose Player A is being interrogated. Player A realizes that, should Player B not confess while he himself does so, he will get a one-year ban rather than two, and should Player B confess, he will get only a five-year ban rather than ten. Clearly, whatever Player B does, it is wise for Player A to confess. When Player B is interrogated, he faces the identical problem, so obviously it is also wise for Player B to confess.

Clearly it is wise for both to confess, resulting in each being banned for five years. The paradox is that if neither confesses, they will each be banned for only two years! Even if they have read this section, and they agree beforehand that neither will confess, it still is rational to betray their partner and confess. There is no honor among cheaters.

The Cheater's Dilemma is just my modification of the very well-known Prisoner's Dilemma. The standard problem involves years in jail rather than the more painful punishment of years banned from bridge. In all cases of the dilemma, individual rational behavior leads to undesirable results for the group.

Chapter 13
Gambling and Expected Value

Is this chapter useful? Why?

Usefulness number: 7. The sections of this chapter that describe and apply expected value are the most useful for bridge players. In any game when there is a choice between several options, it is often wise to examine the expected value for each choice.

To Gamble or Not to Gamble

Society has never figured out how to handle gambling. Many individuals like it, many hate it, many enjoy it and many are destroyed by it. This situation has resulted in governments passing laws to define what forms of gambling are legal and where indulging in them is legal. Usually these laws are illogical and rather arbitrary. A gambling establishment might be illegal in a city but legal on a barge permanently anchored on a river going through the heart of the city.

Gambling laws are continually in flux. In 1910, bridge players in Reno, Nevada could be arrested: playing a social card game was illegal at that time. In Reno of all places! In the 1960s, a rubber bridge club in Toronto was raided, and the proprietor was charged with running a gaming house. World-class bridge player Eric Murray, a prominent lawyer, appeared for the defense and was able to get the charges dismissed on the grounds that bridge is a game of skill. A few years ago, a bridge club in Thailand was raided.

A major problem devising laws to regulate gambling is the result of first having to define 'gambling'. When a homeowner buys fire insurance, that person is in a way gambling. The buyer is placing a small bet that may produce a very large return. Unfortunately, he will win only when part of his home burns. Ironically, the insurance salesman's pitch that you are gambling if you don't buy his insurance is correct. Don't get me started on life insurance. Even though investing in stocks is a form of gambling, all stockbrokers will tell you that you are gambling if none of your assets are in stocks.

Looking back on my academic life, one of my favorite courses was a general liberal arts seminar where students would write and present papers related to gambling in the domain of their major. Gambling is such a rich, broad subject that I found that for any major I could suggest a topic that would be appropriate. For some majors: psychology, political science, economics, ethics, sociology, history, etc., it was easy. Let me mention some of the less obvious ones. Biology (premed) students could summarize articles on brain chemistry changes while one is gambling or why the side effect of many drugs is excessive gambling. Music majors could study the many operas where excessive gambling occurs. Such a plot element can give characters sudden great wealth, or, more often, sudden great poverty. Wonderful drama, either way! For art majors, there are many old paintings where card playing and gambling are depicted. Usually the characters are cheating at the card table.

Chance versus Skill

Eric Murray's defense of the St. Clair Bridge Club took advantage of faulty attempts to define gambling. Many definitions of gambling involve 'games of chance' as opposed to 'games of skill'. Games of skill that include a chance factor may encourage gambling to excess even more than pure games of chance. In a game of skill, a player can easily delude himself into believing that he has the ability to win but is just very unlucky. At an old-fashioned slot machine, such a delusion was not possible. Newer versions of slot machine type games try to make the delusion possible by offering choices in strategy.

I do agree that games of skill can be enjoyed without gambling whereas pure games of chance quickly get boring. Winning a game of skill can be a source of pride, and produce a sense of accomplishment. Our masterpoint system (no-dust trophies) enables that success to linger for all eternity.

Chance enters games and sports in many ways. For example:

1) Dealing cards
2) Dice
3) Human performance (we all have good days and bad)
4) Animal performance (they all have good days and bad)
5) Tiny differences in measurements (balls in or out of court)
6) Computer random number generators (duplicate bridge)
7) Miscellaneous mechanical devices (lotteries, roulette)

Bridge Faces the Gambling Attack

When bridge evolved from whist in the nineteenth century, it almost died in infancy. Decent upstanding citizens labeled the game as a magnet for gamblers and believed the game would only attract players with low moral principles.

There was a lot of truth to this belief. The rules for bridge that appeared in books and pamphlets written between 1886 and 1910 allowed doubling and redoubling to continue without limit. A player could enter a low stakes game but, due to this feature, one hand could quickly become very expensive. Players would get caught up in the spirit of 'You doubled me, I am not scared, I will double again'. Even worse, an innocent player could be asked to be a fourth in a low stakes game where the other three players are working together. The partner of the mark could quickly raise the stakes to a very high level with this doubling feature. Many rounds of doubling could take place without any way for the victim to prevent it. Of course, after he left with empty pockets, the other three players split up the spoils.

This was a terrible feature of the first form of bridge. It enabled the whist fans to justify their strong attack on this new growing game. Bridge often used its alternative name, 'bridge whist', and took up residence in the hundreds of whist clubs in the world. This was a threat to the very game of whist! Even if whist players did not fully believe bridge appealed only to gamblers, they still attacked bridge as a gambling game that was attractive to only players of ill repute. It was a 'talking point' in the battle to save whist from these invaders.

The first American club to play bridge was the New York Whist Club. A member, Henry Barbey, introduced the game in 1892, having learned it in Paris. The game's great success generated two warring gangs. Their battle was documented in *The New York Times* on December 10, 1893, in an article titled 'Couldn't Stand Bridge Whist'.

Some of the members thought that bridge whist fostered a
gambling spirit on too large a scale for the good of the club,
besides, in a certain degree, being the means of casting the
old-style whist into the background.

The article reveals that the club had to split into two clubs, with the new one located a few doors away. Regrettably, some old friendships probably ended. The article leaves the incorrect impression that the old whist players moved out, but other evidence makes it clear that it was the unwelcomed bridge players who formed the new club. This article was the first in *The New York Times* to mention bridge. Bridge went on to have a very long run of regular columns in this paper.

The Whist Reference Book (1899) by William Mill Butler, an encyclopedia of whist, has an entry for 'bridge'. It primarily consists of attacks on bridge.

It is regretted that 'bridge' has found its way also to
America, and that many of our whist-players have yielded
to its temptations. They will undoubtedly live to regret it...

The entry quotes many top whist authorities. The great whist expert and writer Cavendish (Henry Jones) stated, '*It is disgusting, to think that the temple of whist has been thus desecrated.*' (Ibid.)

I need to point out that this must be a pre-1898 quote. In December 1898, a few months before his death, Cavendish wrote an article extolling bridge. He was a convert. Some pro-whist, anti-gamblers saw an odd virtue in bridge: they felt that bridge would take gamblers away from the whist tables, thereby leaving their game pure and clean.

Part of the anti-gambling sentiment was based on the great popularity of duplicate whist and the strength of the American Whist League in the 1890s. It meant whist could be enjoyed without gambling. Even though early bridge players wrote about duplicate bridge, the game was not very attractive in its duplicate form.

The famous whist writer, R. F. Foster, who became an equally famous bridge writer, predicted in 1900 in *Foster's Bridge Manual*.

Some of these days it is hoped that a satisfactory method of playing bridge in duplicate will be found, and when it is we will have something that the world has long waited for, a perfect game of cards, in which skill and judgment are more important than luck, and in which the intellectual pleasure of the play is more attractive than any stake.
(Introduction, p. xvii)

More than one hundred books were written on this first form of bridge. When this first form was evolving into auction bridge, the bridge whist players opposed to auction denigrated it by writing that only gamblers would favor the new form of the game. It was again compared to poker. The same argument surfaced when auction bridge was evolving into contract.

The gambling label never destroyed the game. It probably did not even hurt it. Possibly it even helped bridge develop. Good advertising!

Expected Value at the Roulette Table

Roulette is a very simple game that is ideally suited for casinos. Both the table and wheel are very beautiful. There may be a dozen people at a roulette table (a very social atmosphere) but each individual is playing against a machine that represents the casino. As mentioned in the last chapter, there is no need for game theory. There is no element of the machine trying to outguess a player. This simple game can be fully analyzed using expected value. Different playing options can easily be compared in a search of the most successful line.

Suppose a player places a one-dollar bet on the number 23. Since there are 38 possible equally likely outcomes on an American roulette wheel, the probability of the ball falling into slot 23 is 1/38, and the probability that it falls into a slot other than number 23 is 37/38. The payoff for winning is $36, for a net win of $35.

The expected value, i.e the player's expected return over a long sequence of plays, is $(1/38) \times 35 + (37/38) \times (-1) = -1/19 = -.0526$.

I converted the fraction into a decimal in order to convey the significance of the expected value. This result means that if a player spends twenty-four hours placing bets on a single number, that player should expect to lose approximately 5.26 cents for every dollar bet. If in the twenty-four hours 1000 $1 bets are made, the player should expect to be behind by about $50. Overwhelmingly, the string of results will consist of losses of one dollar but there will be the occasional $35 win.

Suppose a one-dollar bet is placed on a red number. Since 18 of the 38 slots are red, the probability of a red outcome is 18/38, and the probability of an outcome that is not red is 20/38. The payoff for victory is $2, so a net win of $1.

The expected value is $(18/38) \times 1 + (20/38) \times (-1) = -1/19 = -.0526$.

This example yielded the same result as the previous example. Even though each play will now result in either winning $1 or losing $1, the expected value still indicates that, after 1000 plays, the player should expect to be behind by $52.60. Since this is only an estimate, it is simpler to think of approximately $50.

With either example, if a player is down only $30 after 1000 plays, he was quite lucky, even though he lost money. The estimate of an approximate $50 loss will probably be more accurate in the second example than the first. The large but rare payoff for a win makes the final result more susceptible to the vagaries of luck. So, in the first example, the player is more likely to end up winning money after 1000 plays, but also more likely to lose $100 as opposed to $50.

Expected Value at the Bridge Table

For these two modes of playing roulette, we found that the expected value, either way, was –.0526. So, a player should anticipate losing approximately five cents on any dollar bet. At the craps table, different methods of play can be used. With some, the player will lose only approximately one cent on every dollar bet, while with other methods of betting, he can expect to lose ten cents for every dollar bet. Surprisingly, the simplest method, of always betting PASS or DON'T PASS, is very good, resulting in a loss of only approximately one and a half cents for every dollar bet. Even though these different strategies have different payoffs, whatever strategy a player uses, the expected value will be negative.

Let's apply the expected value to look at bridge decisions. Suppose you are at the brink of a decision between playing in 3♡ or 4♡, and you are certain that you will take either nine or ten tricks. To the best of your knowledge, you believe that each outcome is equally likely. Therefore, the probability of each outcome is 1/2. We will first do the calculation when you are vulnerable, so the possible payoffs are 620, 170, 140, and –100.

Expected value when the contract is 4♡
= 1/2 x 620 + 1/2 x (–100) = 310 – 50 = 260
Expected value when the contract is 3♡
= 1/2 x 170 + 1/2 x 140 = 85 + 70 = 155

It is clear that the expected value is much greater with these payoffs when you always bid game. Let's now suppose you believe that there is only a 40% chance of taking ten tricks.

Expected value when the contract is 4♡
= 0.4 x 620 + 0.6 x (–100) = 248 – 60 = 188
Expected value when the contract is 3♡
= 0.4 x 170 + 0.6 x 140 = 68 + 84 = 152

As expected, both values are smaller than when we assumed a 50% chance of winning ten tricks. But even with a 40% chance, it is wise to bid game. Want to try 35%?

Expected value when the contract is 4♡
= 0.35 x 620 + 0.65 x (–100) = 217 – 65 = 152
Expected value when the contract is 3♡
= 0.35 x 170 + 0.65 x 140 = 59.5 + 91 = 150.5

It is still wise to bid game, but by only a very slight margin.

If you try 0.33, bidding 4♡ has an expected value of 204.6 – 67 = 137.6 but bidding 3♡ is 56.1 + 93.8 = 149.9. No longer is it wise to bid game.

With these payoffs, it would be worthwhile to bid game if you anticipate the chance of success is 0.35 or better. It is natural to wonder why bridge books don't mention 0.35. It seems important. *It is not.* The standard forms of scoring for pairs (matchpoints) or teams (IMPs) do not involve these payoffs. In Chapter 17, we will return to these decisions. At least, you are now familiar with expected value. Not to mention, a more realistic assumption would consider that you might take only eight tricks or, on a good day, eleven tricks.

Of course, the same analysis would work with more than two possible outcomes. Suppose, you estimate that there is a 10% chance of making eleven tricks, 30% chance of ten tricks, 45% chance of nine tricks, and 15% chance of eight tricks.

Expected value when the contract is 4♡ = 0.10 x 650 + 0.30 x 620 + 0.45 x (–100) + 0.15 x (–200) = 65 + 186 – 45 – 30 = 176

Expected value when the contract is 3♡ = 0.10 x 200 + 0.30 x 170 + 0.45 x 140 + 0.15 x (–100) = 20 + 51 + 63 – 15 = 119

With these assumptions, it would be better in the long run to play in 4♡ rather than bidding 3♡.

Now let's assume you are not vulnerable. Using the original premise, that you think it is equally likely that you will make nine or ten tricks,

Expected value when bidding 4♡ = 1/2 x 420 + 1/2 x (–50) = 210 – 25 = 185

Expected value when bidding $3\heartsuit = 1/2 \times 170 + 1/2 \times 140 = 85 + 70 = 155$

With this assumption, it is better to bid game.

Fair Games

If the outcome of a game depends only on chance, a mathematical definition exists for labeling it a 'fair' game: a fair game is a game where each side's expected winnings (or 'value') are zero. For example, suppose two people are playing a game and one player is expected to win one-third of the time and the other two-thirds. If the player who wins less often gets $2 for a win and loses only $1 for a loss, this is a fair game for the player since his expected value is zero: $(1/3 \times 2) + (2/3 \times (-1)) = 0$. The payoff of $2 made the game fair. A $3 payoff to the player who wins only one-third of the time would have made the game favorable to the player who loses the majority of the individual plays.

The expected value does not help predict individual outcomes but is useful for predicting the gains and losses over many plays. It is an excellent way to study casino games such as roulette and craps. These are obviously not fair games: the odds are against the players who, in the long run, will lose. A mathematician would say that the expected value of the game to the players is negative. Maybe the excitement of the activity makes up for that difference. I doubt it in the long run. Casino games are virtually always honest but they are not fair – the odds are in favor of the house. Often the words 'honest' and 'fair' are mistakenly used interchangeably.

A Sense of Fairness

The participants of any game *must* feel that they are not being cheated. However, this is not the same as playing a fair game. The question of what is fair is often a personal matter.

I have heard players lament that their team has a total of about 500 masterpoints and they are heading into a match against a team with over 20,000 masterpoints. I have been asked if I think this is fair. I respond, 'Certainly.' I concede that they are unlikely to win but I ask them if a victory would make them very happy. They usually respond that they would be thrilled, on cloud nine. They acknowledge that they would savor the victory for years. I then ask if they think their opponents would be equally ecstatic. They respond, 'Of course not.' I point out that one can therefore argue that the match is not fair to their opponents. Basically, my answer extended the concept of expected value analysis by using pleasure as a payoff rather than a monetary amount. They may rarely win, but when they earn a victory, the payoff is wonderful.

I still remember victories decades ago in seven-board matches against much stronger teams. All of those opponents would probably win nine out of ten matches against my team, but on that particular day, they lost. That is all that counted. Nowadays, I may be on the team that is favored, but I can get an unusual bonus if my team is upset. While watching our opponents celebrate their success, I see them scurry over to the bookseller to buy one of my bridge books. They want to boast to their friends that they beat a bridge author. Sometimes they even ask me to sign a book. They probably will not read the book, but in my case, losing has its rewards beyond being character building.

If one wishes to broaden the standard concept of gambling, duplicate players are really gambling too. The currency they risk for potential gain is 'short-term self-esteem.' This may seem to be of greater value than any financial wager, but self-esteem is easy to replace. A pair with three 40% games followed by a 65% game will have won back all of their self-esteem and then some. While walking to their cars after the 65% game, they will exhibit a triumphant bounce to their step. If financial wagers had been involved, they would have still been well in the red. Actually, if one's supply of self-esteem ever falls too low, one can take a vacation from bridge for a month or two. Self-esteem rejuvenates without even playing. After all, how many players can say that they did not make a mistake in the last month? Giving away one's self-esteem to others at a duplicate event is like giving blood at a local hospital: it replenishes itself quickly.

Chapter 14
Probability of Types of Hands

Is this chapter useful? Why?

Usefulness number: 8. This chapter looks at the probability of picking up a hand that meets some specified condition. Who cares? How can that be at all useful? Once players look at the hand they were dealt, they know exactly the thirteen cards they received. No probability involved! True. But that knowledge is essential for considering the frequency of being able to use a bid or a convention. This chapter provides a background for the next four, which discuss probability-related aspects of bidding.

Every Card Must Satisfy a Requirement

Drawing thirteen cards from the top of a well-shuffled deck of fifty-two cards is equivalent to being dealt a hand of thirteen cards. The actual dealing process is of no consequence. Obviously, it makes no difference whether you look at all thirteen cards at one time or look at each card as you receive it: your hand is the same.

This section will ascertain the probability of obtaining a hand where all thirteen cards must satisfy some requirement.

What is the probability that all thirteen cards will be red cards?

We can imagine a shuffled deck of the fifty-two cards where repeatedly the top card is turned over and removed. The probability that the top card is red is 26/52. After that card is removed, the new top card must also be red. Since there are only fifty-one cards left and twenty-five are red, the probability that this second card is red is 25/51. Likewise, the probability that the third card is red is 24/50. This continues until thirteen cards have been drawn.

So P(thirteen red cards) is 26/52 x 25/51 x 24/50 x 23/49 x 22/48 x 21/47 x 20/46 x 19/45 x 18/44 x 17/43 x 16/42 x 15/41 x 14/40 = 0.0000164

It is interesting to note, but not surprising, that each term is smaller than the last since as each red card gets drawn the supply of undrawn red cards gets depleted.

The final answer was achieved using a shortcut for the arithmetic described in Part III. At least, the procedure should seem straightforward.

What is the probability of being dealt a hand with 0 high-card points?

Since a hand with 0 HCP cannot contain any ace, king, queen or jack, every card must be from the remaining thirty-six cards. Imagine turning over and then removing the top card.

The probability of the first card satisfying the requirement is 36/52. The probability for the second card is 35/51 since only thirty-five of the remaining fifty-one cards meet the requirement. Continuing in this fashion, with two cards removed, the third card has the probability of 34/50. One need only multiply these thirteen values to obtain the probability.

$$P(0 \text{ HCP}) = 36/52 \times 35/51 \times 34/50 \times 33/49 \times 32/48$$
$$\times 31/47 \times 30/46 \times 29/45 \times 28/44 \times 27/43 \times 26/42$$
$$\times 25/41 \times 24/40 = 0.003639$$

Since 1/275 = 0.003636 the odds of being dealt a hand with 0 HCP is approximately 1 to 274. So the odds against are 274 to 1.

Likelihood of a Yarborough

A player can complain about his hand being a yarborough if it does not have a single card higher than a nine. Bridge players often mistakenly refer to any hand containing 0 HCP as a yarborough. You have every right to complain about a hand with 0 HCP, but if it includes a ten, it cannot legitimately be called a yarborough.

What is the probability of being dealt a yarborough?

There are thirty-two cards in the deck that are spot cards from two to nine. The probability of the first card dealt being a nine or lower is 32/52. Similar to the prior two examples, one need only multiply the proper thirteen values to obtain the probability of a yarborough.

P(yarborough) = 32/52 x 31/51 x 30/50 x 29/49 x 28/48 x 27/47 x 26/46 x 25/45 x 24/44 x 23/43 x 22/42 x 21/41 x 20/40 = 0.000547

This value is approximately $\dfrac{1}{1828}$

Legend has it that the Earl of Yarborough offered 1000 pounds to 1 pound against a whist player being dealt such a hand. This was a very favorable bet for the Earl since the actual odds against such a hand are 1827 to 1. In Part III, I will demonstrate a more elegant way to obtain the probability of a yarborough.

Notice that the prior example, which involved hands with 0 HCP, found their chance of occurring to be almost seven times more likely than an actual yarborough. It is surprising that the four tens make such a big difference, but including them does. If the Earl had used that less restrictive condition, he would have quickly lost his castle.

A mathematical whist player should have suggested to the Earl that he would readily accept 500 pounds to 1 pound against a player being dealt such a hand if the four tens were included. As we recently saw the actual odds against this hand are 274 to 1.

How Many of the 635 Billion Hands?

In this chapter, we have so far considered only examples where every card must satisfy some condition. This enabled us to obtain the probability of each card and then simply multiply those thirteen values. Now we will consider the more useful and common situations where the answer cannot be obtained in such a straightforward fashion.

What is the probability of being dealt a hand with exactly seven hearts?

This cannot be done on a card-by-card basis. It is not a requirement that the first card is a heart or for that matter that the first card is not a heart. Of course, this type of requirement may surface when the thirteenth card is drawn. If the first twelve cards include six hearts, the thirteenth card must be a heart, while if the first twelve cards include seven hearts, the thirteenth card must not be a heart. Of course, if the first twelve cards contain fewer than six hearts or more than seven, there is no hope.

We therefore need a more global approach. Consider the examples on page 49. In all of those examples, the numerator (top number of fraction) was obvious and the denominator (bottom number of fraction) was 635,013,559,600.

For all of the probability examples in the remainder of this chapter, the denominator will be the same: 635 billion (or more accurately, 635,013,559,600). We have to figure out how many hands can be formed that satisfy the specified condition of the problem. Let's return to the problem of a hand with exactly seven hearts. For this example, we would perform the steps:

1) Obtain the number of ways in which seven hearts can be chosen from the thirteen.
2) Obtain the number of ways in which six non-heart cards can be chosen from the thirty-nine non-heart cards.
3) Multiply the above values and then divide by 635 billion.

At this time, you have a right to feel disappointed. So far I have not shown how to do Steps 1 and 2; I have merely described how to approach this type of problem logically. In Chapter 19, I will introduce and justify a very powerful formula for that purpose. Till then, I will refer to it as 'the magic formula'.

Does One Multiply or Add?

Students in mathematics courses commonly have trouble on this issue — even math majors! I am only demeaning math majors so that you won't be too offended by my next ridiculously simple example.

Suppose you are politically a card-carrying independent, but cannot find bridge partners who share your leaning. You wish to show no favoritism between the two major political parties. Since you play only on Mondays and Tuesdays, you have a policy that on Mondays, you play bridge with only Republican partners while on Tuesday only with Democratic partners. On Monday, you have a choice of Donald, Ivanka, and Eric. On Tuesday, your options are Bernie, Elizabeth, Kamela, Pete, and Joe. During this coming week, if you are going to play both days, there will be fifteen possible partner options — simply 3 x 5. If, however, you have to babysit your grandchild on one of those two days, you have only eight options. Case 1, you decide to play on Monday (three options) or Case 2, you decide to play on Tuesday (five options) — by adding, a total of eight options. Of course, after rejecting so many partners, you will probably have fewer options in the future. They might use that old excuse, 'I'm in Washington.'

A more general explanation would be: suppose one activity can be done in m ways and a second activity can be done in n ways.

Multiplication Principle: If both activities must be done, the number of ways is obtained by multiplying m *times* n.

Addition Principle: If either the first activity or the second activity must be done, but not both, the number of ways is obtained by adding m *and* n.

These principles can be extended to more than two activities. We will see this throughout the remainder of this chapter.

In the bridge example of a hand with exactly seven hearts, it is not sufficient merely to obtain how many ways one can choose seven hearts from the thirteen hearts, it is necessary also to consider how many ways the six non-hearts can be chosen. Since both must be done, the results must be multiplied.

More Examples of Hand Types

What is the probability of being dealt a hand with exactly four spades and exactly five hearts (Flannery shape)?

1) Obtain the number of ways in which four spades can be chosen from the thirteen.
2) Obtain the number of ways in which five hearts can be chosen from the thirteen.
3) Obtain the number of ways in which four minor-suit cards can be chosen from the remaining twenty-six cards.
4) Multiply the above values and then divide by 635 billion.

Of course, you will need the magic formula to do Steps 1, 2 and 3. Please be patient. In the next two examples, you will need the magic formula before doing Steps 1, 2, 3 and 4.

What is the probability of being dealt a hand with exactly three spades, five hearts, two diamonds, and three clubs?

I will shorten the steps by no longer reminding you that there are thirteen cards in a suit. Sorry about that!

1) Obtain the number of ways in which three spades can be chosen.
2) Obtain the number of ways in which five hearts can be chosen.
3) Obtain the number of ways in which two diamonds can be chosen.
4) Obtain the number of ways in which three clubs can be chosen.
5) Multiply the above values and then divide by 635 billion.

What is the probability of being dealt a hand with exactly four spades and exactly three cards in each of the other three suits?

1) Obtain the number of ways in which four spades can be chosen.
2) Obtain the number of ways in which three hearts can be chosen.
3) Obtain the number of ways in which three diamonds can be chosen.
4) Obtain the number of ways in which three clubs can be chosen.
5) Multiply the above values and then divide by 635 billion.

This is the most common specific hand. The probability of being dealt this specific shape is 2.634%. It is not uniquely the most likely. It is in a four-way tie for that honor with four hearts and three cards in each of the other suits, four diamonds and three cards in each of the other suits, and four clubs and three cards in each of the other suits.

Shape Probabilities

It is time for some useful notation. Rather than writing out these four cases, I will use 4-3-3-3 to indicate that a non-specified suit has four cards and the other suits each have three. I believe *The Bridge World* started the very useful related notation of 4=3=3=3. Using the equal sign instead of the dash indicates specifically four cards in the spade suit and three in each the other suits. Similarly, 3=3=4=3 would indicate four cards in the diamond suit and three in each of the other suits. Consider the prior example with three spades, five hearts, two diamonds and three clubs. That specific shape is 3=5=2=3, but could be described more generally as 5-3-3-2. The general shape notation always starts with the longest suit and proceeds to the shortest.

The following important table provides shape information. In many books the left column is called 'hand patterns' or 'distribution'. Since there is no clear order to the rows determined by the first column of their shapes, I am ordering them by their likelihood in the second column. I am just providing a top fifteen list.

SHAPE	Probability in Percent
4-4-3-2	21.551
5-3-3-2	15.517
5-4-3-1	12.931
5-4-2-2	10.580
4-3-3-3	10.536
6-3-2-2	5.642
6-4-2-1	4.702
6-3-3-1	3.448
5-5-2-1	3.174
4-4-4-1	2.993
7-3-2-1	1.881
6-4-3-0	1.326
5-4-4-0	1.243
5-5-3-0	0.895
6-5-1-1	0.705

Again, this is only the top fifteen. More than 97% of the time, a bridge hand will be one of these fifteen cases. It is interesting that more than 70% of all hands have one of the top five shapes. You can check the ACBL Encyclopedia for all other shapes. The complete list contains thirty-nine general shapes.

Tricky Confusing Issue Alert

In the previous section, it was stated that the hand with four spades and three cards in each other suit is tied for the most popular shape. But if you check the table, it sits in fifth place. What gives?

Using our notation, I stated that 4=3=3=3 was not in sole possession of first place. It is tied with 3=4=3=3, 3=3=4=3, and 3=3=3=4. The table entry for 4-3-3-3 indicates the total probability of the four specific shapes combined. Since these four possibilities are equally likely to occur, the probability of each can be obtained by dividing the table entry, 10.536%, by 4. The result of this division is 2.634%. This is the value provided on the previous page.

Now we can consider 4-4-3-2. In the Shape Table, this entry has the highest probability: 21.551%. But the shape 4-4-3-2 can occur in twelve specific ways: 4=4=3=2, 4=4=2=3, 4=3=4=2, 4=3=2=4, 4=2=4=3, 4=2=3=4, 3=4=4=2, 3=4=2=4, 3=2=4=4, 2=4=4=3, 2=4=3=4, and 2=3=4=4.

So, the probability of four spades, two hearts, four diamonds and three clubs (the fifth entry in this list 4=2=4=3) can be obtained by dividing the table entry, 21.551% by 12. The result of this division is 1.796%. Mystery solved!

Let's consider the general shape 5-4-3-1. The probability entry in the table is 12.931%. If one were to list all specific shapes, the list would contain twenty-four entries. If you don't believe me, simply list the twenty-four as we did for twelve. Therefore, the probability of any specific shape could be obtained by dividing 12.931% by 24. The result is 0.539%. So, even though the general shape is third most likely on the list, any specific shape, such as three spades, five hearts, one diamond and four clubs is only approximately one half of one percent.

As we have seen, it is useful to know how many specific shape cases are described by the general shape notation. When three of the four suits are the same length, as 4-3-3-3 and 4-4-4-1, there are only four specific cases. When all four suits are a different length, as 5-4-3-1, 6-4-2-1, 7-3-2-1 and 6-4-3-0, there are twenty-four specific cases. In the remaining nine shapes, where two suits are the same length, there are twelve specific cases. You can spare yourself the division. The ACBL Encyclopedia has an entry Mathematical Tables that provides the specific shape probabilities.

A useless side note: it is impossible to create a bridge hand where there are an odd number of cards in exactly two suits. Such a hand would add up to an even number of cards — so never thirteen.

This table actually serves a second purpose: it shows not only the likelihood of a hand having some specific shape but also the likelihood of a suit being divided a certain way among the four hands. Therefore, the most likely way for a suit to be distributed to the four players would be for two players each to receive four cards, a third to receive three cards and the fourth to receive two. That will occur 21.55% of the time.

Using the Table for Bridge Purposes

What is the probability that the shape of your next hand will be appropriate to open 1NT?

Let's assume that any hand with the following three shapes would be appropriate for opening 1NT: 4-4-3-2, 5-3-3-2 and 4-3-3-3. Together their likelihood in percentages is 21.6 + 15.5 + 10.5 = 47.6. If we throw in the shape 5-4-2-2, which has a probability of 10.6%, the total rises to 58.2%. For a player who really likes to see himself as a declarer in a notrump contract, one can go a step further and include 6-3-2-2 when the six-card suit is a minor. This generates an additional percentage increase of 1/2 x 5.6 = 2.8, and the total is around 61%. Obviously, this analysis is somewhat misleading because even if you include these borderline last two shapes, it does not mean that all hands with these shapes, no matter where the 15-17 HCP values are located, are appropriate for opening notrump.

What is the probability that your next hand will have a five- card suit or longer?

It is easier to get the probability of a hand *without* a five-card suit. There are only three such shapes: 4-4-3-2, 4-3-3-3 and 4-4-4-1. Together their likelihood in percentages is 21.6 + 10.5 + 3.0 = 35.1. So, the probability of having a five-card or longer suit is 64.9%. The value 65% appeared on page 12.

What is the probability that your next hand will have a void?

In our TOP 15 table there are only three shapes that include a void: 6-4-3-0, 5-4-4-0, and 5-5-3-0. Their percentage total is 1.326 + 1.243 + 0.895 = 3.464. However, many shapes that did not make the TOP 15 list involve a void. Those that did not make the list total approximately 1.6%. This brings the grand total in percentages to 3.5 + 1.6 = 5.1.

What is the probability that your next hand will have a singleton?
In our TOP 15 table, the shapes with a singleton total approximately 30% but approximately 1% did not make the TOP 15 list. Therefore 31% is a reasonable value. The probability of being dealt a hand with a singleton is approximately six times greater than being dealt a hand with a void.

High-card Point probabilities

I will present twenty-six lines of the HCP table. It is very natural to order the rows by HCP.

HCP Probability in percent

0	0.36
1	0.79
2	1.36
3	2.46
4	3.85
5	5.19
6	6.55
7	8.03
8	8.89
9	9.36
10	9.41
11	8.94
12	8.03
13	6.91
14	5.69
15	4.42
16	3.31
17	2.36
18	1.61
19	1.04
20	0.64
21	0.38
22	0.21
23	0.11
24	0.056
25+	0.046

Obviously, the full table would have thirty-eight lines. Remember on page 145, we saw that a hand with 0 HCP has a probability of 0.36%. That is in agreement with the table value. At times like this, mathematics is fun (yes, I said fun). It is fun when solving a mathematics problem produces the value that was expected or when a problem is solved in two different ways and both produce the same answer. Now that I think of it, maybe a better word than 'fun' is 'relief'. If the two answers do not agree, something is wrong and it has to be investigated. More work! Students have often approached me with a troubled look while lamenting, 'I did a problem two different ways; both are correct, but I got two different answers.' I would always first tell them not to look troubled: if their premise is correct, they might have a Ph.D. dissertation. One does not have to worry about mathematics being delicate – it will not break. Mathematical research expands what is known, but virtually never has to fix something.

Tricky Confusing Issue Alert

It is tempting to believe that since the average hand has 10 HCP, a player is as likely to pick up a hand with 9 or fewer HCP as to have a hand with 11 or more HCP. This is not the case. The probability of 9 or fewer is 47%, while 11 or more is only 44%. It is obvious when one considers the fact that all players occasionally receive hands with 23 or 24 HCP. These hands are more than a dozen points above average. However, it is impossible to ever get a hand that is more than 10 points below average. So, to 'average out', it is necessary to have a greater probability of hands 9 HCP or lower than 11 HCP or higher.

The same reasoning is true for the number of aces a player should expect on a deal: the average is one ace, but no aces is more likely than two aces. Actually, no aces is more likely than two or more.

Hands Specified by Shape and HCP

The probability of being dealt the point count to open 1NT when playing the 15-17 range is 4.42 + 3.31 + 2.36 = 10.09%. We saw in the last section that, when using the three possible shapes for notrump, the probability of the appropriate shape was 47%. Therefore, with these crude assumptions, the probability of having the appropriate shape and the appropriate points to open 1NT is 0.47 x 0.10 = 0.047 or 4.7%

Tricky Confusing Issue Alert

The above multiplication of 0.47 x 0.10 is actually a violation of the laws of probability. It is only mathematically correct to multiply the probability of two events when the two events are independent. It is tempting to feel that the shape of a hand has no bearing on the HCP strength of a hand – after all, a hand consists of thirteen cards whether it is 8-3-1-1 or 4-4-3-2. To show that's not the case, let's look at a few extreme shapes. Suppose a hand consists of thirteen cards in one suit. A hand with that shape has exactly 10 points. It is impossible to have more or less than 10. Let's consider a hand with 37 HCP. The only possible shape for such a hand is 4-3-3-3. There are less extreme shape examples. Compare the shapes recently mentioned, 8-3-1-1 and 4-4-3-2. For the first shape, in the eight-card suit there are at least four spot cards that cannot have any HCP, while with the second shape all thirteen cards can have HCP value. The first hand has a maximum of 27 HCP while the second can go up to 36 HCP.

Now that I have convinced you that shape and HCP strength are not independent, we will ignore my reasoning and pretend that they are. The effect of the relationship is minimal, so I feel comfortable with the prior multiplication that set off this discussion. We have already pretended independence on many occasions throughout the book – but only when pretending will not greatly lead us astray. Trust me.

Obtaining the HCP Table Values

The short answer as to how these values are obtained is, 'With an awful lot of work.' The technique is clear-cut but the arithmetic required for considering all cases is not pretty. The historical record produced by Frederick Frost (see Bibliography) indicates the numerous individuals who deserve the credit for doing the arithmetic.

Let's consider the technique. Suppose we want to obtain the probability of being dealt a hand with exactly 15 HCP. One must consider all possible high-card combinations that will produce such a hand. One case is the combination of one ace, three kings, no queens and two jacks. I will use the shorthand AKKKJJ to represent this particular 15 HCP combination. I was surprised to realize that I could write down twenty-three cases:

AAAK	AAAQJ	AAAJJJ	AAKKJ	AAKQJJ
AAKQQ	AAKJJJJ	AKKKQ	AKKKJJ	AKKQQJ
AKKKQJJJ	AKQQQQ	AKQQQJJ	AKQQJJJJ	AQQQQJJJ
KKKKQJ	KKKKJJJ	KKKQQQ	KKKQQJJ	KKKQJJJJ
KKQQQQJ	KKQQQJJJ	KQQQQJJJJ		

The last case involves nine face cards but comes to only 15 HCP. If the four spot cards were all tens, the hand would have thirteen honor cards but still only 15 HCP. Since the king can be in any suit, there are four hands that meet this condition. So, we can create a 15 HCP hand with as few as four honors and as many as thirteen. Another observation of limited usefulness involves the total number of kings and jacks in each sequence. We see, for any 15 HCP hand, that sum is odd. For any 16 HCP hand, that sum would be even.

I did not expect to find so many different ways a 15 HCP hand could be generated. When I introduced the shorthand, I used the case AKKKJJ. It is ninth on my above list. For this one case, one would have to obtain the number of ways one ace can be chosen from the four, the number of ways three kings can be chosen from the four, the number of ways no queens can be chosen from the four, the number of ways two jacks can be chosen from the four and the number of ways seven spot cards can be chosen from the thirty-six spot cards. These five values can then be multiplied together to obtain the number of 15 HCP hands that can be formed with one ace, three kings, and two jacks. A similar calculation would have to be done for all twenty-three of the above cases. Since the cases are mutually exclusive, all twenty-three values could then be added together.

Despite all this talk about how to do it, I still have not provided readers with the total technique. In Chapter 20, I will return to this example and complete the calculations for the above case AKKKJJ. I promise! By this point, I am sure, I have convinced you to use the values either in the table that I provided or in the ACBL Encyclopedia rather than doing the arithmetic on your own. In the next few chapters, we can call on the information in this chapter's tables in order to study aspects of bidding. In Chapters 20 and 21, I will compute several values in these tables in order to prove their accuracy.

Chapter 15
Bidding Maxims and Partnership Holdings

Is this chapter useful? Why?

Usefulness number: 9. There are many ways that probability can be an aid to a bridge player during the auction, but this topic has been largely ignored. The next several chapters will focus on bidding issues, such as the average support to expect from one's partner. In this chapter, we'll look at some well-known maxims and how our bidding systems implement them — usually quite successfully, but not without some failures.

Partnership HCP Holdings

The most important maxims deal with the joint holding of a partnership, both in high-card strength and the quality of the trump-suit fit. The last chapter focused only on individual hand likelihood. Now we will deal with the probability of joint holdings. This first table is only a partial table.

North-South HCP	East-West HCP	Probability (percent)
17	23	6.831
18	22	7.566
19	21	8.047
20	20	8.222
21	19	8.047
22	18	7.566
23	17	6.831

The symmetry is obvious, so the identical pairs of lines can be combined to save space. This results in the following full table:

Partnership HCP Split	Probability (percent)
20-20	8.222
21-19	16.094
22-18	15.132
23-17	13.662
24-16	11.814
25-15	9.784
26-14	7.767
27-13	5.886
28-12	4.248
29-11	2.926
30-10	1.910
31-9	1.176
32-8	0.682
33-7	0.371
34-6	0.186
35-5	0.086
Even more extreme splits	0.053

The most common HCP split between the partnerships is 20-20. No surprise! But if you combine the two cases North-South 19, East-West 21 and North-South 21, East-West 19, the split 21-19 appears to be more likely than the 20-20. This conclusion can erroneously be drawn from the second table. It should remind you of the table on page 39 where we saw that a 2-2 split is the most likely four-card split but when adding together the two ways a suit can split 3-1, that split erroneously seems the most likely.

26 HCP? 25 HCP? How Much is Enough for Game?

In Part I, I mentioned that many maxims based on probability have been passed down to modern players from our bridge forefathers. The top players and authors generated 'rules' from their observations and analysis of the game. In the 1950s, new players were told that with 26 HCP, they should aim to end up playing in game in either notrump or a major. The Goren system preached this so well, it became the eleventh commandment and was followed religiously. Many books still use 26 but several popular books advocate 25. Which is right? This is actually not an answerable probability question. If Bob Hamman were playing the hand against average defenders, 23 might be adequate most of the time. If a duplicate beginner were playing against excellent defenders, 28 might be the magic number. This question cannot be answered by studying our double-dummy hand records. Declarer's knowledge of where every card is located is usually much more important than the defenders' knowledge of where every card is located. Probably 23 or 24 would be the right number at double-dummy. In general, even though declarer gains more from double-dummy analysis than the defense, it also occasionally allows the defense to come up with peculiar, 'brilliant' opening leads.

The change to 25 HCP for game may be an example of the 'tail wagging the dog'. Virtually all teachers and books have switched their opening notrump range from 16-18 to 15-17, but they still say that a responder with 10 points should push to game. Therefore, after providing 26 as the magic number, it is awkward to contradict oneself by stating that 15 + 10 = 25 is enough. Students quickly object!

HCP hand evaluation is most useful when evaluating the trick-taking potential of flat hands that result in a notrump contract. More than a dozen HCP systems were studied between 1902 and 1948. These systems were considered appropriate for trick-taking potential in only notrump contracts. I will make additional comments on those systems in Chapter 18.

Let's consider the traditional maxim of a partnership needing 26 or more HCP for game in notrump. Based on the table, that strength, for either partnership, will occur only on approximately 25% of hands. If we lower the requirement to 25 HCP, the frequency jumps up to approximately 35% — a big difference generated by a change of 1 HCP in the maxim. In Chapter 18, I will address, with a different approach, the answer to the question about what HCP strength is needed to have a good chance of making 3NT.

If we use 33 HCP as our requirement to bid a notrump small slam, that number or more will occur on approximately 0.7% of the deals. This implies that deals with the HCP strength being that uneven between the two partnerships will occur on approximately one hand every five sessions. This seems remarkably low. Don't forget that we are looking at the strength for notrump slams with balanced hands — having a very shapely hand will yield slams with far less HCP strength. In Chapter 18, we will look at data on the frequency of slam bidding.

Eight-card Fits and Seven-card Fits

The search for an eight-card major fit and, if found, choosing it for trumps is another cornerstone of all modern bidding systems. On many occasions, I have checked the hand records after receiving +120 in a notrump partscore. Often, double-dummy analysis hand records would indicate that the best possible score was three of a major for plus 140. My partnership had a 4-3 fit (called a 'Moysian fit'). Such fits usually require excellent declarer play, and having double-dummy knowledge certainly helps the computer. One should not be misled by studying hand record results of double-dummy play.

If I were questioned as to my favorite common convention, I would answer 'support doubles'. My second-place finisher would be 'new minor forcing'. The goal of these two conventions is to help find eight-card major-suit fits.

Does my partner have support?

This may appear to be a silly question, since the main objective of bidding is to discover the answer to it. The solution is found through partnership communication rather than through probability. Your partner will tell you if he has support. True – but many factors may limit communication, such as:

1) Preemptive bids by one of your opponents.
2) Preemptive bids by your partner.
3) A very weak hand held either by you or your partner.

The more restricted the communication, the greater the role that probability plays.

When you pick up your hand before any bidding, on the average your partner has one-third of what you do not have. For example, if you pick up a hand with 15 HCP, on average your partner will have 8 1/3 HCP. If you have a seven-card heart suit, your partner on the average has two hearts.

We have seen that 65% of bridge hands have at least one suit that is five cards or longer. This certainly is a desirable suit to recommend to your partner as a potential trump suit. If you hold a five-card heart suit, your partner on the average has 2 2/3 hearts. The actual probability breakdown: 0 or 1 hearts is 16%, 2 hearts is 29%, 3 hearts is 31%, 4 hearts is 17% and 5 or more hearts is 7%. So, there is a 55% chance of three-or-more-card support (eight-card or better fit).

If you hold a six-card heart suit, your partner on the average holds 2 1/3 hearts. The actual probability breakdown: zero or one hearts is 24%, two hearts is 33%, three hearts is 28%, four or more hearts is 15%. Even though there is now a reduced chance of three-card support or better (43%), the chance of an eight-card fit or better has risen to 76%.

If you pick up a five-card suit, the likely ways for the other eight cards to be split between the three players are: 3-3-2 with probability 31%, 4-3-1 with probability 26%, 4-2-2 with probability 21%, and 5-2-1 with probability 13%. These are the four most likely splits for the eight cards. They total over 90%.

If you pick up a six-card suit, the likely ways for the other seven cards to be split between the other three players are: 3-2-2 with probability 34%, 4-2-1 with probability 28%, 3-3-1 with probability 21%, and 4-3-0 with probability 8%. These are the four most likely splits for the seven cards. They total over 90%.

The numbers for a seven-card suit are surprising. The most likely split for the six cards in the other three hands is 3-2-1 and the second most likely is 2-2-2. That result, in itself, should be expected but the margin of difference is the shocker. The probability of 3-2-1 is a whopping 53.3% while 2-2-2 is only 14.5%.

If you pick up a hand with two five-card suits, the chance of an eight-card fit or better in one of the two suits is a very high 83%. This is not surprising, since if your partner has two or fewer cards in one suit, he must have eleven or more cards in the other three suits.

When you pick up a hand with three four-card suits, the chance of an eight-card fit in one of those suits is 80%. This probability might seem higher than expected, but even though you need four-card support from your partner, there are three possible suits where your wish for a fit may come true.

This section is uncomfortable to write in the sense that these values may be used as too much of a crutch. They are perfect when a player only has knowledge of his own hand, but that accuracy deteriorates quickly as information becomes available. The expected support is not relevant once you bid a suit and your partner tells you about his support or lack of it. But sometimes the opponents' aggressive bidding will rob your partner of the opportunity to communicate. Over the past several decades, players have become more aggressive preemptive bidders. The resulting lack of communication forces their opponents to turn to probability, somewhat out of desperation.

Nine-card Fits

We are nicely equipped with our maxim that an eight-card major-suit fit is a fine choice for trumps. Obviously a nine-card fit is even better — more accurately, much better! Let's consider two different trump holdings:

Case 1

Dummy   8 7 6

Declarer A 5 4 3 2

Case 2

Dummy   9 8 7 6

Declarer A 5 4 3 2

There are many reasons Case 2 is much better than Case 1. With Case 1, declarer can never draw trumps before doing any ruffing in dummy. Therefore, declarer can never ruff in dummy with the peace of mind that he will not be overruffed. In Case 2, if trumps split 3-1, declarer can draw trumps and then ruff once with that peace of mind. If trumps split 2-2, declarer can ruff twice with impunity. Big difference.

An important feature for approximately half (crude estimate) of all endplays involves drawing trumps, stripping the hand, and with trumps in both declarer's hand and dummy, being well positioned for a ruff and sluff. In Case 1 above, declarer can never draw trumps and still have a trump card in dummy. In Case 2, 90% of the time, declarer can draw the defender's trumps and still have at least one trump card in dummy.

We can use the tables in Chapter 4 to obtain the expected number of losers in the trump suit.

For Case 1

If the suit splits 3-2, there are two losers, while 4-1 results in three losers and 5-0, four losers.

Expected number of losers = 0.68 x 2 + 0.28 x 3 + 0.04 x 4 = 2.36.

For Case 2

Expected number of losers = 0.40 x 1 + 0.50 x 2 + 0.10 x 3 = 1.70.

For these example suits, the expected number of trump losers for the eight-card suit was two-thirds of a trick more than for the nine-card suit.

Reasonable Bidding that Misses a Nine-card Major Fit

We will now look at the easiest way to miss a nine-card fit in a major (not that a partnership would want to!). With a 5-3-3-2 shape, where the five-card suit is a major), it is common to open in notrump with the appropriate point count. Responder may have a four-card holding in the same major but, with a weak hand, may not be able to communicate his holding. The nine-card fit is only revealed by declarer's face when dummy lands on the table. Neither player did anything wrong. Bidding systems have holes. It is equivalent to playing baseball when a batter hits a gentle pop-up that happens to land between the first baseman, second baseman and right fielder. The ball was poorly hit but it found a seam in the defense. Our bidding systems cannot be perfect for all hands; they also have seams.

Some players are uncomfortable about opening notrump with a five-card major but they are also uncomfortable with the bidding problem generated by opening the major and then finding a later bid to describe the hand strength. Pick your poison: either communicate your strength on the first bid but not your major, or communicate the major but not the strength.

Let's obtain the probability of this problem occurring. Of course, many players with a five-card major and 15 HCP will search for a rationale to downgrade the hand to 14 HCP so that the major can be opened. Likewise, with 17 HCP, they will search for a rationale to upgrade to 18 HCP. For our purposes, let's assume there is no downgrading or upgrading. So, any hand with 5-3-3-2 shape with a five-card major and 15 to 17 points will be opened 1NT. The table on page 154 indicated that the point range will occur on 10% of all hands. The table on page 151 indicates that 5-3-3-2 occurs on 15.5% of hands. The twelve specific shapes corresponding to 5-3-3-2 include six with a five-card minor and six with a five-card major. Since 0.10 x 0.155 x 0.5 = 0.008, 1NT will be opened with a five-card major only once every 130 hands. Of course, probably no damage will be done if partner has little support for that major. However, we saw on page 163 that when a player opens a five-card major, his partner will hold three-card support or more 55% of the time. So there is a real possibility of harm.

Reasonable Bidding that Finds a Six-card Minor Fit

When playing a forcing 1NT response to one of a major, it is possible for declarer to play at the two-level in a six-card minor fit — a poor six-card fit at that, since it involves a three-card suit both in declarer's hand and in dummy. Please don't lose sleep in fear or this occurrence — it is rare. The opener must hold five spades, three hearts, three diamonds and two clubs. With 5=3=3=2 shape and responder 1=4=3=5, reasonable bidding may result in the auction 1♠ – 1NT (forcing); 2◇, all pass. Using the shape table on page 151, the probability that the opener has that specific shape is 1/12 x 0.155 = 0.013. The probability of the responder holding that specific shape is even smaller, 1/24 x 0.129 = 0.0054. The probability that both specific shapes occur can be estimated by multiplying these values. This will result in a probability of 0.00007 or 0.007%[‡‡‡].

In short, we see that there is little reason to fear that this bidding sequence will land a partnership in a six-card fit. It is very rare if we merely consider the two shapes. If we include the point range requirements for the opener and responder, the likelihood gets much smaller. It is already small enough that bridge players can sleep well at night. One may ask oneself: why not just end up in the 5-1 spade fit since that would probably be better than the 3-3 fit? Yes, but when responder passes the 2◇ bid, he hopes that partner has at least four diamonds. Not unreasonable.

[‡‡‡] I hope you realize that the multiplication of those two values is not mathematically acceptable since the two shapes are not independent. But they are almost independent. We have pretended independence before, so why stop now? Pretending independence is less of an issue than my rounding.

Partnership Suit Holdings

Even though maxims about trump fits extol the virtue of searching for an eight-card fit in a major, of course, nine or ten would be even better. Dare we dream of eleven? Eight cards create a fit – fewer than eight is a disappointment.

We just witnessed an example where reasonable partnership bidding resulted in a trump suit where both declarer and dummy each held three cards. One consolation is that they did not miss a great fit. The partnership's twenty-six cards consisted of six spades, seven hearts, six diamonds and seven clubs. We will refer to this with the notation 7-7-6-6. (Notice that this notation does not refer to specific suits.) They did not have an eight-card fit in either a major or a minor. Clearly, their opponents held seven spades, six hearts, seven diamonds and six clubs. This is represented identically as 7-7-6-6. So, their opponents also lacked an eight-card fit.

For any suit holding of one partnership, their opponents' suit holding is obviously determined. Here is a table with the probability of different partnership suit holdings and the corresponding opposing partnership holdings. I will list only the top ten. This covers all possibilities that have a 4% or greater chance of occurring.

Your Partnership's Holding	Probability	Opponents' Holding
7-7-6-6	10.49%	7-7-6-6
7-7-7-5	5.25%	8-6-6-6
8-7-6-5	23.60%	8-7-6-5
8-7-7-4	6.56%	9-6-6-5
8-6-6-6	5.25%	7-7-7-5
8-8-6-4	4.92%	9-7-5-5
9-7-6-4	7.29%	9-7-6-4
9-6-6-5	6.56%	8-7-7-4
9-7-5-5	4.92%	8-8-6-4
9-8-5-4	4.10%	9-8-5-4

The first two lines (holdings) are the only combinations where the best fit for your partnership is a seven-card suit. They total 16%. Therefore, at the time you pick up your cards, there is an 84% chance that you and your partner will hold an eight-card fit or better.

The next four lines correspond to holdings where your partnership's best fit is eight cards in a suit. These four lines total 40% but if we include other holdings not frequent enough to make the table where the best fit is exactly eight cards, the total is 46%.

The last four lines correspond to holdings where your partnership's best fit is nine cards in a suit. These four lines total 23% but again, if we include other holdings not in the table where the best fit is exactly nine cards, the total is 28%.

It is not surprising that the 8-7-6-5 holding is the most frequent one, but it is surprising that it wins that title by so great an amount. Almost one hand in four, your partnership will have this holding. Many probability values are repeated for different holdings; this is not surprising since holdings sort of come in pairs. Compare Lines 2 and 5. Your partnership's holdings and your opposing partnership's holdings are switched. Shouldn't their probabilities be the same? Of course – and, thankfully, they are.

This table will be used in Chapter 17. Robert MacKinnon's two books (see Bibliography) extensively study bridge decision-making through an examination of partnership holdings.

Opening 1NT with 12 to 14 HCP

Let's assume the same shape constraints as opening a strong 1NT (15-17). We saw in the last chapter that the probability (in percentages) of having 15, 16 and 17 HCP are respectively: 4.42, 3.31 and 2.36. These values total 10.09. So, on 10% of hands, the opener is in the proper point range. The probability (in percentages) of having 12, 13 and 14 HCP are respectively: 8.03, 6.91 and 5.69. These values total 20.63. So, with this weak notrump range, slightly more than twice as many hands will be appropriate for opening 1NT. Allowing just the three shapes 4-4-3-2, 5-3-3-2 and 4-3-3-3 as appropriate for notrump, we saw that 47% of all hands are one of those three shapes. Since 0.47 x 0.206 = 0.097, almost 10% of hands are appropriate in terms of both shape and points to open 1NT when using the 12-14 range.

Some may feel that partnerships are really putting their heads on a chopping block by playing a weak notrump. It is not as risky as it seems since weak notrump players are well-equipped with escape mechanisms when doubled.

When the auction starts with a strong 1NT, particularly if the partnership is playing four-suit transfers and Stayman, the probability is very high that opener will eventually become the declarer. This is still true, but to a lesser extent, when using a weak notrump range with transfers and Stayman, since there is a greater chance of the opposing partnership entering into the auction.

Don't get excited thinking that playing 12-14 HCP notrump solves the problem we have seen for strong notrump players when opener holds 15-17 HCP with a five-card major. Ideally, weak notrump bidders show a strong notrump range by opening a minor and then, after the likely one-level response, bidding 1NT. But suppose the weak notrump player has 16 HCP and a five-card major? Clearly, the bidder must open the major but if responder bids 1NT (whether forcing or not), opener has trouble showing that strength without overstating it.

Is the Hideous Hog an ethical player?

The Hideous Hog provides the following advice to his partner's, 'Please, please, partner – let me play the hand. I assure you that it is in your own interest.'[§§§] Clearly, the Hog was called a hog for good reason. His statement carries many messages – I am a much better declarer than you are; you stink as a declarer; don't bid notrump; try to bid a minor rather than a major. The Hog often becomes declarer because of the excellent hands he is dealt. This is a result of his modified point-count system, which is described in *Bridge in the Menagerie*: 'He weights his point count by adding

---

§§§ "Table Up," Victor Mollo, p.18. In *Bridge in the Menagerie*, 2013, Master Point Press.

20% to get his values into perspective."¶¶¶ How else can he factor his ability into hand evaluation?

The Hog's comments do hit on a rarely discussed bridge topic. In any basketball game, be it a high school team or a professional one, the better players take the majority of the shots. What about bridge partnerships when one player is substantially stronger than his partner? Wouldn't it be beneficial if the stronger player used weak notrump and the weaker one used strong notrump? We saw that 12-14 point hands occur more than twice as often as 15-17 point hands. This approach would result in the stronger player becoming declarer more often than the weaker player. The rules of bridge prevent such an obvious devious plan: both members of a partnership are required to play the same system. It would be unethical for a partnership to have an understanding that the better player will often open 1NT with 14 but the weaker player will stick with the traditional 15-17. Recently it has become acceptable to open notrump with a singleton ace, king or queen, but would be similarly unethical to have an understanding that the stronger player will take advantage of this new acceptability, while the weaker player will never open notrump with a singleton honor.

¶¶¶ Ibid., p. 26.

Chapter 16

Bidding Conventions

Is this chapter useful? Why?

Usefulness number: 8. This chapter is useful for analyzing probability-related questions that pertain to conventions. Most of the mathematical issues are not matters that arise suddenly in the middle of a bridge hand. They are primarily related to deciding what conventions you wish to put on your convention card, and how religiously you wish to follow the standard form of the convention. Thankfully, such discussions do not happen at the bridge table, so you can employ any computing device or refer to any mathematical table that you wish.

Frequency Issues

There are several frequency issues:

1) How often will the convention come up?
2) Relaxing a requirement of a convention will often reduce its usefulness and/or clarity, but will result in greater usage. What is the resulting increase in frequency?
3) How often does the convention or the bid it replaces come up?
4) Some conventions are used in the hope of finding something in partner's hand. What is the chance of finding it?

Let me give an example of Item 2: the well-known Weak Two-bid. It is so common among duplicate players, it is hardly appropriate to classify it as a convention, but it is. The standard treatment requires a six-card suit with either two of the top three honors or three of the top five. Especially when non-vulnerable but even sometimes when vulnerable, most players take liberties with these rules, for example reducing honor requirements, allowing five-card suits in third seat or allowing five-card suits in all seats. When players relax the requirements, they increase the frequency of use but, unfortunately, they convey less clear information to partner. In general, we will see that the more specific a convention, the rarer the usage but the greater the amount of information conveyed.

Around 1900, bridge books often recommended that a dealer should make spades trumps when their hand had no winnable tricks – even if holding few or no spades. I am not going to attempt to explain why, but merely tell you that it related to the rules and scoring at that time. Trust me, the strategy had a great deal of merit, and most authors strongly recommended it. One author surprisingly felt the system was good but he did not want to recommend its use. He feared that players would like it, use it successfully, and then would attempt to use it on hands where it would not be appropriate. I often think about that since modern bridge players tend to expand the usage of conventions that they like to a dangerous level.

In the next two sections, I will look at two popular conventions, Gambling 3NT and Flannery. Both conventions involve the opening bid, and we will assume that the bid is made by the dealer. There is no point in the book where I feel more honest in using mathematics. The other three players have not had any opportunity to communicate any information about their hands by either bidding or passing. So, these conventions are totally appropriate for mathematical analysis. The less information there is available, the greater the role of probability.

Both conventions are rarely used, but when the opener has an appropriate hand to employ either, a great amount of information is communicated.

MAJOR WARNING: Before describing any conventions I want to provide this warning: please do not start playing any convention simply because you read about it in this book. I only present conventions for the purpose of examining their frequency of occurring or some aspect of probability related to the convention. A very limited purpose.

Before playing any convention both you and your partner should read about it in the same book on conventions since different books have similar but often not identical descriptions. Let the agreed upon book establish your partnership understanding. A very common expression in team sports for the last decade is for teammates "to be on the same page." If two bridge partners are not using the same book, obviously, they cannot be on the same page. I want to recommend two books on conventions by Barbara Seagram: *25 Bridge Conventions You Should Know* (with Marc Smith), and *25 More Bridge Conventions You Should Know* (with David Bird).

Gambling 3NT Convention

Suppose you are the dealer and pick up:

♠ Q   ♡ J 7   ◇ A K Q J 9 8 4   ♣ 7 5 2

If you are playing the Gambling 3NT Convention, you will open 3NT. That shows a running seven-card minor (rarely, eight) but no outside ace or king. Partner then can either leave you to play in 3NT or can bid 4♣ for you to pass or correct to diamonds. At times, partner may even bid 5♣ or 6♣ for you to pass or correct. With just your one bid of 3NT, you have actually almost totally described your hand. An added bonus is that you have made it hard for your opponents to search for their very likely major-suit fit.

When your partner opens 3NT, an example of a perfect dummy to leave in the 3NT contract, rather than pull to the minor, is a hand with three aces and nothing else of value. You can count ten tricks. But, of course, you don't pass 3NT if you are void in either minor — there will be no entries to partner's hand! Your partner may take only three tricks, with the three aces, rather than the eagerly-anticipated ten.

So far, I have described the convention, but what are the probability issues?

1) Some books specify AKQJxxx in the minor, some just AKQxxxx, and some just say a seven-card running minor. What is the probability that the minor will in fact run in each case?
2) How much greater is the likelihood of using the convention if the requirement of AKQJxxx is reduced to AKQxxxx?

Let's start with Question 1. If declarer is left to play in 3NT, dummy must have at least a singleton in the minor (see above), so declarer will have at least an eight-card fit in the minor. With AKQJxxx, the only way the suit will not run is if dummy has a singleton, the seven-card suit does not include the 10-spot, and the suit splits 5-0. Even assuming declarer does not hold the 10-spot, the probability that dummy has a singleton is 0.28 and the probability of a 5 0 split is 0.04. Since 0.28 x 0.04 = 0.011, there is approximately a 99% chance the suit will run. Without the jack, i.e. AKQxxxx, the suit will not run if dummy has a singleton and the suit splits 4-1 or 5-0. It also will not run if dummy has a doubleton and the suit splits 4-0. The probability of a singleton is 0.28 and of a doubleton is 0.38. So, the probability that this suit will not run is 0.28 x (0.28 + 0.04) + 0.38 x 0.10 = 0.13. So, even without the jack, the suit will run 87% of the time.

The above result was based on the implied guarantee that your partner held at least a singleton. If you had been dealt AKQxxxx in a minor and opened 3NT, until your partner passed thereby guaranteeing at least a singleton, the probability that the suit will run is only 84%.

Now for Question 2. The probability of holding a seven-card club suit is 0.88%. So, the probability of being dealt a seven-card suit in either clubs or diamonds is 1.76%. But once we place the restrictions of holding AKQJxxx and no outside ace or king, the probability falls to 0.029%. With the less restrictive constraint of not requiring the jack, the probability leaps up to 0.073%. The mathematics to obtain this value appears in Chapter 20.

This convention replaces an opening bid of 3NT that shows a balanced 25-27 HCP. The probability of a hand in that point range is only 0.043% — an even rarer occurrence than holding the right hand for a Gambling 3NT. Besides, the big hand can be described by starting with 2♣, and then rebidding 3NT.

The Flannery Convention

When playing this convention, an opening bid of 2◊ shows a hand with exactly four spades, exactly five hearts, and four cards in the minors. It also requires 11 to 15 HCP. This shape includes any of these five specific shapes: 4=5=2=2, 4=5=3=1, 4=5=1=3, 4=5=4=0 and 4=5=0=4. From the shape tables we see that the corresponding probabilities for these five specific cases are 0.88, 0.54, 0.54, 0.10, 0.10. Let me remind you how each of these five values can be obtained. For the first specific shape (4=5=2=2), just take the proper value in our shape table (10.58) and divide it by 12; this will result in 0.88. For the second and third, divide 12.93 by 24; for the fourth and fifth, divide 1.24 by 12. So, by adding these five values, we see that there is a 2.16% chance of having the proper shape for using this convention. Since you will have the appropriate point range only on 34% of the hands, there is less than a 1% chance you will be able to open a hand with a Flannery 2◊. Remember, too, that I am assuming you are the dealer. Often, it seems, when I have the perfect hand for Flannery someone else opens the bidding before I get my opportunity.

When a player opens a Flannery 2◊, his partner feels flush with knowledge. It is immediately clear to responder whether the partnership has a fit in either major, as well as the exact number of cards in that fit.

At the beginning of the chapter, I provided a list of four questions on frequency issues. Question 4 indicated that many conventions are used when a player hopes to find something. The Flannery bidder hopes that his partner has at least four spades or at least three hearts. The probability that at least one of these hopes is fulfilled is 74%.

Flannery does replace a very common bid: the weak two-bid in diamonds. You may feel that this weak-two does little to prevent the opponents from finding their major-suit fit. However, the drawback of Flannery is that the opponents now know a great deal about your hand too, and may be able to defend or compete much more accurately. Probability can only indicate the frequency with which the opportunity to use the convention occurs – after that your bridge judgment must help you decide whether to adopt it.

Conditional Probability

The topic of conditional probability is an important one for bridge players. Even though we have actually been using it since Chapter 2, I have not formally defined it, and now is as good a time as any to do so, at least semi-formally. Conditional probability is needed when a probability is determined based on the certainty of some given condition. Let's look at an example where we can obtain a probability without a given condition and then obtain the probability of the same event when there is such a condition.

When picking up a hand, the probability that we have 15 HCP is:

$$P(15 \text{ HCP}) = 4.42\%$$

But should it become known that the hand is in the 15-17 point range this probability jumps dramatically:

$$P(15 \text{ HCP, given } 15\text{-}17 \text{ HCP}) = 44\%$$

How would one know that partner holds a hand in the range 15 to 17? Easy – he opens 1NT. Why is the probability 44%? We will justify that value in the next chapter. Even though that 44% figure first surfaced in Chapter 6, I still have not justified the value.

I mentioned that we encountered conditional probability way back in Chapter 2. It was the example that involved the likelihood of opening 1◊ with a three-card diamond suit. I pointed out that there is often confusion between the two different but similar interpretations: P(opening 1◊ with a three-card diamond suit) and P (three-card diamond suit given a 1◊ opening).

As communication takes place during the bidding, using conditional probability is essential.

Stayman or Not

An interesting and common (all too common) decision arises when you hold two four-card majors, with fewer than 8 points, and your partner opens 1NT. You are caught between a rock and a hard place. You don't have the strength to invite game but realize that there is a high likelihood of missing an eight-card major-suit fit, or for that matter a nine-card major-suit fit (remember the last chapter). Don't you wonder how likely it is that you are missing a major-suit fit?

Let's investigate the three basic shapes that partner may have. For each, we can figure out the probability of missing a fit. Partner may be 4-3-3-3, 4-4-3-2, or 5-3-3-2. In Chapter 14, we saw that the probabilities of these shapes are 0.105, 0.216 and 0.155 respectively. These values total 0.476. Just these three shapes encompass almost half of all possible hands. Therefore, we will assume partner, with 15-17 HCP, will open 1NT on only these three shapes but will open all hands with these shapes:

P(4-3-3-3 given partner opens 1NT) = 0.105/0.476 = 0.22
P(4-4-3-2 given partner opens 1NT) = 0.216/0.476 = 0.45
P(5-3-3-2 given partner opens 1NT) = 0.155/0.476 = 0.33

In the case 4-3-3-3, there are only four specific shapes. In two of these possibilities the four-card suit will be either hearts or spades so the probability will be 2/4. In the case 4-4-3-2, there are twelve specific shapes, and ten of those twelve will have a four-card major. The only way it will not happen is if the notrump bidder has three spades, two hearts and four cards in each minor or two spades, three hearts and four cards in each minor. In the case 5-3-3-2, the good news is that you cannot miss an eight-card major fit, but the bad news is that you may miss a nine-card major suit fit. The five-card suit is just as likely to be one of the majors as one of the minors.

P(missing an eight- or nine-card fit) = 2/4 × 0.22 + 10/12 × 0.45 + 2/4 × 0.33 = 0.11 + 0.375 + 0.165 = 0.65

So, there is roughly a 65% chance of finding an eight-card or better fit in a major. This is another example of Question 4 on the first page of this chapter.

P(missing a nine-card fit) = 0.165

Indeed, there is a realistic chance of missing a major-suit fit.

Before continuing, it is necessary to point out the two ways that I was playing somewhat loosely with the mathematics involved in my analysis. In the case of the 5-3-3-2 shape, I stated that the five-card suit was as likely to be in a major as in a minor. In the last chapter, I pointed out that players downgrade 15 HCP hands so that they can open the major and likewise upgrade 17 HCP hands. So, I told a slightly innocent lie. In Chapter 1, I mentioned that once you look at your own hand, certain probabilities relating to the opener's hand need to be modified. Since, in this example, you hold eight cards in the major suits and only five cards in the minor suits, the notrump opener is slightly more likely to hold more cards in the minors than the majors. Another slightly innocent lie. Both lies slightly increased my above probability values, so the actual probability of missing a nine-card fit is a little less.

I am happy to report that I can suggest a rather fine solution, a convention called Garbage Stayman. It allows responder (you) to bid 2♣ without implying any strength. If the notrumper bids a major, which you expect and are praying for, you will pass. If your partner bids 2♢, thereby denying a four-card major, you bid 2♡, asking partner either to pass or to bid 2♠ if spades are his better major. You can feel certain of at least a seven-card major fit unless your partner opened 1NT with a doubleton in each major.

Transfer or Not

After your partner opens 1NT, it is desirable for you to transfer into your five-card suit even with no HCP. Yes, you may end up in a seven-card fit but it is not too likely. I will provide some analysis and then apologize, as usual, for cheating with my mathematics. My lies are more blatant in this section than the last one: not my proudest moment.

If the notrump bidder is 4-3-3-3, it is impossible to end up in a seven-card fit after a transfer. If he is 4-4-3-2 or 5-3-3-2, the chance of playing in the seven-card trump suit is still only 25% in each case. Therefore, by using values obtained in the last section for the probability of each shape, P(seven-card fit) = 0.22 x 0 + 0.45 x 1/4 + 0.33 x 1/4 = 0.19.

So, the probability that you will end up in an eight-card or longer fit is 81%. Even if you end up in a seven-card fit, it may be the best place since the trump suit will provide some entries to dummy, therefore providing an opportunity to lead toward the strong hand rather than being forced to lead away from it. Of course, there is no problem if the responder has the strength of an invitational hand or better since subsequent bidding will enable the partnership to establish whether or not it has an eight-card fit in a major.

The two lies in the last section, in a modified form, interfere with the accuracy of my analysis of transfer bids. If the responder holds a five-card suit, it is more likely to be in the suit of partner's doubleton than in the other suits. But the chance of finding three-card support after partner opens one notrump is considerably better than the general situation of finding three-card support for a five-card suit. On page 163, we said that, for the general situation, the probability was only 55%. The difference is easily justified. In general, opposite a five-card suit a player can hold a void or singleton, but after the 1NT opener, that cannot happen. Even though the 81% is misleadingly large, the actual value is still much larger than that 55% value.

Overcalling Unusual 2NT, Michaels, others

The bridge world is rich in conventions that show two-suiters. Typically, they show 5-5, or if the bridge powers are on your side, 6-5. Even 5-4 may be workable at times. When you pick up a hand, the chance of it being 6-5 is only 1.4%, but the chance that your partnership has an eight-card or better fit in one of those two long suits is 92%. The chance of your hand being 5-5 is 4%. Now the chance that your partnership has an eight-card or better fit in one of those two long suits is 84%. The chance of your hand being 5-4 is a healthy 25%. In this case, the chance that your partnership has an eight-card or better fit in one of those two long suits is 74%. We did encounter the 74% value earlier in this chapter when we looked at the Flannery convention.

The percentages in the last paragraph were based on the likelihood of support before any bidding took place at the table. The values are accurate for Flannery since the convention involves an opening bid. However, the two-suiters in this section involve conventional *overcalls*. When an opponent opens with a suit bid showing five cards or more (at any level), the probability of you finding a fit are obviously changed by the opening bid. I have good news and bad. The good news (assuming an opponent did not bid one of your long suits) is that your partner is more likely to have support for at least one of your suits. The bad news is that if your partnership declares the hand, you will likely face a bad trump break.

Conventions that show two suits are particularly useful when an opponent opens a strong notrump. You should feel empowered to come into the bidding when you have methods for showing a two-suiter.

Memory, Wakefulness and Conventions

Probably the most important likelihood question for any partnership when deciding whether or not to play a convention is, 'Will either player forget the convention?'

One would think that conventions that rarely occur, like Gambling 3NT, would be the most forgettable. But I believe the conventions that one can sleep through are the most forgotten. Usually it is not really a case of 'forgetting a convention' but simply not being awake enough to recognize it at the table. My favorite example is Drury. It's easy to miss the significance of the opening bid of one of a major being in third or fourth seat, so that a 2♣ response now has a different meaning. Those passes prior to the opening bid are easy to sleep through. The bidding is just too ordinary. By contrast, a 3NT opening is an alarm clock going off.

Chapter 17
Bidding Decisions

Is this chapter useful? Why?

Usefulness number: 8. There are many bidding situations where the use of probability can aid decision-making. Some probability-related decisions arise in constructive auctions where the issue is whether to bid game or slam, while others are in competitive auctions.

Bids that Show HCP Ranges

When a bidder shows a range of points, his partner should not mistakenly believe that all possibilities are equally likely. In Chapter 6, I indicated that when the opening bid is 1NT (15-17 HCP), the probability that the bidder holds 15 HCP is 44%, 16 HCP is 33%, and 17 HCP is 23%. In Chapter 14, the HCP table shows that you will pick up 15 HCP on 4.42% of hands, 16 HCP on 3.31%, and 17 HCP on 2.36%. Since these values total 10.09%, we need only divide each value by 10.09%. The division by 0.10 (equivalent to a multiplication by 10) is so simple it obscures the technique.

In the last few chapters, I assumed for simplicity that all 15-17 HCP hands with the three balanced shapes are opened 1NT. Suppose we assume instead that, for those three balanced shapes, only 80% of the 15 HCP hands are opened 1NT, that all 16 HCP are, and that 90% of the 17 HCP are opened 1NT. Now if your partner opens 1NT, what is the probability he has 15 HCP? 16 HCP? 17 HCP? We can answer these questions with Bayes' Theorem. It is necessary to identify the result and the potential sources.

Result: Partner opens 1NT
Potential Sources: Three potential sources — holding 15 or 16 or 17 HCP
P(partner opens 1NT) = 4.42 x 0.8 + 3.31 x 1 + 2.36 x 0.9
= 3.54 + 3.31 + 2.12 = 8.97 (values in percentages)

P(15 HCP given partner opens 1NT) = 3.54 / 8.97 = 0.39
P(16 HCP given partner opens 1NT) = 3.31 / 8.97 = 0.37
P(17 HCP given partner opens 1NT) = 2.12 / 8.97 = 0.24

Not surprisingly, compared to our prior example, the probability of the source being 15 HCP decreased, while 16 HCP increased, and 17 only slightly changed. 15 is still the most likely source, but by a slender margin. We could apply Bayes' Theorem with more complicated assumptions, such as that 15% of all 14 HCP are upgraded and opened 1NT, while 10% of all 18 HCP hands are downgraded and opened 1NT. Same technique. Why didn't we use Bayes' Theorem on the original problem in this chapter? I sort of did, but since we were assuming that all 15-17 HCP hands with the proper shape were opened 1NT, there would have been some unnecessary multiplications by 1. Try it and see for yourself. The actual formula for Bayes' Theorem appears in Appendix 2. Since you know the technique, the formula is not that important, but it should be understandable.

In the same section of Chapter 6, we considered the sequence 2♣ – 2◇; 2NT showing 22-24 HCP. It was indicated that the probability was 55% for 22 HCP, 30% for 23, and 15% for 24. The Chapter 14 table showed that a player would pick up 22 HCP on 0.21% of hands, 23 HCP on 0.11%, and 24 HCP on 0.06%. These total 0.38; therefore, the probability of each after showing 22-24 HCP can be determined by dividing each value by 0.38. Since 0.21/0.38 = 0.55, 0.11/0.38 = 0.29, and 0.06/0.38 = 0.16, we now have justified these values. (Some rounding errors crept in.)

This approach would also work for two-point ranges, such as a 2NT opener which shows 20-21 HCP. The probability from the HCP table of picking up a hand with 20 HCP is 0.64 and with 21 HCP is only 0.38. Since the two values total 1.02, when 2NT is opened the probability that the opener has 20 HCP is 63% (0.64/1.02) and 21 HCP only 37% (0.38/1.02).

Often, one must consider the average strength of partner's hand. If the opener shows 15-17 HCP, the average count is not 16, but it can be obtained by expected value.

Expected HCP = 0.44 x 15 + 0.33 x 16 + 0.23 x 17
= 6.60 + 5.28 + 3.91 = 15.79

When opener shows 20-21 HCP:

Expected HCP = 0.63 x 20 + 0.37 x 21 = 12.60 + 7.77
= 20.37

When opener shows 22-24 HCP:

Expected HCP = 0.55 x 22 + 0.30 x 23 + 0.15 x 24
= 12.10 + 6.90 + 3.60 = 22.60

In summary, when partner promises a big hand, the hand is probably toward the bottom of the range. And the better your own hand is, the greater the chance that your partner's big hand is at its lower end of the range.

Suppose your partner passed your opening suit bid, thereby limiting his hand to a maximum of 5 HCP. Consider the two-point ranges 0-1 HCP and 3-4 HCP. The range 3-4 is more than five times more likely than 0-1. The range 3-4 is about three times more likely than 1-2. (I ignored 5 HCP because most players figure out how to count that hand as 6.) We see from these examples that when one is dealing with hands with fewer than 10 HCP, the upper end of the range is more likely.

Obviously, decisions such as going to game and slam are based on partner's described strength. These probabilistic considerations shed some additional light on what that strength is likely to be.

Bids that Show Shortness

After a trump fit is found, many conventional bids show shortness and indicate either a void or a singleton, but these two options are not equally likely. Being dealt a hand with a singleton is six times more likely than being dealt a hand with a void. So, if your partner shows shortness, base your subsequent bids on the assumption that your partner has a singleton rather than a void. I am sure that no readers are surprised by this remark.

Don't Miss Games, Even Not Vulnerable

At Swiss Team events, when a team splits up to head into battle at two tables, the title of this section will often be shouted. In this section, we will use expected value calculations to justify this pronouncement.

In Chapter 13, we already looked at expected value calculations for bridge scoring. But at that time, we studied bridge values rather than the payoffs that occur in team events. Now we have to consider what result occurs at each of the two tables in order to obtain payoffs.

Suppose you must decide between passing your partner in 3♡ or going to 4♡. Based on your knowledge, you feel declarer is equally likely to take nine or ten tricks (a tossup). Maybe it will depend on whether you win or lose a finesse. Assume the same number of tricks will be made at both tables. Assume that you are aggressive and under these circumstances will bid game 70% of the time but you know that at the other table the timid players will bid game only 40% of the time. First, let's suppose that you are not vulnerable.

We can separately consider the two cases: when game makes and when it does not. Each has a probability of 0.5.

When declarers take ten tricks:

If both tables bid game, the swing = 0. The IMP (International Matchpoint Scale) result is 0. The probability of this situation is 0.5 x 0.7 x 0.4 = 0.14. If you bid game but the opponents do not, the swing is 420 – 170 = 250. The IMP result is +6. Probability of this situation is 0.5 x 0.7 x 0.6 = 0.21. If you don't bid game but the opponents do, the swing is 170 – 420 = –250. The IMP result is –6. The probability of this situation is 0.5 x 0.3 x 0.4 = 0.06. If neither you nor your opponents bid game, the swing is 170 – 170 = 0. The IMP result is 0. The probability of this is 0.5 x 0.3 x 0.6 = 0.09.

When declarers take only nine tricks:

If both tables bid game, the swing is –50 – (–50) = 0. The IMP result is 0. The probability of this situation is 0.5 x 0.7 x 0.4 = 0.14. If you bid game but opponents do not, the swing is –50 – 140 = –190. IMP result is –5. The probability of this situation is 0.5 x 0.7 x 0.6 = 0.21. If you don't bid game but your opponents do, the swing is 140 – (–50) = 190. The IMP result is +5. The probability of this situation is 0.5 x 0.3 x 0.4 = 0.06. If neither you nor your opponents bid game, the swing is 140 – 140 = 0. The IMP result is 0. The probability of this is 0.5 x 0.3 x 0.6 = 0.09.

Expected value = 0.14 x 0 + 0.21 x 6 + 0.06 x (–6) + 0.09 x 0 + 0.14 x 0 + 0.21 x (–5) + 0.06 x 5 + 0.09 x 0 = 1.26 – 0.36 – 1.05 + 0.30 = 0.15

We see that the aggressive bidding pair was rewarded on the average by 0.15 IMP.

Before moving on, it is a good habit to check that the eight probabilities add up to 1. The eight possibilities cover all cases and are mutually exclusive, so any value other than 1 for the sum of their probabilities would be an obvious error. Since we assumed that ten tricks would be made 50% of the time, the first four probabilities should add up to 0.5 and the second four should also add up to 0.5. They do. The first four probabilities are identical to the last four.

Well, if being aggressive is good with this scenario, let's carry it a little further to bidding game 90% of the time. The eight probabilities will all change, but the IMP payoffs will remain the same. With this modification, the eight probabilities become 0.18, 0.27, 0.02, 0.03, and of course the same four values are repeated. I will leave out the four cases where the payoff is 0.

Expected value = 0.27 x 6 + 0.02 x (–6) + 0.27 x (–5) + 0.02 x 5 = 1.62 – 0.12 – 1.35 + 0.10 = 0.25 IMP

This improvement correctly demonstrates that when you have a 50% chance of success, bid game. The argument is even more powerful when declarer is vulnerable. The payoff possibilities change to 620 – 170 = 450 (+10 IMP), 170 – 620 = –450 (–10 IMP), –100 – 140 = –240 (–6 IMP), and 140 – (–100) = 240 (6 IMP).

When you go to game 70% of the time, the computation involves these payoffs but the same probabilities as our first example. I will again ignore the four cases where the payoff is 0.

Expected value = 0.21 x 10 + 0.06 x (–10) + 0.21 x (–6) + 0.06 x 6
= 2.10 – 0.60 – 1.26 + 0.36 = 0.60 IMP

When you go to game 90% of the time, the expected value
= 0.27 x 10 + 0.02 x (–10) + 0.27 x (–6) + 0.02 x 6
= 2.70 – 0.20 – 1.62 + 0.12 = 1.00 IMP

There is nothing novel in these calculations but they demonstrate that, with IMP scoring, if you believe that there is a 50% chance that game will be made, you should bid game 100% of the time.

The expected value does not involve game theory. You are not trying to outguess an opponent who is trying to outguess you. But suppose you feel your team is ahead in the match. Now you would want to be in the same contract as the opponents and make the same decisions as they do during the play. This would result in a push rather than a swing board. Of course, if your opponents realized that they were behind, they would have a different goal: they would want a swing board. So possibly it becomes a guessing game.

Another form of team play is Board-a-Match. It is rarely played. On every board, if your team gets a better score than your opponents, you receive 1 point. A poorer score gets 0, an equal score 1/2. The margin of outscoring the other team on that board is of no importance. Does it still pay to bid all games that are a 50-50 chance?

No. Consider our last calculation. When vulnerable, you bid game at a 90% rate, while your opponents bid at a rate of 40%. Now with these payoffs:

Expected value = 0.18 x 1/2 + 0.27 x 1 + 0.02 x 0 + 0.03 x 1/2 + 0.18 x 1/2 + 0.27 x 0 + 0.02 x 1 + 0.03 x 1/2
= 0.09 + 0.27 + 0 + 0.015 + 0.09 + 0 + 0.02 + 0.015 = 0.50

The result of 0.5 shows that an average result is expected. This same result of 0.5 will arise no matter what probability is plugged in for bidding game by either team. There is no gain or loss in being the more aggressive team playing against a less aggressive team. What is important is being lucky on a tossup decision.

Even though Board-a-Match is rarely played, I am providing this example because of its obvious carryover to duplicate pairs events. Your matchpoint score has little to do with bridge scoring but is totally dependent on how many pairs you beat or tie on each board. When playing duplicate pairs, the important thing to remember is to bid game whenever it makes, and not bid game when it does not make. How is that for useless advice?

Slam Bidding

Slam bidding can be analyzed in the identical fashion as game bidding. First, I will make several assumptions: using IMP scoring, you will take either eleven or twelve tricks, and during the bidding you believe the probability of each outcome is 50%. Under that assessment, you will bid a small slam 90% of the time but believe that your opponents will only bid it 40% of the time. I am sure these values seem familiar. The eight outcomes are identical to the last example with IMP scoring. But four of the cases can be ignored since the payoff is zero: when both partnerships bid and make slam, both bid but do not succeed, neither bids slam but take 12 tricks, and neither bids slam while they take only eleven tricks. This leaves four cases. First let's assume you are not vulnerable. If the slam suit is a major the four interesting cases are: 980 − 480 = 500 (+11 IMP), 480 − 980 = −500 (−11 IMP), −50 − 450 = −500 (−11 IMP), and 450 − (−50) = 500 (+11 IMP).

The next line is almost identical to the prior example with IMP scoring where declarer goes to game 90% of the time:

Expected value = $0.27 \times 11 + 0.02 \times (-11) + 0.27 \times (-11) + 0.02 \times 11 = 0$ IMP.

There is no benefit to bidding aggressively or for that matter bidding meekly with these payoffs. It is just like duplicate pairs: a partnership is equally rewarded for the correct decision as it is punished for the wrong one.

If we did this example with a vulnerable declarer, the result would be the same. The only change would be that 11 would become 13 and −11 would become −13.

For a strong partnership playing in a typical club duplicate pairs game, it is not essential to bid slams aggressively. Club players are more timid than top players when it comes to slam bidding. If an excellent partnership recognizes the likely prospect of a slam, and therefore bids the slam, which makes on a double squeeze, they will receive a top board. But this is sort of getting two tops on the same board, one for bidding the slam, and the other for the excellent declarer play. If they had not bid slam but merely made an extra trick in the play, they would still have got the same top.

It Is Rare Not to Have a Fit

In Chapter 15, a table appeared that provided the probability of various partnership holdings. The only way for neither partnership to hold an eight-card fit is if both partnerships hold two seven-card fits and two six-card fits. The probability of this situation is 10.5%. If your opponents have an eight-card fit, the only way that your partnership does not also have an eight-card fit is if you have three seven-card fits and one-five card fit. The probability of that is 5.3%. In summary, the probability of your partnership holding an eight-card or better fit is 84%. If your opponents have an eight-card fit, the probability of your partnership having one as well is 94%.

Typically, when the opponents find a good fit, your chances of a good fit with partner improve. Even more emphatically, if the opponents find a great fit, your chances of a great fit with partner improve. Therefore, your opponents' fine bidding may reveal your fit. Admittedly, you may not know which suit, but the knowledge that you have a fit will give you license to search aggressively.

The Law of Total Tricks and Bergen Raises

Consider the following suit:

Dummy

A 7 5

Declarer

Q J 10

Declarer has already drawn trumps and declarer has to play this suit. How many tricks will declarer take in this suit? This is a probability question. Assuming this is not a trick question about tricks, the answer is three tricks 50% of the time and two tricks 50% of the time. It all comes down to where the king is located. What if the question were asked from the viewpoint of the defense? How many tricks will the defense take in this suit? The answer is zero tricks 50% of the time, and one trick 50% of the time. Again, it all comes down to which defender holds the king.

Now I will ask a third question. How many tricks in total will declarer and the defenders take in this suit? This is not a probability question. The answer is always three. Either the finesse loses and 2 + 1 = 3 or the finesse wins and 3 + 0 = 3. Simply, if cards are positioned well for the declarer, they are badly positioned for the defense and when they are positioned badly for the declarer, they are positioned well for the defense.

Suppose your opponents have passed throughout the bidding. Do they have an eight-card fit? Who knows? Well, actually, you may be the first to know. Suppose your partner opened the bidding 1♥ and you have a four-card heart suit. Since your partnership has at least a nine-card fit, you are certain that your opponents have at most four hearts so they have must have at least 22 cards in the other three suits. Therefore, they must have at least one suit with at least eight cards. It is interesting that you are the only player with this information. If your partner opens 1♥ and you hold five hearts, you are certain that your opponents have at most one loser in the heart suit. One of the opponents will definitely be aware of that fact and will be motivated to bid courageously.

This is all background information for the Law of Total Tricks, which plays a major role in competitive bidding decisions. It became famous through Larry Cohen's classic book, *To Bid or Not to Bid* (1976). A must read! Cohen acknowledges that the Law of Total Tricks was described by Jean-René Vernes in the June 1969 issue of *The Bridge World* and that Marty Bergen was the first top player to appreciate its importance fully.

In his 1969 article, Jean-René Vernes provides the description: 'The number of total tricks in a hand is approximately equal to the total number of trumps held by both sides, each in its respective suit.'[****]

This implies that if one side has a ten-card fit and the other a nine-card fit, combined they can take a total of approximately nineteen tricks. I almost hate to mention the Law since I cannot do it justice in a few lines. I want to make it clear that I know my explanation is grossly inadequate and I am truly embarrassed by it. Please read Larry Cohen's book or at least a long journal article on applying the Law. Vernes' article describes tests on the correctness of the Law from World Championships (1954-1963) and double-dummy play. A large double-dummy study of the Law was conducted by Matt Ginsberg, and the results were published in the November 1996 issue of *The Bridge World*. It demonstrated that the Law performed very well for all examples when the number of total tricks was not greater than 20.

This leaves open some question as to the Law's relevance for typical bridge players who play in a duplicate club once or twice a week. Certainly, they may not be able to take the maximum number of tricks that are in theory possible. But even more important is that they often stay out of the auction and never realize that they have a fit. I believe that in club games many more hands have a final contract in a major at the two-level than in a Flight A Regional event. Better players come into the auction without much

---

[****] Jean-René Vernes, "The Law of Total Tricks", *The Bridge World* (June 1969), p. 5.

provocation. They do not allow their opponents to be left in peace at the two-level in a major (particularly in 2♡).

Vernes' article also states an important practical maxim that is generated by the Law: 'You are protected by 'security of distribution' in bidding for as many tricks as your side holds trumps.'[++++] For example, if your side holds nine hearts, it is usually wise to compete to the three-level. (Note that this does not imply that your side can necessarily take nine tricks – a common misunderstanding of the Law.)

One consequence of the Law of Total Tricks is Bergen Raises. This popular convention consists of a variety of raises to the three-level used when your partner opens a major and you hold four-card support. In summary: if partner opens 1♡ and if you hold four hearts with fewer than 7 points bid 3♡, if you hold four hearts and 7-9 points bid 3♣, and if you hold four hearts and 10-12 points bid 3♢. With fewer than 7 points, 3♡ is often a very successful preemptive bid. With 10-12 points, the knowledge of four-card support will often help your partner make the correct decision on whether to go to game. For example, if partner has a two-suiter, the ruffing power in dummy rates to be very useful. A friend, Richard Braunstein, whom I see regularly at the American Bridge Teachers' Association yearly convention, studied Bergen Raises for club-level players. He was disappointed by the performance of the 3♣ bid. He found that it often resulted in a contract that went down at the three-level but would have been successful at the two-level. Since the opposing pair has at most half of the points, they will probably never get into the auction and find their fit. With duplicate scoring, advanced players will find some way to leap into the fray.

Some interesting studies are available online that point out how different the world-class game is from the club game. Some look at players of different ability levels and measure their game and slam frequencies. I will return to this in Chapter 18.

++++ Ibid., p. 6

Why are weaker players less eager to enter the bidding? A major reason is that their poor declarer play will increase their likelihood of being punished: a hard argument to refute. Sometimes I think the name of our game, 'contract bridge', encourages beginners to be timid bidders. If one looks up the word 'contract' in a thesaurus one finds 'pledge', 'promise', 'binding agreement'. Any honest person, or at least most honest people, do not want to violate a contract. If one promises to take ten tricks, one is morally bound to take ten tricks. Three decades ago, an elderly man, who had played auction bridge as a child, asked me if I felt embarrassed when I failed to fulfill a contract. I think I gave him some self-deprecating flip answer, 'I am used to it since I go down very often.' But his question did make me consider not only the meaning of the word 'contract' but its role in the history of contract bridge.

The form of contract bridge that was born around 1919 provided very miserly points for fulfilling a contract but severely punished players who failed to do so. Points per trick were spades 2, clubs 4, diamonds 6, hearts 8 and notrump 10. The reward for a small slam was 50 points and for a grand slam was 100. But for each undertrick, the defenders would get 50 — if they had doubled, 100. Often the undertrick points were called 'fines' or 'penalties'. Sounds awful — like a violation of the rules. With these values, players would only want to be in a contract that they were certain to fulfill. In 1925, Harold S. Vanderbilt introduced modified values, which quickly became the standard scoring method. When the scoring for our game changed in the late 1920s, the strategy of our game was also altered. Not fulfilling a contract was no longer a tragedy.

Chapter 18
Statistics for the Human Element

Is this chapter useful? Why?

Usefulness number: somewhere between 4 and 10. Obviously, I am unable to judge its usefulness. Right now I would not rate it useful, but some of the content of this chapter may prove in a few years to be very useful – perhaps it will even become a 10. At the heart of the problem is that this chapter describes a very new subject. Not statistics – that subject is several centuries old – but bridge performance statistics, which is in its infancy. One might question whether it has even been born.

25 or 26 HCP – Which is Enough?

Let's return to a very common topic in this book: the idea that a partnership needs 26 HCP (25 in some books) for bidding 3NT. That one point makes a surprisingly big difference. We saw that an uneven HCP split of 26-14 or more only occurs on about 25% of all hands, whereas 25-15 or more will occur on 35% of hands. I commented that what Bob Hamman can accomplish with 23 HCP, a beginner may need 28 HCP for. What about the typical reader, who is not quite Bob Hamman but is superior to a beginner? That's a large crowd. Just keep track of your performance on 25 HCP hands. After a large number of hands, if you are only successful on 20% of the hands, your personal maxim should not be 25; maybe it should be 26 or 27. Then try the same experiment with 26 HCP, and see how you fare. What if your success rate is 90% with 25 HCP? Maybe you should try 24. I can see three valid objections to my proposal.

1) Too much work keeping track of personal performance.
2) Since I play very little, the statistics will not mean much.
3) The results may be embarrassing.

Objection 1 response: You are correct. Few players would want to do the required record keeping. To be honest, I would not respect anyone who did. But with our computer-generated hands and computer records of results, no serious work should be involved. The computer will know with 100% accuracy how many HCP a partnership had and whether or not declarer was successful.

Objection 2 response: You are again correct. With a small sample, statistics can be very misleading. An alternative approach is to study players at different ability levels. For lack of any rating system more enlightening than our masterpoint system, we could have categories, such as 0-49, 50-499, 500-4999, and 5000+. It would be interesting to learn what the maxim would be for the different categories. One can even obtain the probability of success against different levels of opponents. In general, top players play against tougher opponents than beginners. The computer knows your opponents' masterpoint holdings. It could be that as a declarer, your success rate is 70% against defenders who each hold between 50-499 masterpoints, but the rate drops to only 40% against opponents who each hold between 500-4999 points.

At the table a close decision might be based on the perceived level of your opponents. However, you can't simply ask whether they have a good knowledge of bridge. This is not the type of information covered by 'full disclosure'. If they answer with more than a dirty look, they are probably lying anyway.

Objection 3 response: You are again correct. It could be embarrassing. An individual should be able to opt out of having his personal statistics generated or else have the data stored as securely as humanly possible. The statistics generated for players at your level should provide you with some useful information even without your personal data.

Old Statistics, and New Bridge Performance Statistics

Statistics deals with observing data, describing data and drawing inferences from the data. Even though this subject is many centuries older than our game of bridge, only recently have we had computers at our local clubs capable of being able to conduct the type of study mentioned in the last section. Computers can kibitz, record and point out our weaknesses as well as our strengths. For club games they obviously do not record the trick-by-trick play, but when playing online even that information is known and recorded.

Even though I have not used the word 'statistics' till this chapter, I actually introduced the idea at the start of the book. I mentioned relative frequency and suggested an experiment of keeping track of every hand you play in order to tally what percent contain a five-card or longer suit. That experiment would involve generating a statistic in order to estimate a probability. It would actually be a silly experiment since we have easy methods to compute the probability of that event, and that is true of any totally card-based decision. But when a problem does not lend itself to straightforward mathematics, statistical values may jump to the rescue. In summary, for problems that deal only with playing cards, one can calculate the probability of any event. No experiment that generates statistics is required. But for studying human performance, statistics is an essential tool.

After playing duplicate bridge for many years, I can make very accurate statements about the hands that I received. Probability provides me with surprisingly reliable information. I know that my average hand had almost exactly 10 HCP. But I have no idea what contract I played in the most. Is it 1NT, 3NT, or something else? Likewise, I have no idea of my success rate in 3NT contracts. Or more specifically my success rate in 3NT when holding exactly 25 HCP. But for my recent results, the computer knows!

Baseball Statistics

When I watch sports on TV, I am treated to a plethora of statistical information. Fifty years ago, baseball players had batting averages. They still do. But now graphics come up revealing the batting average against left-handed pitchers, right-handed pitchers, during day games, during night games, in their own stadium, on the road, against a particular pitcher, against a particular team, etc.

Home runs produce many measurements: distance traveled, height, launch angle, exit velocity. Fifty years ago, the announcer would merely shout that the ball went way over the outfield fence. It is clear why there are so many statistics: modern technology made these values easy to obtain, organize and display.

Statistics have changed sports strategy. In baseball, the placement of the fielders and the reduced innings of starting pitchers result from various studies. Teams have their departments of analytics which study statistics. I can only speculate whether bridge will soon be studied with a more statistical approach. Individual statistics from actual results may in the future play a greater role in determining the 'correct' bid or play. I hope it doesn't change the game in an undesirable way.

Using Statistics to Study Bridge Strategy

Bridge has been conducting statistical studies since the arrival of computer- generated hands. One option is to use double-dummy analysis. I am familiar with two books that do this: *Winning Notrump Leads* (2011) and *Winning Suit Contract Leads* (2012), both by David Bird and Taf Anthias. The books contain a short chapter comparing different simulation methodologies. As their titles indicate, these books study the opening lead, a reasonable topic to study since it is the only card play decision made by a player before the dummy is revealed. Selecting the opening lead is a decision made with very little information, so chance plays a major role in its success – a prime situation for statistical analysis. A computer can quickly generate and analyze tens of thousands of deals. The large sample is a great virtue, particularly when studying rare events.

An alternative is to study hands that are actually played in clubs and tournaments. This type of analysis would observe human results rather than double-dummy results. The analysis could consider the different levels of human opponents. What might be a very successful guideline in a weak club game may be a losing strategy in a stronger event. On page 113, I provided a hand where the percentage play for a contract might, in the long run, be less successful than taking a line where a defense error is likely to occur. In the last chapter, the section on the Bergen Raises considered the issue of unnecessarily playing at the three-level when weak opponents will sell out and let you play at the two-level.

Our example for obtaining the success rate of 3NT contracts is not a rare event. We have seen that there is a 10% chance that a deal will have exactly a 25-15 HCP split between the partnerships. If they cannot find an eight-card major fit, most will end up playing in 3NT. If the study involved the success rate of 6NT contracts with 33 HCP, it would require observing many more hands since such an uneven HCP split is quite rare.

In between these two options there is a third option: single-dummy analysis and robots playing. They are unaware of the location of all fifty-two cards but simulate a certain level of play. Both books on opening leads mentioned above contain a chapter on the pros and cons of the three approaches.

Experts often describe bridge as a game of mistakes. The trick to winning is making fewer mistakes than your opponents. Are these experts merely being humble? I doubt it. After all, they are bridge players! Using double-dummy analysis totally ignores mistakes. Even worse, it often makes bad bridge decisions from a mathematical point of view because it knows that these decisions will succeed on a particular deal. Remember, you don't need probability if you know where all fifty-two cards are located. If any player made the exact plays of a double-dummy analyzer, that player would quickly be banned from the game for cheating.

Two interesting studies were conducted by Matthew Kidd. They appear online under two titles: 'Partial, Game, Slam, and Grand Slam. Statistical Breakdown' (May 19, 2015) and 'Slam Statistics' (November 8, 2013). These studies compare the bidding at different levels of bridge ability. (The studies use masterpoint holdings of partnerships to rate ability.) They also compare human bidding with double-dummy analysis. Not surprisingly, beginners bid and make more partscores than experienced players. This is an obvious result of both not aggressively bidding game and not having the opponents outbid their own partscore. An interesting result from these articles is that with double-dummy analysis, a small slam can be made on 10.65% of the deals and a grand on 2.94%. Both are rather surprisingly large results. Don't forget that this is for either pair on a given deal. So, on a given deal, your partnership's probability of being able to make a small slam or grand is roughly half of these values: 5.33% and 1.47%, respectively. This is still large, but remember it is double-dummy. This means that the computer will be wise enough to always play in the slam that makes. It will not go down a trick in 6♡ when 6◇ is a lock for twelve tricks.

Squeeze Frequency

After my first book, *A Bridge to Simple Squeezes*, was published, I was often asked about the frequency of squeezes. This question cannot be answered by either mathematical methods or a statistical study of relative frequency. The essential problem is the difficulty in defining whether or not a squeeze occurs on a hand. Consider the questions:

1) Is a hand a squeeze hand if a squeeze occurs but the defense could have prevented the squeeze by destroying communication or threat cards?

2) Is a hand a squeeze hand if the same result can be achieved by taking a finesse, but if the finesse fails several tricks will be lost?

3) Is a hand a squeeze hand if the early defense is so poor that the squeeze is no longer needed?

Rather than admitting my ignorance in establishing a number for squeeze frequency, I would answer a different question: 'On what percentage of hands should declarer be considering a squeeze?' I would point out that many elements are required for a squeeze. These elements do not mean that a squeeze is possible – they only mean that a squeeze might be possible. Then I would suggest a ballpark figure that 15% of the hands have squeeze potential, but only a small fraction of these will result in a squeeze. When a declarer recognizes these elements, he must be on the lookout for a squeeze. So, in summary, I answered a more important question – how do you recognize those elements? Most players have never been taught to look for the elements, so they don't even consider squeezes.

Important Experiments in Bridge History

Bridge has had a long history of experimentation. The first well-documented duplicate event was a whist match in 1857. Its goal was not to learn which team was stronger but to learn how much luck was involved in the duplicate game. A team of four top experts played against a team of four poor players. (I wonder whether it was hard to recruit four players who were willing to go down in history as poor whist players. Their names are known and at least some had very successful careers.) The results were reported in the weekly British paper, *Bell's Life*, on March 6, 1857. The conclusion was not a surprise. The article states: 'It will be observed that this experiment does not altogether eliminate luck, as bad play sometimes succeeds. But by far the greater part of luck, viz., that due to the superiority of winning cards, is, by the plan described, quite got rid of.' That was the first publication on whist written by Henry Jones (alias 'Cavendish'). He went on to be the greatest whist writer and authority.

The famous Culbertson matches in 1930 and 1931 appeared on the surface to be a competition between players but the events were actually a competition between bidding systems. With the world watching, the winner of these matches (particularly in the Culbertson-Buller and Culbertson-Lenz events) was certain to have hot-selling books describing his system. The world watched these experiments. During the Culbertson-Lenz match[‡‡‡‡], 879 deals were played. The Culbertson partnership bid and made nine small slams and the Lenz partnership eight. So, on slightly less than 2% of the hands a small slam was bid and made. No grand slams were bid and made. These values are sharply in contrast to the Kidd results mentioned earlier.

---

‡‡‡‡ A 1933 movie *Grand Slam* starring Loretta Young and Paul Lucas is a fictional depiction of the Culbertson-Lenz match. The movie reveals the world of bridge and the wealth generated by bridge book sales at that time.

As contract bridge was only a few years old, slam bidding methods were very primitive, and only experts would even try to bid a slam. Recorders at the match kept track of the aces and kings each side was dealt. Each partnership should have expected on the average two aces per deal with a total of 879 x 2 = 1758 aces and, of course, an equal number of kings. So, the combined total of aces and kings for each partnership should have been approximately 3516. In actuality, the Culbertson partnership received 3520 and the Lenz 3512. Remarkably close! Don't feel sorry for Lenz, his partnership received 1771 aces while Culbertson received only 1745; but Lenz received 34 fewer kings than Culbertson. Multiplying each ace by four and each king by three, Lenz received 12,307 HCP counting only aces and kings, while Culbertson received a total of 12,305. Neither side could even try to argue that their partnership received poorer cards. Statistics corresponding to their match appeared in several bridge books in the 30s and 40s and in all editions of the ACBL Encyclopedia.

ACBL Member Statistics

Let me provide you with a very positive piece of information: ACBL members have been given the gift of longevity. I find this quite comforting and therefore make sure to renew my membership on time so as not to leave any gaps. When my doctor attacks me for not exercising enough and even goes so far as to recommend joining (and using, I guess) a health club, I point out that the average ACBL member will live to an older age than the average health club member. I even recommend that he join the ACBL.

For anyone who doubts my facts, the average ACBL member is around age seventy, while the average health club member is around forty. Based on any actuarial table a seventy-year-old has a greater chance to live to ninety than a forty-year old. Actuarial studies on life expectancy were first performed by John Graunt (1620-1674) in London.

This demonstrates a misleading statistical argument. It is always necessary to ask if the conclusion makes sense before accepting its correctness. It is similar to what I indicated when using tables of numerical values. Even though one doesn't know the correct value, one must ask oneself whether the value passes the smell test. I have taught a course on how to lie (mislead) with statistics. Of course, it was not my goal to teach lying but rather how to detect misleading statistical information. In the early computer days (fifty years ago), it was common to believe that we were entering an 'information age'; unfortunately, it can now be described as a 'misinformation age'.

The ACBL provided me with some membership statistics. The impressive data includes: 90% hold a college degree, more than half of those with a college degree have a postgraduate degree, and over 30% have a household annual income in excess of $200,000. Bridge has always been a game that attracted wealthy participants. The first journal on bridge appeared in 1906. It was titled *Bridge* with the subtitle *A Monthly Magazine Published for Lovers and Students of the Game.* (I find the subtitle confusing, but I assume it meant lovers of the game.) The first page had a large announcement for advertisers: 'Bridge Players are People Who Spend Money.' Advertisers clearly believed this announcement. The journal contained advertisements for clothes, cigarettes, theater tickets, country homes, apartments, soap, sugar, fire-proof hotels and even wallpaper. At that time bridge players were sometimes called 'bridgers'. Sounds strange! But the term is reasonable — consider: golfers, bowlers, dancers, singers and skiers.

It is interesting to examine the table of percentages of ACBL members in different total masterpoint categories. It is available at the ACBL website. Far and away, the most common masterpoint total is 0. Surprising! But more than 7000 ACBL members (that is more than 4%) have 0 points. No rounding involved. I would not be surprised if several thousand maintain their membership but have not played duplicate for many years. That, however, would not explain 0 points. My guess is that many serious foreign players from countries not under the jurisdiction of the ACBL wish to receive the Bulletin and follow the happenings and results of tournaments sanctioned by the ACBL.

Computing the 'average' masterpoint holding can be very misleading. There are three main measures of 'average'. The *mode* is the most frequent number of points held. That is clearly 0. The *median* is the masterpoint total where the same number of players have fewer points as have more points. At the time of writing this, the median is approximately 190 masterpoints. The *mean* would involve adding up the total masterpoints of all members and dividing by the total membership (or at least approximating the value). That value would be greatly influenced by the almost 1000 players with more than 10,000 points. These outliers would result in an artificially high value for the 'average' – misleading but accurate.

At the beginning of this chapter, I suggested an experiment that involved a split of ACBL members into four categories: 0-49, 50-499, 500-4999 and greater than 5000. These categories do not reflect partitioning the ACBL membership into four equal size groups. The top category only consists of 2% of the membership while the other three groups are each over 30%. In fact, even though the top category has very few members, by the measure of hands played per year, particularly in Regional and NABC events, this group is probably underrepresented when using these four categories.

Upon leaving club games, I would often overhear, 'We were the strongest pair, we should have won.' At any bridge event, I believe many partnerships, maybe most, think that way. We have our egos! But even if a pair is the strongest, it is far from a guarantee of winning. It would only mean that the partnership's probability of winning is greater than any other pair. This can only be ascertained by studying the partnership's winning relative frequency.

At the other end of the spectrum, even the poorest pair will occasionally win. Given enough time, with very long, healthy lives, they will have a session with twenty-four top boards. It is similar to a monkey typing a work of Shakespeare – but it will take the bridge players less time than the monkey.

Let me give a scenario that goes against intuition. You are driving to a Sectional with your wife and another couple. You make an agreement that whichever couple has the lower overall percentage for the tournament pays for dinner on the drive home. The first day, you and your wife are at 55% and the other couple 54%. On the second day, you and your wife have a 63% game and the other couple a 62%. As you prepare for the drive home, anticipating the dinner and which fine bottle of wine you wish to order, the other couple does the arithmetic and happily states, 'Looks like you are paying for dinner.' What happened? How can that be possible?

Your average was 1/2 x 55 + 1/2 x 63 = 59.

Your friends only played one session the first day.

So, their average was 1/3 x 54 + 2/3 x 62 = 59 1/3.

I'm afraid that you are paying for dinner. Sorry! Weighted averages can be tricky.

Alternative Hand Evaluation Methods

Throughout this book, I have used the standard HCP system (4-3-2-1). This system is often criticized for undervaluing aces, kings and tens while overvaluing queens and jacks. The criticism of undervaluing aces and kings is truer for suit contracts than for notrump contracts. But during the process of bidding one is often communicating one's strength without knowledge of whether the final contract will be in a suit or notrump. Tricky business.

Between 1900 and 1955 more than a dozen alternative systems were tried. The most shocking appeared in Edmund Robertson, *The Robertson Rule and Other Axioms of Bridge Whist* (1902). In this system, the ace = 81, king = 54, queen = 36, jack = 24, and ten = 16; the average hand has 211 points. Robertson realized the arithmetic would be a bit complicated and advocated a rather reasonable simplification (ace 7, king 5, queen 3, jack 2, and ten 1). One can design an experiment that would compare the ability of this system and our standard one for predicting success in 3NT. One can run an experiment in order to ascertain the best cutoff for game with the 7-5-3-2-1 system. Since the average hand has 18 HCP, game in notrump would require about 46 points. My own view is that this experiment is not worth the effort. To a great extent the appeal of the 4-3-2-1 system is its simplicity: no fractions, no large numbers, no great effort to use.

A short historical note: Our 4-3-2-1 system was first described in Bryant McCampbell's book *Auction Tactics* (1916). It was popularized by Milton Work around 1930. Till mid-century, it was seen only as a system for evaluating notrump strength. In 1949, Fred

Karpin and Charles Goren (with the help of an actuary, William Anderson) each published small books adapting the 4-3-2-1 system for suit contracts by assigning point values for distribution. The rest is history!

Player Ability Evaluation Methods

Our masterpoint system has certainly been a success. Many players incorrectly believe it was created by the ACBL, but in fact a similar point system was used in the mid-1930s by several bridge organizations. The bridge world was like a country with several currencies. We needed a standard currency (I mean masterpoint). The ACBL was formed by merging the two largest masterpoint-awarding organizations, the American Bridge League (ABL) and the United States Bridge Association (USBA). So, we see, the ACBL didn't create the masterpoint system; quite the opposite – the multiple masterpoint systems created the ACBL! To its credit, since its birth in 1937, the ACBL has done a great job managing the system. Prior to the direct computer recording of points, club results were entered on small slips of paper and given to a player. After the player got tired of showing off a shoebox full of slips to friends, he would mail a few dozen at a time to the ACBL to be recorded.

The American Bridge League had a monthly publication called *American Bridge League Bulletin.* Sound familiar? The August 1936 publication listed the point holdings of over 200 players. The top five were David Burnstine 607, Howard Schenken 506, Oswald Jacoby 472, Waldemar von Zedtwitz 379 and P. Hal Sims 326. The already famous Ely Culbertson had 96 points and the soon to be famous Charles Goren had only 32. How does your masterpoint holding stack up against these greats? I cannot resist including a few sentences from this 1936 publication that are still relevant. 'If you are conducting a local bridge tournament, Master Points increase the attendance from 10% to 50% and double the prestige. Your tournament attracts players from distant regions 'on the hunt' for Master Points, and the results of your tournaments are published in official records. The ultimate aim of the American

Bridge League is to place a Master Point tournament in every community...' In 1936, the word 'masterpoint' was two separate words.

Over my fifty-five years of ACBL membership, I am quite sure the most common topic in the 'Letter to the Editor' section of the *ACBL Bulletin* is how to create a better rating system. But the masterpoint system was not created as a rating system. It is a trophy system without the actual physical trophy. If a player plays once a week in a club game and does only well enough to receive a masterpoint award for one game each month, he is not doing exceptionally well. But on the bright side, he will be reaching a new personal record lifetime masterpoint total a dozen times a year. Now that sounds and feels like a major accomplishment. Who could not love such a system? Unfortunately, young players often feel that the system does not fairly reflect their ability. This was described in an editorial by Paul Linxwiler in the October 2019 *ACBL Bulletin*.

Let me return to baseball. Even though it is a team game, the majority of the statistics measure individual performance. Jacob DeGrom recently won his second straight Cy Young Award. Over those two seasons his earned run average (ERA) was wonderful (slightly over two runs per game) even though his win-loss team statistic over those two years was an unimpressive twenty-one wins and seventeen losses. With computer-generated hands and scoring one could easily generate a variety of measures for studying declarer performance. Should those statistics be used to form a rating system? Do we want that? I have no idea. I just want to point out that it is doable.

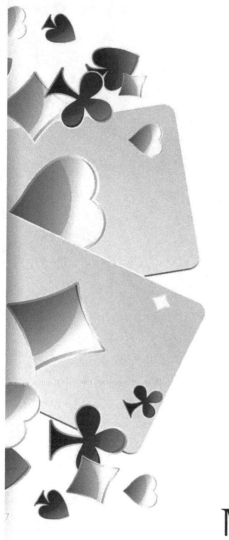

PART 3

*The bidding and play
of each hand must
be diagnosed from its
individual symptoms; and
a player whose main guide
is the "mathematical"
percentages will no more
succeed than a doctor who
diagnoses his patient's
illness as a cold simply
because a cold is more
probable than a cancer.*

Ely Culbertson

MUCH MORE
THAN YOU EVER
WANTED TO KNOW
ABOUT PROBABILITY

Chapter 19

Number of Ways Events Happen

Is this chapter useful? Why?

Usefulness number: 8. This chapter is on a subject called *combinatorics*. In it, I present a very powerful formula, provide numerous examples, and justify the correctness of this tool. The formula is essential for understanding Chapters 20 and 21 where you will discover how the values in virtually all bridge tables can be obtained. In the last few chapters, I referred to this tool as 'the magic formula'.

Combinatorics

The suit split tables in Chapter 4 can be found in probably a hundred books on declarer play, so most players are familiar with these values. Understandably, those books do not provide a justification of the values. Occasionally a bridge player asks me how the values in the suit split tables were obtained. In the next few chapters, my goal is to provide a clear answer to that question and similar ones.

The term *combinatorics* refers to a branch of mathematics where one studies how many ways an event can occur. Sometimes it is called by the less impressive name *counting*. As we have seen in Chapter 5, many probability problems can be solved by simply obtaining the numerator and denominator of a fraction. Easier said than done! It usually requires a basic knowledge of combinatorics.

In Chapter 14, I introduced the Multiplication Principle and the Addition Principle. At that time, I used examples about a player having Democratic and Republican bridge partners. I will not repeat those examples but will repeat the Principles.

Suppose one activity can be done in m ways and a second activity can be done in n ways.

Multiplication Principle: If both activities must be done, then the number of ways this can happen is obtained by multiplying m by n.

Addition Principle: If either the first activity or the second activity must be done, but not both, then the number of ways is obtained by adding m and n.

Both principles can be extended to more than two activities.

Consider a poker hand consisting of five cards. How many different arrangements can be made with the five cards?

Any arrangement of five cards can be viewed as the placement of a card in each of the five positions. Suppose the five cards are the ♡2, ◊Q, ♠9, ♣J and ◊3.

- Any of these five cards can be placed in the first position. Suppose the ♠9 is placed in the first position.
- Any of the remaining four cards can be placed in the second position. Suppose the ◊Q is placed there.
- Any of the remaining three cards can be placed in the third position. Suppose the ◊3 is placed there.
- Either of the remaining two cards can be placed in the fourth position. Suppose the ♣J is placed there.
- Only one card (the remaining ♡2) can be placed in the fifth position.

Each time a card is placed in a position, an activity is performed. Therefore, one is performing five activities. The total number of possible arrangements of these five cards is 5 x 4 x 3 x 2 x 1 = 120.

Unfortunately, whatever order you put the cards in, it is still a crummy poker hand.

Suppose you are playing bridge with a slow partner and to kill time while waiting for him to bid, you randomly start rearranging your thirteen cards. How many different ways can the thirteen cards be arranged?

Use the same method as with the Poker hand. With the thirteen cards the number is:

13 x 12 x 11 x 10 x 9 x 8 x 7 x 6 x 5 x 4 x 3 x 2 x 1
= 6,227,020,800

To the left of the equals sign, we certainly have a long expression. It would have been worse if the question involved how many arrangements could be made of the entire fifty-two-card deck. The answer would involve writing 52 x 51 x 50... all the way down to 1. Ridiculous! Mathematicians saw a need for a shorthand notation. Instead of writing out these long expressions, one can represent the three expressions in the compact forms: 5!, 13! and 52!

For example, 5! = 5 x 4 x 3 x 2 x 1 = 120.

This representation with an exclamation point is called *factorial notation*: 5! is read '5 factorial.'

Returning to the example of a bridge player rearranging his thirteen cards, we saw that 13! = 6,227,020,800. This number is too big to be relatable. If you form a new arrangement every second and work nonstop twenty-four hours a day, it will take 197 years to form all arrangements of those thirteen cards. Seems unbelievable, but it is not a misprint. Let me convince you.

There are sixty seconds in a minute and sixty minutes in an hour, so 3600 seconds in an hour. Working twenty-four hours a day and 365 days a year, there are a total of 3600 x 24 x 365 = 31,536,000 seconds in a year. When 6,227,020,800 is divided by 31,536,000 the result is 197.46.

Suppose you pick up your hand and think about the order in which those thirteen cards will eventually be played. How many ways can this happen? The answer would again be 13! = 6,227,020,800. During the play, you don't really have all of those options due to the restriction of having to follow suit. But if you have a great hand with 37 HCP, there are 13! different orders in which you could choose to play your winners.

We saw that 5! is only 120 while 13! is more than six billion. A moderate increase in n, from 5 to 13, had an enormous effect on the resulting factorial value. Prior to the year 2000, when the world's population was smaller, I could have stated that the number of ways thirteen cards can be arranged exceeded the entire world population. This is an example of 'factorial growth'. Certainly, such fast growth is a challenge to one's intuition. The result of the multiplications required to compute 52! is a number with 68 digits.

Exponential growth is also extremely fast, but not as fast as factorial growth. As an example, suppose a bridge player decides that in the following month he will teach four friends to play and thereby starts a game. The four beginners are each required for their free bridge lessons to in turn create four beginners in the following month. So, during the first month, four people will learn the game, during the second month sixteen people will learn the game, during the third month sixty-four new people, etc. During the seventeenth month, more than seventeen billion people will learn the game. Since this is more than twice the world population, many household pets would have to take up the game.

It is interesting to note that this phenomenal growth is achieved so quickly with no player ever teaching more than four people, and the seventeen billion only represents the number of individuals learning the game in the seventeenth month, not the total number of players. In many ways this is at the heart of how bridge grew between 1898 and 1908. Even though several dozen books were published, and many professional teachers emerged, players primarily learned the new craze from friends and relatives who had recently learned the game.

At a Regional, how many ways can six people form a line to buy an entry?

Since any of the six can be first in line, any of the remaining five can be next in line behind that person, and so on, the total is:

$$6! = 720$$

Please don't fear the arithmetic for computing factorials. They require no effort. I will explain in the next section. All books need some mystery.

The Magic Formula (Combination Formula)

The study of the number of different ways in which objects can be arranged is not particularly important to bridge players but the factorial notation is necessary for the following very important formula, previously referred to as the 'magic formula'.

The number of ways r objects can be chosen from n objects is:

$$_nC_r = \frac{n!}{r!(n-r)!}$$

In many books an alternative notation is used, $\left(\begin{array}{c} n \\ r \end{array}\right) = \dfrac{n!}{r!(n-r)!}$

Occasionally 0! will be encountered. It cannot be obtained in the standard fashion, but by definition 0! = 1. So whenever 0! appears, just replace it with 1. Let's do a few examples where nCr provides the solution.

Six guests at your home want to play bridge. As the all-powerful host, you can choose which four will play. How many ways can four be chosen to play?

$$6C4 = \frac{6!}{4!(6-4)!} = \frac{6!}{4!2!} = \frac{6 \times 5 \times 4 \times 3 \times 2 \times 1}{4 \times 3 \times 2 \times 1 \times 2 \times 1} = \frac{6 \times 5}{2 \times 1} = 15$$

Note that the order in which the players were chosen is unimportant. The only important result that the people care about is which four are playing, not the order of selection.

This arithmetic can be done by hand in three ways. Either 6! can be divided by the product of 4! and 2!, or 6! can be divided by just 4!, and the result can then be divided by 2!, or the order of the two divisions can be reversed (first divide by 2! and then 4!). Usually it is easier to divide by the larger, here 4!, and then the smaller since cancellation simplifies the arithmetic. It is useful to carry out the arithmetic of the first two or three examples – but no more. We will see simple ways to avoid the arithmetic.

You have seven cards. How many five-card poker hands can be formed?

$$7C5 = \frac{7!}{5!(7-5)!} = \frac{7!}{5!2!} = 21$$

It is easiest to first divide by 5! since it will cancel out all numbers in the numerator that are 5 or smaller. This will leave $(7 \times 6) / (2 \times 1) = 21$.

How many ways can you choose thirteen cards from fifty-two cards to form a bridge hand?

$$52C13 = \frac{52!}{13!(52-13)!} = \frac{52!}{13!39!} = 635{,}013{,}559{,}600$$

I am sure this value of just over 635 billion looks familiar to you. It has appeared throughout the book.

Tricky Confusing Issue Alert

How many ways can your partner be dealt the thirteen cards to form his hand?

One would think the answer would be the same as the previous example, 635 billion, and that answer would be correct before you look at your own hand. However, once you do that, it is clear that your partner cannot have any of your thirteen cards. So, your partner's thirteen cards are chosen from the remaining thirty-nine cards.

$$39C13 = 8,122,425,444$$

Still a large value, but eight billion is much smaller than 635 billion.

Don't be put off by mistakenly thinking that obtaining nCr involves a lengthy computation. No arithmetic is necessary. A \$15 scientific calculator is capable of evaluating the function nCr. Actually, you can save the \$15 by just googling 'combination calculator'. Many options will appear. The letter C is used to indicate that one is obtaining the number of Combinations that can be formed. You will only need to provide n and r. You should always do a test example in which you know ahead of time the correct value. You may face a strange-looking number since for very large values calculators and computers will display a result using scientific notation (part of the answer may involve 10 raised to an exponent). If you just want to compute a factorial, such as 26!, just google 'factorial calculator'. Again, first try an example (such as 5!) where you know the correct answer.

Very old books on bridge probability introduce some shortcuts for doing the required arithmetic. Some were written in the early days of computers and calculators. There is no shortcut in arithmetic that is superior to totally avoiding it with a computational device.

Now that we have the most important formula in combinatorics and have seen how to use it, we are capable of obtaining more involved probabilities. It is natural to wonder whether the formula works as well as I have claimed. I must convince you of my truthfulness.

Justification of the Combination Formula

We can consider the last example for possible bridge hands:

$$52C13 = \frac{52!}{13!(52-13)!} = \frac{52!}{13!39!} = 635,013,559,600$$

Imagine turning over one card at a time from a fifty-two-card deck.

There are fifty-two possibilities for the first card. Suppose it is the ♡8. There are fifty-one possibilities for the second card. Suppose it is the ♢7. There are fifty possibilities for the third card. Suppose it is the ♡5. There are forty-nine possibilities for the fourth card. Suppose it is the ♢A.

In this fashion, suppose the next eight cards that are drawn are ♣6, ♠A, ♠4, ♣A, ♢8, ♢2, ♡K, and ♠7.

There are forty possibilities for the thirteenth card. Suppose the ♠5 is that thirteenth card.

The above steps can be done in:

52 × 51 × 50 × 49 × 48 × 47 × 46 × 45 × 44 × 43 × 42 × 41 × 40 ways

We would like a convenient shorthand. Obviously, this is not 52! We only have the above thirteen terms. But there is a convenient shorthand. Just divide 52! by 39!. The 39! will cancel out all the terms from 39 on down, leaving just 52 × 51 × 50 × .... × 40.

But we are not done. Consider the thirteen cards that were drawn to form a hand. Suppose the third card drawn was not the ♡5 but the ♢A. Suppose the fourth card drawn was not the ♢A but the ♡5. I just reversed the order in which these two cards were drawn but did not change any other drawn cards. Has my bridge hand changed? Not at all! It is still the same thirteen cards. Both scenarios produce the same hand. But reversing the time of drawing the two cards resulted in counting that hand with those thirteen cards twice.

When a player picks up a bridge hand, the only important feature is the thirteen cards it contains. The order in which the cards were dealt is of no consequence. But the procedure that has just been described is affected by the order in which the cards were dealt. This means every bridge hand will be counted multiple times. It will be counted for all possible arrangements of thirteen cards. Fortunately, we just saw that thirteen playing cards can be ordered in 13! ways. We have our answer.

Putting it all together, we just need to divide 52! by 39!. Take that result and divide by 13!. The process described by these last two sentences is described by the mathematical expression (nCr) at the beginning of this section.

A Few More Examples and Relationships

Place the thirteen spades face-up on the table. How many ways can you select four spades? (All bridge players will greedily select ace, king, queen and jack.)

$$13C4 = 715$$

Place the thirteen spades face-up on the table. How many ways can you select nine spades?

$$13C9 = 715$$

Are the last two examples an odd coincidence? Not really. Suppose you go to your local grocery store to purchase four apples. The store has six for sale. Shouldn't the number of ways you can choose four apples to purchase be the same as the number of ways you can choose which two apples to reject? Therefore, we are not surprised that the following relationship will always hold:

$$nCr = nC(n - r)$$

You have 12,000 masterpoints but no partner. You go to the partnership table at a local Regional. Eight bridge players are on their knees begging you to choose them as your partner. The whole scene is rather disturbing for witnesses — but flattering for you. How many choices do you have?

$$8C1 = \frac{8!}{1!(8-1)!} = \frac{8!}{1!7!} = 8$$

This answer is obvious. You don't need the magic formula since common sense produces the same answer as the formula. The following relationship is obvious:

$$nC1 = n$$

Suppose you have had a bad month of bridge, never finishing above third. Obviously, all seven of your regular partners played poorly. One solution is to play with all seven this coming month, so that you can get the bad taste out of your mouth. Obviously, the choice of seven from seven can be done in only one way. Since there is no freedom of choice, this is logical. It is useful to note that the mathematics is consistent with the obvious since 7C7 = 1 way. An alternative solution is to give up playing bridge for a month. In this case, you would need 0 partners which can be done in 7C0 = 1 way. Likewise, choosing no partners can be done in only one way. This, too, is logical. For any value of n:

$$nCn = 1 \text{ and } nC0 = 1$$

Any of the above four relationships can be justified by plugging values into our formula for combinations. The last two require evaluating 0!. It is necessary to remember that we defined 0! = 1.

At a Regional, your team is competing in a Bracket 3 round robin event. There are eight teams, so seven rounds will be played. How many matches will take place in Bracket 3?

An easy and obvious way to solve this is to reason that during each round four matches will be played. So, after seven rounds 7 x 4 = 28.

An alternative way is to reason that every match will involve choosing two of the eight teams to play each other. With this approach, the answer is 8C2 = 28. Thankfully the answer is the same with either approach. Why solve it two different ways? To check that the answers agree. It builds confidence. Sometimes, there is only one obvious way.

You run the friendliest club in the ACBL. One club rule is that, at the end of a session, every single player must shake hands with every other player. At a ten-table game, how many goodbyes will be exchanged?

40C2 = 780

Each goodbye requires two people. So, every way two people can be chosen from the forty would involve a handshake. Notice that the method is identical to the round robin team event example. In both examples, one wants to learn how many ways two items can be paired up. Even though, on the surface, the problems look very different, it is another example of two very different problems really being mathematically the same.

Chapter 20
Probability of Types of Hands (Again)

Is this chapter useful? Why?
Usefulness number: 9. You may recall that Chapter 14 has the same title, but without the word 'Again'. We saw procedures to obtain solutions, but lacked a crucial tool necessary to carry them out. Chapter 19 introduced the combinations formula, which was the tool we needed. In this chapter we will use it to justify several probability statements in the book and to compute bridge table entries for shape and HCP.

What is the probability of being dealt a yarborough?
There are thirty-two cards in the deck that are the spot card nine or lower. From these thirty-two cards, 32C13 bridge hands can be formed. Therefore:

$$P(\text{Yarborough}) = \frac{32C13}{52C13} = \frac{347,373,600}{635,013,559,600} = 0.000547$$

This value is approximately $\dfrac{1}{1828}$

This same example was solved using a less elegant method at the beginning of Chapter 14. At that time, it was done without the use of the tool for obtaining the number of combinations. The answers agree. Great!

Computing Shape Probabilities

How many hands can be formed containing a heart suit with exactly seven cards?

Since there are 13C7 ways of being dealt seven hearts from the thirteen hearts, and 39C6 ways of being dealt six cards that are not hearts from the thirty-nine cards that are not hearts, the total number of hands that can be formed with seven hearts is 13C7 x 39C6 = 1716 x 3,262,623 = 5,598,661,068.

What is the probability of a hand containing a seven-card heart suit?

On page 147, the procedure for this problem was provided. It involved three steps. In the last example, we have just completed two and a half of those three steps. All we need to do is divide the above result by 635,013,559,600.

In summary,

P(hand containing a seven-card heart suit) =

$$\frac{13C7 \times 39C6}{52C13} = \frac{1716 \times 326,623}{635,013,559,600} = 0.0088$$

P(hand containing any seven-card suit) =

$$\frac{4 \times 13C7 \times 39C6}{52C13} = 4 \times 0.0088 = 0.0352$$

I am pleased to announce: If the probabilities of all possible shapes with a seven-card suit were totaled in a complete shape table, the result would be this value.

How many hands can be formed with four spades, five hearts and four cards in the minors? What is the probability of being dealt a hand with this shape?

There are 13C4 ways to choose four spades, 13C5 ways to choose five hearts and 26C4 ways to choose four cards in the minors.

The number of hands is 13C4 x 13C5 x 26C4 = 715 x 1287 x 14950 = 13,757,064,750. For the probability, simply divide this value by 635,013,559,600. The result is 0.0217.

How many hands can be formed with three spades, five hearts, two diamonds and three clubs? What is the probability of being dealt such a hand?

There are 13C3 ways to choose three spades from the thirteen, 13C5 ways to choose five hearts from thirteen, 13C2 ways to choose two diamonds, and 13C3 ways to choose three clubs.

The number of hands is 13C3 x 13C5 x 13C2 x 13C3 = 286 x 1287 x 78 x 286 = 8,211,173,256.

To obtain the probability of the described hand, we merely divide by 52C13 = 635,013,559,600. The result of the division is 0.01293.

The procedure to obtain this probability was described in five steps on page 149. More mathematically, we can now summarize the five steps as shown below.

P(hand containing three spades, five hearts, two diamonds, three clubs) =

$$\frac{13C3 \times 13C5 \times 13C2 \times 13C3}{52C13} = \frac{8,211,173,256}{635,013,559,600} = 0.01293$$

You may be surprised that the value is only about 1.3% since a 5-3-3-2 shape is quite common. It is important to realize that this is the probability of one specific shape. If we want to compute the probability of being dealt any hand with the general shape 5-3-3-2, we must consider that any of the four suits can be the five-card suit, any of the remaining three suits can be the two-card suit and the two remaining suits must both be three-card suits. Therefore, we must multiply the previous answer by 4 x 3 = 12. Therefore, P(5-3-3-2 shape) = 12 x 0.01293 = 0.155. This value of approximately 15% is quite reasonable. But we can require more than obtaining a reasonable value. The result should be identical (except for rounding) to the value that appears on page 151 for the general shape 5-3-3-2. It is. Wonderful!

Here is a summary of our procedure to obtain the probability of any general shape. First obtain the probability of any specific shape that is included in the general shape, such as (3=5=2=3), multiply that value by the number of specific shapes represented by the general shape, and compare the result to the table entry. In this fashion, you can compute all the entries in the shape table. But, please don't. For any bridge probability problem, use the table rather than computing each probability from scratch. I hope you find it comforting to know how the values were obtained; should a table entry look strange, you know how to check it.

Computing HCP Probabilities

What is the probability of a hand containing exactly three aces and two kings?

There are 4C3 ways to choose three aces from the four, 4C2 ways to choose two kings from the four, and 44C8 ways to choose eight cards that are neither an ace nor a king from the forty-four such cards.

Therefore, P(exactly three aces and two kings) =

$$\frac{4C3 \times 4C2 \times 44C8}{52C13} = \frac{4 \times 6 \times 177,232,627}{635,013,559,600} = 0.0067$$

We do not know the HCP of the described hand since we do not know if the eight cards contain any queens or jacks. If we further stipulate that it contains no queens and two jacks, the numerator would become 4C3 x 4C2 x 4C0 x 4C2 x 36C6 = 280,482,048. Of course, the denominator would not change. You should not be surprised that the numerator is much smaller. In this example, the added requirement of no queens and two jacks is much more restrictive.

The only question of this type that I can recall ever being asked concerned the probability of being dealt all four aces. The number of hands containing all four aces is 4C4 x 48C9 = 1 x 1,677,106,640 = 1,677,106,640. By dividing this number by 635 billion, we find the probability to be 0.00264.

On page 157, we considered all ways in which a 15 HCP hand could be created. We found twenty-three alternatives. The option AKKKJJ was considered. We know that there are 4C1 x 4C3 x 4C0 x 4C2 x 36C7 = 801,377,280 hands that can be formed meeting our requirement. When this value is divided by 635,013,559,600, the resulting probability is 0.001262. This is a far cry from the table value for 15 HCP. We have to obtain the probability of the other twenty-two possibilities and then add them.

Another way to generate a hand with 15 HCP is with three aces, a king, and nine spot cards. The number of ways to form a hand with three aces, one king, no queens or jacks, and nine spot cards is 4C3 x 4C1 x 4C0 x 4C0 x 36C9 = 4 x 4 x 1 x 1 x 94,143,280 = 1,506,292,480. After the standard division by 635 billion, we find the probability of picking up a 15 HCP hand with three aces and one king is 0.00237. This result is almost twice the probability of the 15 HCP case AKKKJJ. Consider a third case, AAKKJ. The number of ways a hand can be formed is 6 x 6 x 4 x 30,260,340 = 4,357,488,960. After the division, its probability is 0.00686. In short, the twenty-three ways of being dealt 15 HCP have very different probabilities of occurring. Those twenty-three values vary considerably, so I cannot even pretend that they are all the same value. It is far too much work to carry it out with reasonable accuracy! I will happily trust the table value for 15 HCP.

What is the probability of being dealt a 2 HCP hand?

I will work through this example in order to justify the value in the table. Thankfully, there are only two situations that yield a 2 HCP hand. One situation is no aces, no kings, one queen and no jacks. The other situation is no aces, no kings, no queens and two jacks. Therefore, the numerator is:

$(4C0 \times 4C0 \times 4C1 \times 4C0 \times 36C12) + (4C0 \times 4C0 \times 4C0 \times 4C2 \times 36C11) = 5,006,710,800 + 3,604,831,776 = 8,611,542,576$

When this value is divided by 635,013,559,600, the result is 0.01356. I am very pleased. This value is in agreement with the table value.

Computing HCP Probabilities is Harder than Shape

It is interesting to note that the methods used for computing shape and HCP probabilities are very similar, but the work involved for HCP is usually much greater. We saw that with 15 HCP, twenty-three cases had to be considered. All twenty-three cases yielded different probabilities. Don't be misled by the example for 2 HCP. This is easy — that is why I chose to do it. It only involved two cases. Justifying values in the general shape table is always very easy. Even if the general shape corresponds to twenty-four specific shapes (such as 5-4-3-1), all twenty-four cases have the same probability, so you need to compute the probability for one specific shape and multiply that value by 24.

In the next chapter, when we are concerned with the combined holdings of a partnership and partnership support, we will again see that that it is much easier to obtain the probabilities of joint suit holdings than joint HCP holdings.

Let's play around with a very different hand evaluation system, for the fun of it. Yes, you read it right — for the fun of it. We will count 1 point for every card that is either an ace, king, queen or jack. With this system, players would just count the number of cards in their hand which are an ace or a face card. A four-year-old could do hand evaluation. Certainly, this is not a very sophisticated or accurate system. All hands would correspond to a numerical value in the range from a minimum of 0 to a maximum of 13. Now it would be extremely easy to obtain the probability of any of those fourteen possible values for a hand. For example, the number of ways a hand could have a numeric value of 4 is $16C4 \times 36C9 = 1820 \times 94,143,280 = 171,340,769,600$. After dividing by 635 billion, we see that the probability of the value 4 is 0.27. This is a large value, but no great surprise since 4 is expected to be the most likely value when using this hand evaluation method. We could vary this example by evaluating hands based on their combined number of aces and kings. The best possible hand would be an 8. The number of possible hands holding exactly two cards that are either an ace or a king is 8C2 x 44C11.

A Few Stray Comments Finally Justified

On page 14, I promised that the hand ♠Axxx ♡Kxx ♢Axxx ♣Ax was more than two million times more likely than ♡AKQJxxxxxxxxx. Why?

For the first hand, three spade spot cards are needed to be selected from the nine; in the heart suit, two spot cards have to be selected, in diamonds three spot cards, and in clubs, one spot card. So, a hand with this specific shape can be formed in 9C3 x 9C2 x 9C3 x 9C1 = 84 x 36 x 84 x 9 = 2,286,144 ways. For the thirteen-heart suit hand, all nine heart spot cards must be used so it can represent only one specific hand. It is silly to even represent this as a combination, but I do not mind being silly. Since there are nine heart spot cards and all nine are needed to fill out the heart suit, the number of ways is 9C9 =1. This justifies the Chapter 1 statement.

On page 23, I stated that the probability of opening 1♢ with a three-card diamond suit is slightly less than half of 1%, while if your partner opens 1♢, the probability that he has only a three-card suit is approximately 5%. Why?

First, let's justify the first statement about opening 1♢ with a three-card suit. It will happen only with the specific shape 4=4=3=2 and a hand holding 12, 13, 14, 18 or 19 HCP. One can obtain the probability of each of the five values. Their total probability is 0.233. What about 15-17 HCP? With 15-17, a player holding that shape would happily open 1NT. In summary, the probability of this specific shape is 0.01796, and the probability of one of those HCP values is 0.233. Therefore, the probability can be obtained by multiplying those values, 0.01796 x 0.233 = 0.0042. Let me remind you of a few of the assumptions flying around. The major mathematics assumption is the independence of shape and HCP.

The bridge assumptions are numerous. For example, I am assuming that one would not open 1♦ with 11 points even when holding the ace and king in one suit and another ace, but would open 1♦ with 12 points composed of only queens and jacks.

Now for the second question when you are given that partner opened 1♦. We have to obtain the probability of opening 1♦. First, let's consider points. For balanced hands, the possible HCP values are 12, 13, 14, 18 and 19. As above, their total probability is 0.233. For unbalanced hands, when 1NT cannot be opened, the possible HCP values are 12 to 21. Now there are ten HCP values where a declarer may open 1♦. Their total probability is 0.344. Let me first make a list of the specific shapes for balanced hands (in the appropriate point range) where we can assume 1♦ would be opened: 3=3=4=3, 4=4=3=2, 4=3=4=2, 4=2=4=3, 3=4=4=2, 3=2=4=4, 2–4–4=3, 2=3=4=4, 3=3=5=2, 3=2=5=3, and 2=3=5=3. For unbalanced hands, the list of specific shapes that would usually open 1♦ would include: 4=4=4=1, 4=1=4=4, 1=4=4=4, and any hand with a five- (except the general shape 5-3-3-2 which has already been counted) or six-card diamond suit that does not contain a second five-card suit (except a five-card club suit). I am assuming that, with four in both minors, you always open 1♦. The same is true for five cards in both minors, but not for three cards in both minors. I am guilty of never considering suit quality with these assumptions.

We already obtained the probability of opening 1♦ with a three-card suit. This can only occur with the specific shape, 4=4=3=2. With considerable effort, we can obtain the probability of opening 1♦. One has to obtain the probability of all shapes where 1♦ would be opened when holding a balanced hand, and multiply that value by 0.233. One has to obtain the probability of all shapes where 1♦ would be opened when holding an unbalanced hand, and multiply that value by 0.344. After adding these two results, one finds that the probability of opening 1♦ is 0.091 (approximately 9%). By dividing 0.0042 by 0.091, we obtain the probability that a player who opens 1♦ has a three-card diamond suit. The resulting probability is approximately 0.046. This value represents the likelihood that given your partner opened 1♦, he holds a three-card diamond suit. This value is still small but more than ten times greater than the alternative problem that sounds similar. As mentioned in Chapter 2, the number of diamonds in your own hand has an impact on this probability.

The September 2009 *ACBL Bulletin* included a column by Paul Linxwiler on the frequency of opening 1♦ with a three-card suit. The article referred to a computer simulation of ten million hands in the 12 to 21 HCP range performed by Tim Goodwin. Only hands strong enough to qualify as an opening bid were considered. Using standard bidding methods, the probability breakdown was 1♣ 27.7%, 1♦ 28.2%, 1♥ 16.6%, 1♠ 17.2%, 1NT 9.2%, 2NT 1.0%. For the hands that were appropriate to open 1♦, 4.3% held exactly three diamonds, 44.1% held exactly four diamonds and 51.7% held five or more diamonds. This simulation is in reasonable agreement to our mathematical solution for opening 1♦ with a three-card suit. Don't be surprised that Goodwin's probability of opening 1♦ is 28% and my figure was 9%. He considered only hands strong enough to open the bidding. Goodwin's simulation also studied the probability of different club lengths being held by your partner when he opens 1♣. The results were: the probability that your partner holds exactly three clubs is 23.4%, exactly four clubs 26.5%, and five or more 50.1%.

Gambling 3NT and Flannery

In Chapter 16, I mentioned that a hand appropriate for Gambling 3NT is very rare. Even if we do not require holding the jack in that minor, the probability is only 0.073%. Assume the long suit is clubs. We need to include the club ace, king, queen, four cards chosen from the other ten club cards and six cards from the other three suits − not including either the ace or king in these three suits. That is 10C4 x 33C6 = 210 x 1107568 = 232,589,280 hands. When this large number is divided by 635 billion, we find that the probability is only 0.000366.

You may be a little troubled by 10C4 x 33C6. In almost all of our previous examples, the numbers preceding the capital C totaled 52 and the numbers following the capital C totaled 13. But, in this example, they only totaled 43 and 10, respectively. Why the difference? The answer is not hard to understand. The hand must include the club ace, king and queen. Those three cards can be chosen in 3C3 = 1 way. We must not include an ace or king from the other three suits. From these six cards we must choose no cards, 6C0 = 1. Now the expression could be written as 3C3 x 10C4 x 6C0 x 33C6. Indeed, in this form, the four numbers preceding the C total 52 and the four numbers following the C total 13. But the product of the four terms has not changed since the two additional terms are both equal to 1. The expression only looks different. Because of the way I did this example, it is possible that the six non-club cards are all in the same suit. Quite a hand: 7-6-0-0. Very unlikely. Not a hand where you would use Gambling 3NT. I did it to make the analysis easier.

Before moving on, I must remind you that we considered only a seven-card club suit. We must not forget the diamond suit. So, the probability of the Gambling 3NT is 0.000366 x 2 = 0.000732.

Let's revisit Flannery. In Chapter 16, we considered the five specific shapes where the Flannery 2◇ bid could be made. I used the table for each shape and added the five values in order to get the probability of being dealt a hand with an appropriate shape for Flannery. The sum was 2.16%. On page 222, I obtained the probability of being dealt a hand with four spades, five hearts and four cards in the minors. The result was a probability of 0.0217. The very slight difference is the result of rounding. I am pleased. We did the problem in two ways and got the same answer. Great! Don't misinterpret this result. It only represents the probability of being dealt the necessary shape for Flannery. Only 34% of these hands will be in the point range for the convention.

Chapter 21
Probability of Partnership and Defensive Holdings

Is this chapter useful? Why?

Usefulness number: 8. This chapter is indirectly very useful. It is similar to the last chapter, which demonstrated the mathematics for computing the value of any table entry (shape or HCP) pertaining to an individual hand. In this chapter the same will be done for joint partnership holdings and the suit splits in the defenders' hands. The tables are directly useful. But there is no need to recompute table values: you should use and usually trust the tables. My goal is for you to have the comfort of knowing how the table values were obtained.

This chapter also demonstrates the method for computing the suit split probabilities when the declarer knows how another suit is splitting. A few books contain such tables — I will mention two in this chapter. On the surface this sounds very useful but we know that declarer cannot refer to a probability table in the middle of a hand or perform the mathematics while playing.

Combined Partnership Holdings

In this section we will consider both the shape and HCP holdings for a partnership rather than a single player.

We have usually used for obtaining a single player hand probability the denominator of 52C13 = 635,013,559,600, which represents the number of possible thirteen card hands. But a partnership receives twenty-six cards. Now we have to consider how many ways twenty-six cards can be dealt from fifty-two. The denominator will be 52C26 = 495,918,532,900,000, a much larger number.

What is the probability that a partnership has a combined shape of 8-7-6-5?

Carrying over our notation for single player general shapes, this means the eight-, seven-, six- and five-card suits can be any of the four suits. Let's consider the specific case of five spades, seven hearts, six diamonds and eight clubs (5=7=6=8). We can compute the probability for this specific shape and then multiple by 24. Why 24? There are four ways to choose which suit has eight cards, three ways to choose which suit has seven cards, two ways to select the six-card suit and then of course only one suit is left to be the five-card suit (no choice). In summary, 4 x 3 x 2 x 1 = 24.

The numerator for the holding (5=7=6=8) will be 13C5 x 13C7 x 13C6 x 13C8 = 1287 x 1716 x 1716 x 1287 = 4,877,436,914,000.

Wow! This looks wrong. The repetition of the same values for different items, such as the numbers 1287 and 1716, looks suspicious. Often an unexpected repetition of a value is an indication of an error. Must be a Julian mistake. No, I'm okay. Remember nCr = nC(n-r). The repetition is not an indication of an error, but quite the opposite. It should be expected.

The denominator will be 52C26 = 495,918,532,900,000. The result of the division is 0.009835. When this value is multiplied by 24, the result is 23.604%. This is a surprisingly high value. Almost one quarter of the deals. Note that this value agrees with the table entry on page 168.

What is the probability of a partnership being dealt a total of 2 HCP?

We just have to use our HCP computation method from the last chapter, but modified for the twenty-six cards held by a partnership. So the denominator will be, as in the last shape example, 52C26 = 495,918,532,900,000. We still have to consider the possibilities of the partnership holding either one queen or two jacks. The numerator will be (4C0 x 4C0 x 4C1 x 4C0 x 36C25) + (4C0 x 4C0 x 4C0 x 4C2 x 36C24) = 2403221184 + 7510066200 = 9913287384. The result of the division will yield the answer of

0.00002. Note that the 36C25 represents the number of ways of choosing twenty-five of the thirty-six spot cards.

Computing Partner Support Probabilities

You just picked up a hand that has exactly five hearts. What is the probability that your partner has exactly three hearts?

You hold five of the thirteen hearts in the deck and eight of the thirty-nine cards that are not hearts. Therefore, the other three players have a total of eight cards that are hearts and thirty-one cards that are not hearts. The thirty-one is obtained by subtracting their number of hearts from their total number of cards, $39 - 8 = 31$.

The number of ways in which your partner can have three of the eight missing hearts is 8C3. The number of ways in which your partner can hold ten cards that are not hearts from the remaining thirty-one cards that are not hearts is 31C10. Your partner can hold 8C3 x 31C10 different hands with exactly three hearts.

Since you have in your own hand thirteen of the fifty-two cards, the total number of hands your partner can hold from the remaining thirty-nine cards is 39C13.

P(partner has three hearts)

$$= \frac{8C3 \times 31C10}{39C13} = \frac{56 \times 44{,}352{,}165}{8{,}122{,}425{,}444} = 0.306$$

Likewise, P(partner has four hearts)

$$= \frac{8C4 \times 31C9}{39C13} = \frac{70 \times 20{,}160{,}075}{8{,}122{,}425{,}444} = 0.174$$

These results agree with the values indicated on page 163.

Computing Suit Split Probabilities

In this section we will turn our attention to the time when dummy has landed on the table. Declarer (South) knows his own thirteen cards and dummy's thirteen cards. Ignore the opening lead. So, declarer knows the location of twenty-six cards. The remaining twenty-six cards are in one of two places. The number of ways in which those twenty-six cards can be split is equivalent to figuring out how many hands can be formed for West. We can ignore East, since East will get whatever thirteen cards are not in the West hand.

How many possible hands can West hold if you don't look at the lead?

$$26C13 = \frac{26!}{13!(26 - 13)!} = 10,400,600$$

Not that large of a number since we are only dealing with the location of twenty-six cards.

Tricky Confusing Issue Alert

We have not had a 'tricky confusing issue alert' in some time. It is tempting to reason that each card can be in one of two places (West or East). Therefore, one can use the multiplication principle repeatedly for the twenty-six cards held by the defense. This would yield 2 x 2 x 2 x 2 x 2... for all twenty-six cards, resulting in the value of 67,108,864. The mistake with this approach is obvious when one considers that this result would include situations such as West receiving fifteen cards and East eleven or West receiving twelve cards and East fourteen. There is no requirement that both West and East each receive exactly thirteen cards. I probably set you up for this confusion. Several times in the book, I have stated that with four cards missing, the number of possibilities was 2 x 2 x 2 x 2 = 16. With five cards missing, it would be 32. I could do this kind of calculation when I was dealing with a small set of cards and was not restricted by the thirteen-card requirement. Actually the thirteen-card requirement played a role in the sense that the more balanced specific splits were more likely to occur than the less balanced specific splits.

The total number of deals is that staggering twenty-nine-digit number on page 62. I will now justify that value. Suppose you are South. There are 52C13 possible hands that you could receive. There are 39C13 possible hands your partner (North) could receive. West could receive any of 26C13 hands. East can only receive one hand consisting of the remaining thirteen cards.

In summary, there are 52C13 x 39C13 x 26C13 x 1 possible deals. If you wish to multiply it out, you will obtain that twenty-nine-digit number. I would recommend that you simply trust me.

Dummy has just appeared. Suppose declarer and dummy have seven spades combined. What is the number of ways in which West can have exactly two spades? Don't try to draw any inferences from the opening lead.

The number of ways in which West can have two of the six missing spades is 6C2. The number of ways in which West can have eleven cards that are not spades from the twenty missing cards in the other three suits is 20C11. Therefore, the total number of hands that West can hold with exactly two spades is 6C2 x 20C11. Earlier we found that the total number of hands that West could hold is 26C13 = 10,400,600.

Therefore P(West has two spades)

$$= \frac{6C2 \times 20C11}{26C13} = \frac{15 \times 167,960}{10,400,600} = 0.242$$

Obviously, if we figured out P(East has two spades), the calculations would be the same and the value would be 0.242. Since a 4-2 split requires that either West has two spades or East has two spades:

P(4-2 spade split) = P(West has two spades) + P(East has two spades)
= 0.242 + 0.242 = 0.484.

This is the value that appears in Appendix 1 for a 4-2 split in the table for six cards held by the defense.

Likewise, P(West has one spade)

$$= \frac{6C1 \times 20C12}{26C13} = \frac{6 \times 125{,}970}{10{,}400{,}600} = 0.073$$

P(5-1 spade split) = P(West has one spade) + P(East has one spade)
= 0.073 + 0.073 = 0.146

This roughly corresponds to the value in Appendix 1 for a 5-1 split.

Similarly, P(West has no spades)

$$= \frac{6C0 \times 20C13}{26C13} = \frac{1 \times 77520}{10{,}400{,}600} = 0.075$$

P(6-0 spade split) = P(West has no spades) + P(East has no spades)
= 0.0075 + 0.0075 = 0.015

P(West has three spades)

$$= \frac{6C3 \times 20C10}{26C13} = \frac{20 \times 184{,}756}{10{,}400{,}600} = 0.355$$

The probability of East having three spades can be ignored since it occurs only when West has three spades. Therefore, P(3-3 spade split) = P(West has three spades) = 0.355. It is important to appreciate why we did not have to double the value as was done for the other table entries.

We have completed the whole table for the case when declarer is missing six cards. These computed values are in line with the table values. If you want to impress bridge players with this technique, tell them that it is based on the *hypergeometric distribution*.

Declarer and dummy have five spades combined. What is the probability of a 4-4 split?

P(4-4 split) = P(West has four spades)

$$= \frac{8C4 \times 18C9}{26C13} = \frac{70 \times 48{,}620}{10{,}400{,}600} = 0.3272$$

In Appendix 1, I included a table for eight cards held by the defense. This value appears.

Declarer and dummy have eight spades. What is the probability of a 4-1 split?

P(West has 1 spade)

$$= \frac{5C1 \times 21C12}{26C13} = \frac{5 \times 293{,}930}{10{,}400{,}600} = 0.141$$

P(4-1 spade split) = P(West has one spade) + P(East has one spade)
= 0.141 + 0.141 = 0.282

This result agrees with the table value for a 4-1 split.

Suppose declarer believes a suit is splitting 6-1 based on a weak two-bid made by a defender. We know that the values in the tables for the other three suits are no longer appropriate. However, the technique introduced in this chapter can still be used in the post-mortem to figure out the probabilities of the splits in the other suits. On the surface this might seem rather useless since the hand is finished before these calculations can be carried out. It appears only to help you defend your chosen line of play to your partner. I believe understanding the formula and applying it yourself will improve your intuition about suit splits. When you can appreciate how a tool works, you are not only comfortable using it but are more likely to use it correctly.

Declarer and dummy have a total of eight diamonds. West opened the bidding 2♡. Suppose declarer and dummy hold six hearts. Since the defenders don't use a weak two-bid with a five-card suit, declarer can reasonably assume that hearts are breaking 6-1. What is the probability of a 4-1 diamond split?

The probability of West having one diamond and East four is not the same as East having one diamond and West four. Both values must be obtained.

P(4-1 split with West holding one diamond)

$$= \frac{5C1 \times 7C6 \times 14C6}{7C6 \times 19C7} = 0.298$$

- 5C1 is the number of ways to choose one diamond from the five missing diamonds.
- 7C6 is the number of ways to choose six hearts from the seven missing hearts.
- 14C6 is the number of ways to choose six cards that are neither hearts nor diamonds.
- 19C7 is the number of ways to choose seven cards that are not hearts.

P(4-1 split with East holding one diamond)

$$= \frac{5C1 \times 7C1 \times 14C11}{7C6 \times 19C12} = 0.036$$

East would have to hold one diamond, one heart and eleven cards that are neither hearts nor diamonds.

P(4-1 split) = P(4-1 split with West holding one diamond) + P(4-1 split with East holding one diamond) = 0.298 + 0.036 = 0.334

We see that the 2♡ bid by West increased the likelihood of another suit breaking 4-1. East having four diamonds is eight times more likely to occur than West having four diamonds. We have seen that their probabilities are 0.298 and 0.036, respectively.

Tables have been produced that indicate how some particular suit is likely to split when given information on how another suit is splitting. The Vivaldi/Barracho book, *Probabilities and Alternatives in Bridge* (see Bibliography), contains twenty pages of suit split tables where the reader is provided with information on splits in other suits. Rubens (see Bibliography) also contains suit split charts.

Since most bridge players consider it sacrilegious to open a weak two-bid with a side four-card major, I chose diamonds rather than spades as a possible four-card suit in the last example. It is totally inappropriate to apply our mathematics when it violates a bridge principle. Of course, bridge principles and guidelines are in flux; I believe sins are on the rise.

One must be careful when trying to base decisions on certain biased information. For example, suppose declarer is in a notrump contract and the opening lead by West indicates that East started with a singleton and West with a seven-card suit. This extreme split would be clear evidence that West is more likely than East to be short in the other suits. Now suppose the opening lead indicates that West has four cards in the suit and East three. Remember, West will usually lead a long suit, so West probably does not have a five-card suit. East is more likely than West to hold a five-card suit. Certainly, declarer should not get excited that he learned that West has one more card than East in the led suit. Declarer should expect that the opening leader will usually lead a suit in which he has more cards than his partner.

Chapter 22
Probability of Hand Repetition

Is this Chapter Useful? Why?

Usefulness Number: 6. This chapter describes a technique for handling problems where one is interested in how often an event should be expected to occur when bridge hands are repeated. I will show a few bridge-relevant examples, but, to be honest, the bridge applications are not that significant. Therefore, the low usefulness number. But the technique that uses the binomial distribution has many important applications in the non-bridge world.

Two pre-alerts

FIRST PRE-ALERT: The next few pages may appear to involve a lot of calculations. Don't worry. This is not the case. All the calculations can be avoided.

SECOND PRE-ALERT: The rest of this chapter describes a method for conducting an experiment that involves repeated trials. On each trial either an event will occur or it will not occur. The words 'success' and 'failure' are just assigned labels for whether the event occurs or not; they have no relation to the standard use of these words. In a particular example, dying could be labeled a success. On each trial, either the event will occur (success) or will not occur (failure).

Computer Hand Generation

In Chapter 6: Equally Likely Outcomes, I indicated that the goal of having all 635 billion hands occurring equally often and independent of prior hands is a dream rather than a reality when humans do the dealing. I mentioned that I would talk about computer-generated hands in this chapter.

A few decades ago, players tended to blame computers for creating interesting but tricky distributional hands. I would defend computers by pointing out that it is rather easy to generate random hands but much harder for a computer to differentiate whether a hand is interesting or not. The beauty of bridge is that randomly generated hands are interesting and tricky. As the bridge world has grown accustomed to computer-generated hands, players no longer ask. During the transition to computer-generated hands the following question/complaint was very common.

Common Question (Opinion) Alert

Players would approach me with more of an opinion than a question, such as, 'I don't think the hands created by the computer are fair and honest. What do you think?' The player was not really asking a question but searching for agreement. It often included an implication that the computer very personally wanted to make him look foolish.

For players who seemed threatening, rather than giving them my short answer that I think computers have a great deal of integrity, I provided a more cowardly diplomatic answer. I would ask them, based on their experience, what they believed was different. Often, they responded that the computer-generated hands produced distributions that were too extreme. Actually, I am willing to concede that their observations are correct, but only because human shuffled hands are too flat. We discussed this in Chapter 6.

One can test certain characteristics of hands. But one has to first determine what types of hands are believed to occur too often or too rarely. For example, one can think 'too distributional' means too many hands with a six-card or longer suit. We know from our distribution table that 79% of all hands do not have a six-card or longer suit, so 21% have a six-card or longer suit. To shorten my verbiage (not easy), I will call having a six-card or longer suit a 'success' and not having such a suit a 'failure'. Suppose you play a 24-board session and keep track of the number of successes. If, on all 24 boards, you never have a success, it means that none of your hands had a six-card or longer suit. What a boring session! You should ask the director to return your entry fee. Obviously, the extreme opposite would be for all 24 boards to meet our criteria for success. That would produce a wild session. So, the minimum number of successes is 0 and the maximum is 24. This yields a total of 25 possible values. Suppose we wish to obtain the probability of exactly eight successes. How likely is that? But we can first answer an easier question: how many successes do you expect on the average?

We just need the product of the number of hands times the probability of a success. For this example, you should expect to have 24 x 0.21 = 5.04 successes. Therefore, in most 24 board sessions, one should expect either four, five, or six successes. Having eight successes is several successes more than average. But is it rare? Do you have any grounds to question the honesty of our random hand generator? No to both questions. The probability of eight successes is 0.064. Therefore, during your next session of bridge, there is a 6.4% chance of being dealt exactly eight hands that include a six-card or longer suit. Being dealt so many long suits should make for a rather exciting session.

As already mentioned, don't worry about how that 0.064 probability was obtained. I will show both an easy way and a hard way to obtain the value. Why the hard way? It facilitates understanding.

One can obtain any number of successes for this example. The probability of 0 successes is 0.0035, 1 success is 0.022, 2 successes is 0.068, 3 successes is 0.133, 4 successes is 0.185, 5 successes is 0.197, 6 successes is 0.166, 7 successes is 0.113, 8 successes is 0.064 and 9 or more is 0.048. These values should add up to 1. Happily for me, they do. Not surprisingly, the most likely result is 5 successes followed closely by 4 successes and 6 successes. If we add the probability of 8 successes to 9 or more, we obtain 11.2%. We are not too surprised that one third of our hands had a six-card or longer suit. Nothing seems shockingly abnormal by this test when eight of the 24 trials were successes.

What if we change the previous computer-generated hand example to five sessions of bridge? Now we will observe 120 hands. The expected number of successes is 120 x 0.21 = 25.2. This result is no surprise since we are considering five times as many hands as the prior example. Let's now consider the probability that one-third or more of our hands contain a six-card or longer suit. That would correspond to 40 or more successes on the 120 hands. The probability of that is 0.00115. This value is roughly one-tenth of 1%. A shocking result. Something looks wrong. Certainly, this would be suspicious and would require serious testing of the random hand generator.

The Binomial Distribution

The binomial distribution provides a technique for handling the above type of example. Actually, the example is typical of a large category of problems involving repeated trials. Certain features must be satisfied in order for a problem to be appropriate for applying the binomial distribution. The five key features are:

1) The problems involve repeated trials (represented by n). In our example, we first used n = 24, then n = 120.
2) Either an event happens or does not happen (labeled 'success' and 'failure'). In our example a success was a six-card or longer suit.
3) On every trial, the probability of a success is the same (represented by p). In our example p = 0.21.
4) All trials are independent of prior trials.
5) We wish to obtain the probability of a certain number of successes (often represented by k).

What is the probability in your next thirty hands that you will have shortness (void or singleton) on exactly nine hands?

Perfect for the binomial distribution. The number of trials is thirty while the number of successes is nine. We can use our shape table to figure out that the value for p for this example is 0.35. Plugging these three numbers into the binomial distribution yields a probability of 0.133.

What is the probability in your next twenty-four hands that you will have 13 or more HCP on twelve or more hands?

The number of trials is twenty-four while the number of successes is twelve. We can use our HCP table to obtain the probability of being dealt 13 or more HCP. We find that the probability of a success is 0.268. So, p = 0.268. Plugging those three numbers into the binomial distribution yields a probability of 0.013. You may find this result surprisingly small. The event of a hand with 13 or more HCP is not rare, but to have it occur on half of your hands in a 24-board session is quite rare.

What is the probability in your next 200 hands that you will have a two-suiter (5-5, 6-5 or 6-6) on ten or more hands?

The number of trials is 200 while the number of successes is ten or more. We can use our shape table to figure out that the value for p for this example is 0.055. Plugging these three numbers into the binomial distribution yields a probability of 0.666.

The last three examples are perfect for applying the binomial distribution. Now I will give some flawed examples. (They are flawed because they deal with percentages based on human performance rather than playing cards.)

During your next 24-board session of bridge, what is the probability that you will be declarer exactly eleven times?

It is clear that n = 24 and the number of successes is eleven. However, the probability that you are declarer on a hand is not clear-cut. Are you more aggressive than the average player? Are you timid? Most players cannot answer these questions about themselves with any certainty. Possibly in the future, personal statistics will generate such information. Typically, we can do no better than use some estimate. There is another problem: even if in the long run you become declarer 25% of the time, you might not satisfy the requirement of independent trials. That is, if you are brilliant on the first hand in which you are declarer, you aggressively try to become declarer the rest of the session. But if you look foolish on that first hand, you might try to avoid becoming declarer for the rest of the session. Even with the flaws that I have mentioned, go ahead and use the binomial distribution. I won't tell anyone.

If you want to know the probability that your partnership will be declarer on fifteen hands during the next 24-board session, the same technique can be used. You will likely have to assume that the probability of the event on each hand is 50%.

Very Easy Way to Compute Values

At this point it should be clear as to the type of problem that can be solved by the proper application of the binomial distribution. In all examples, I performed the computation without indicating the method and merely provided the result. But how can you do it? Simple. Follow the four steps:

1) Google 'Binomial Distribution Generator' and pick any option.
2) Enter number of trials, probability and number of successes.
3) After pressing 'computation', you will see the result for that exact number of successes. You often will find a result for the exact number and more, as well as the exact number and less. It may even display a graph for all possible numbers of successes.
4) Check a few examples to see if your results are the same as mine. Mine should be correct.

Very Hard Way to Compute Values

When I was a child, we did not have these newfangled computers to do our work for us. The world used old-fashioned computers. The word 'computer' was in the 1950s a job title for a human occupation, not unlike: teacher, doctor, and engineer.

It is useful to see how values for the binomial distribution can be computed without any computational device. The explanation builds our understanding of the binomial distribution.

Let's return to the first example in this chapter, where $n = 24$, $p = 0.21$, and you want to obtain the probability of eight successes. Imagine you get a success on the first eight hands. This requires a failure on the next sixteen hands. We need to multiply 0.21×0.21 ....x 0.21 (8 times), which is equal to 0.00000378. We need to multiply $0.79 \times 0.79 \times .... \times 0.79$ (16 times), which is equal to 0.023016. The product of these two values is 0.000000087. This very small number is not surprising since it represents the probability of a success on the first eight hands played and then a failure on the next sixteen hands. But the eight successes can occur on any of the 24 boards, so we must obtain the number of ways we can choose eight boards from the 24 boards. No problem. Just obtain 24C8 = 735471. This number must be multiplied by 0.000000087. The product is 0.064. The value 6.4% agrees with the answer we obtained earlier in the chapter.

In a 24-board session, what is the probability of being dealt exactly five hands with a six-card or longer suit?

This problem is very similar to the previous example. What we labeled a success has not changed and, of course, what we labeled a failure has not changed. The probability of a success on any hand is still 0.21 and the probability of a failure is 0.79. All that has changed is that now we only have five successes, thus nineteen failures. Therefore, we need to obtain 0.21 x 0.21 x 0.21 x 0.21 x 0.21 = 0.000408 and 0.79 x 0.79 x ..... x 0.79 (19 times) = 0.01135. After multiplying those two values we need to consider how many ways we can select five boards where a success will occur. Easy: 24C5 = 42,504. After multiplying that number to the prior product, the result is 0.197. So, the probability is 19.7% that you will be dealt exactly five hands that contain six-card suits or longer when you play a 24-board session. This seems like a large value but it is not surprising.

Based on these examples, it is easy to understand the mathematical representation of the binomial distribution.

P(k successes) = nCk multiplied by $p^k(1 - p)^{n-k}$ for n trials with success probability p for each trial.

This representation of the binomial distribution would look strange to a mathematician, or for that matter, most anybody else. It is usually expressed with the alternative combination notation mentioned on page 213. Typically, the binomial distribution is:

P(k successes) = $\binom{n}{k} p^k (1 - p)^{n-k}$ where k = 0, 1, 2, ...n for n trials with success probability p.

Bridge Scoring is Almost Always Incorrect

After a session of bridge, my non-bridge-playing wife often asks me how I did. When I respond, 'Poorly,' I am asked a follow-up question as to who played poorly? I would find it painful to blame my partner and even more painful to blame myself. At times, I can honestly blame our conventions. The weak notrump (11-14 HCP) will occasionally produce poor results for a session: we might miss a major-suit fit or wrong-side a hand. When this response is incorrect, I have my fallback explanation, 'There was almost certainly a mistake in the scoring, otherwise we probably would have won.' I can justify the first phrase of my statement, but maybe not the second part.

Consider a 24-board ten-table session. At each table, twenty-four scores have to be recorded. Therefore, 240 scores are entered into the computer or placed on a travelling slip. Suppose we assume that 1% of the scores are entered incorrectly. (I spoke to a number of directors who felt that 1% was a low estimate.) Here we can use the binomial distribution with 240 trials and p = 0.01. For this example, a success is actually a mistake. The average number of mistakes is 240 x 0.01 = 2.4. By using the binomial distribution, one finds that the probability of no successes is 0.090, one success is 0.217, two successes is 0.262, three successes is 0.210, four successes is 0.126 and five or more success is 0.095. I checked that these values add up to 1. In summary, there is only a 9% chance that the scores have been entered with no errors. Therefore, I can state the first part of my comment with confidence.

In short, when you have many repetitions, even if an event is very unlikely, it should be expected to occur on a trial or several trials. A good baseball example is pitching a perfect game. When a batter comes to the plate he dreams of hitting a home run or, at a minimum, getting on base. Roughly 70% of the time, he returns immediately to the dugout where his only hit is smashing his bat against the dugout steps. But should this very likely occurrence take place twenty-seven straight times for a team, history is made. Not good history for that team, but great history for the opposing pitcher.

Chapter 23
History and Future of Bridge Probability

Is this chapter useful? Why?
Usefulness number: 5. The history of bridge is only slightly useful at the bridge table but, I hope, it is interesting. I had to include a section on the future of bridge probability in order to get the rating number up to 5.

Probability of Games, before 1743

Back in the seventeenth and eighteenth centuries, a mutually beneficial relationship existed between gamblers and mathematicians. Gamblers would bring interesting problems and some financial support to mathematicians. Mathematicians would help gamblers design new games and tell them which side was favored in existing games. The early days of probability treated the subject as a science, and the mathematicians would test their theories through experimentation. The gamblers did much of the lab work for the experiments and would notice unexpected results and bring them to the attention of the mathematicians.

Many of the greatest mathematicians were involved. The French were great gamblers, which helped them dominate the early study of probability. A famous correspondence between Blaise Pascal (1623-1662) and Pierre de Fermat (1601-1665) took place in 1654. It was prompted by the gambler Chevalier de Méré (Antoine Gombaud) (1607-1684) who approached Pascal with questions about probability when rolling dice.

Prior to their correspondence, the Italian Gerolamo Cardano (1501-1576) had already written about games. He was a mathematician, a gambler, and in his spare time a highly respected physician. He wrote his groundbreaking *The Book on Games of Chance* at about the age of twenty but it was not published until 1663!

More than a century after it was written. Boy – did he pick the wrong publisher. Cardano truly deserved the label of 'genius'. But he was not a stable genius; unfortunately, he led a sad, self-destructive life. Gambling helped bring this about. It is all described in *Cardano: The Gambling Scholar* by Oystein Ore.[§§§§] This book also includes an English translation of Cardano's work on probability.

In Cardano's book, he studies dice games more than card games. This is not surprising since dice had already been used for several thousand years in gambling games, while playing cards had only recently arrived in Europe. Some of the predecessors of whist already existed; their common feature was a trump suit or some form of very powerful cards. An interesting 500-year-old quote, provided by Ore, compares dice with the new world of cards: 'There is a difference from play with dice, because the latter is open, whereas play with cards takes place from the ambush, for they are hidden.'[¶¶¶¶] This comment shows great insight about the future world of whist and bridge. In both games, all cards are dealt out. There is no chance of future dealt cards changing the value of a hand, as in poker. For duplicate bridge players, the chance factor only pertains to the location where the previously dealt cards are hiding.

By the time Cardano's book finally appeared, it had lost some of its originality. Fermat and Pascal were already studying dice. Around 1620, Galileo (1564-1642) was writing about dice games. He would not have been fooled by the game that I described on page 76.

Jacques Bernoulli (1654-1705) wrote on probability in the 1690s. His important book, *Ars Conjectandi*, did not appear till 1713. There were more than a dozen mathematicians with the name Bernoulli. It was really the family business. The binomial distribution described in Chapter 22 involved a sequence of independent trials often called Bernoulli trials.

---

§§§§   Oystein Ore, Cardano, the Gambling Scholar (Princeton, NJ: Princeton University Press, 1953).

¶¶¶¶   Qtd. in ibid., p. 206.

The great mathematician, Abraham de Moivre (1667-1754), was the first to write about the English card game Whist (Whisk). At that time, few Frenchman were familiar with Whist. De Moivre was a French Protestant, so his world changed after the Edict of Nantes was revoked in 1685. Historians believe he was imprisoned for a few years and then ended up in London at the age of twenty or twenty-one. France's loss was England's gain. This is an early example of a country rich with experts losing its advantage via a 'brain drain'. In England he became a mathematics teacher and tutor. His office appeared to have been the London coffee houses. I picture him sitting behind a sign, MATHEMATICIAN FOR HIRE. CHEAP WORK. I'm sure when business was slow, he would kibitz a few hands of whist; he was at least in the perfect setting. This enabled him to be aware of probability problems that whist players were encountering.

De Moivre's famous work, *The Doctrine of Chances...* (1718), on games and gambling was a classic. It was greatly enlarged in 1738 and enlarged again in 1756. The 1738 edition not only dealt with games of cards and dice but also included several sections on annuities and insurance. One could justify calling this book the start of actuarial science.

This section enabled me to name drop a half dozen of the greatest mathematicians. If you include the full Bernoulli family, the number jumps to almost two dozen. Did I leave out Huygens, Newton and all the others? In any case, I have made my point (with overkill) that the study of games and gambling drew the top mathematical scholars. If you want more, please look at F. N. David's *Games, Gods, and Gambling* (1962).

Probability in Whist, 1742-1900

I choose an odd cutoff date of 1742 because in that year the book, *A Short Treatise on the Game of Whist...*, by Edmond Hoyle (1672?-1769) was published. By 1743 it had revolutionized the world of games. I shortened the title since the full title describes the contents of the book and is almost as long as it – the type of information one would expect to find on the back cover of a modern-day paperback. The book primarily provides readers with maxims for playing whist skillfully, but at the very start, several pages are devoted to whist probability issues. Within a decade of this book's publication, Hoyle had written a half dozen small books on games (such as backgammon, piquet, quadrille, brag), and a large book that contained all of the small books. These books were extremely popular and for the past 277 years, books that describe a collection of games are often given a title that includes the name Hoyle. The expression 'according to Hoyle' infers playing by the rules, but it is not limited to games. It is often used in business, law, and politics. Actually, it is often used in those fields in a negative form: 'not according to Hoyle'. Hoyle's books never actually provided the method of playing these games since he apparently assumed his readers would know that, but he did provide laws for punishing a player who violated proper play.

I should say a few words about whist before continuing. It differs in two major ways from bridge: no dummy is placed on the table and there is no bidding. Some readers may have played 'bid whist' where there is some bidding, but I am describing the pre-1900 version of whist, at a time when bid whist did not exist. Trumps were determined by the dealer turning face up the last card that he had dealt himself: the suit of that card became the trump suit.

Hoyle's 1742 book dealt with several types of probability issues. One natural question was related to who had a card or cards. Some examples are: What is the probability that partner holds exactly one out of two specific cards? What is the probability that partner holds one or two out of three specific cards?

Hoyle's book also addressed questions that gamblers had to answer concerning unfinished games. Suppose A is ahead of B by some score and is likely to win. B suddenly falls ill or remembers it is his wedding anniversary; he has to immediately terminate the game and head home. What should B pay A? The answer is obviously dependent on the score and the likelihood of each player winning from that point forward.

There is a variant to suddenly terminating a game. Suppose someone enters a room where whist is being played. That individual is eager to start betting. Imagine partnership A is ahead of partnership B and more likely to win. What should be the odds to enable bets to be placed in the middle of a game? This would enable even the players themselves to place bets when there is a break between hands. Of course, the odds will be primarily influenced by the present score. Hoyle's book on whist included tables that indicated the probability of either pair going on to win for all possible scoring possibilities. With some new online forms of gambling, it is possible to place a bet on a game or sporting event that is already in progress. Hoyle had apparently realized that in 1742.

In 1743, a satirical play was written about Hoyle and his book. It demonstrates the immediate success of Hoyle's book. The anonymous author of *The Humours of Whist* makes fun of a player who enjoys stating the probability of any card holding but is a big loser at the whist table. As the top players enjoy themselves while gathering in his money, he feels greatly rewarded when the winners compliment his skill at mathematics. They know this will bring him back to the table for future fleecing. The player's name is usually referred to as Sir Calculation, but his full name is Sir Calculation Puzzle.

Hoyle wrote a small book in 1754 on probability, *An Essay Towards Making the Doctrine of Chances Easy to Those who Understand Vulgar Arithmetick Only...* (As you can see, even the abbreviated title is long.) It demonstrates the arithmetic needed to obtain different odds. Several pages describe how to compute combinations. Even though Hoyle's name lives on 250 years after his death, little is known about his life. Some writers have conjectured that he may have been a lawyer.

Hoyle's mathematics was accurate although there is no record of any personal training in the subject. The natural question is, 'Who helped Hoyle with his mathematics?' Abraham de Moivre is almost certainly the answer, since Hoyle and de Moivre frequented the same London coffeehouses. In Hoyle's 1754 book, he acknowledges de Moivre's publication.

William Payne was an early writer on whist. The first edition of his book, *Maxims for Playing the Game of Whist...*, came out in 1770. It is thought that he was a mathematics teacher. I was, however, less impressed by William Payne's mathematics than Hoyle's. He covers the same issues, but in his effort to simplify he introduces some ambiguity. For example, his first statement is 'It is about 5 to 4, that your partner holds one card out of any two.' Does this mean exactly one card or at least one of the two cards? When Hoyle wrote 'That he has One of them only, is 31 to 26', the word 'only' indicates exactly one.

I occasionally think of the first sentence in the Preface in Payne's old book, 'The Game of Whist is so happily compounded betwixt chance and skill, that it is generally esteemed the most curious and entertaining of the cards, and is therefore become a favourite amusement to persons of the first consequence, and most distinguished abilities,...' This one sentence continues for a whole paragraph. Payne appreciated the probability aspects generated by chance.

The best book explaining whist probabilities was written by William Pole in 1883. The book's title is rather pompous: *The Philosophy of Whist: An Essay on the Scientific and Intellectual Aspects of the Modern Game*. Probability is explained in Part II (150 pages) with an almost equally pompous title, 'The Philosophy of Whist Probabilities.' Even though bridge had not yet surfaced, even in its most primitive form, much of the mathematics needed for the game was developed in this excellent whist probability book.

Many whist book titles included words like 'scientific' and 'philosophy'. Their authors embraced the academic and intellectual features of the game. The title of the book just mentioned certainly demonstrates that tendency.

The American Whist League, which promoted duplicate whist, profited from publishing an excellent journal with a short title but long subtitle, *WHIST: A Monthly Journal Devoted to the Interests of the Game*. From Dec. 1893 through May 1894 it ran a monthly column written by Edwin Howell titled, 'The Probabilities of Whist'. These articles were extremely well written but Howell's main impact came a few years later when his duplicate movement became popular. He died in 1907 but his movement lives on. Quite remarkable!

Probability in Bridge, 1890-Present

Until 1920, the laws and scoring of bridge (called 'auction' at that time) were changing so quickly that no one delved into bridge probability. In his book, *Correct Auction*, E.V. Shepard included several chapters on probability. The 1934 book *Mathematical Odds in Contract* by Eugene Northrop and Arthur Stein (see Bibliography) was the first contract bridge book that was devoted entirely to probability.

The groundbreaking work in this field was written by Émile Borel and André Chéron in 1940, *Théorie mathématique du bridge...* (see Bibliography). Borel was a superstar in the field of probability during the first half of the 20th century. As we saw, the French started probability theory. With their love of gambling, how could they not? A few centuries later, Borel continued their mathematical legacy. As already mentioned, the second edition in 1955 included a discussion of Restricted Choice. Many publishers have produced different editions and printings over the years in both French and English; the most recent English publication (2017) is listed in the Bibliography. Don't be misled by Borel's book title using the word 'mathematics' rather than 'probability' or 'odds'. It does not consider any mathematical topics other than bridge probability. Many bridge players might find my last sentence peculiar since they would associate the mathematics of bridge merely with probability. However, different areas of mathematics were used for generating and studying alternative duplicate movements. Edwin Howell, who had graduated with honors in mathematics from Harvard, was respected as a top authority on both probability and the mathematics behind duplicate movements. The areas of mathematics related to duplicate movements are excellently described in Ian McKinnon's work *Duplicate Bridge Schedules, History and Mathematics* (see Bibliography).

None of these books mention HCP since their role in bridge bidding only took off around 1950 when they were expanded to count distributional points. Several authors (Frederick Frost, Robert Kibler, Roy Telfer and Alec Traub) combined their studies to produce *Bridge Odds Complete* (see Bibliography). This book contains a very large set of useful tables.

In the past few decades, when a bridge player asked me what book I would recommend for learning about bridge probability, I would endorse *Bridge Odds for Practical Players* by Kelsey and Glauert (see Bibliography). An easy, clear choice. Now, of course, I would instead recommend this one, but not just for selfish reasons. The Kelsey book never discusses the probability issues related to bidding and starts with a chapter on combinatorics. This I fear could scare readers away when they are only in the middle of that first chapter.

Whist Probability Differs from Bridge Probability

The mathematical tools of probability were more applicable to the game of whist than the game of bridge. Here is an example to justify this statement.

As already mentioned, whist did not have any bidding. The trump suit was usually determined by the dealer turning over the last card he had dealt to himself. While the cards were being played, no hand was placed on the table. All four players played their own hands. The opening lead in bridge, made without the dummy being visible, is a carryover from whist.

As a present-day bridge player, suppose you are on opening lead defending against a spade contract. You hold two small trumps and king-doubleton in hearts. Envisioning your partner holding ace-third in hearts, your adrenalin starts flowing at the thought of leading the king, continuing with the small heart and ruffing the third round. You can already anticipate the look of admiration on your partner's face and the word 'brilliant' flying through his lips. But what if partner holds three small hearts? Now words may still be flying through your partner's lips but 'brilliant' will not be one of them – unless he's giving you the advice, 'Don't try to be so brilliant!'

The gambler lurking in any cardplayer's head will be tempted to try. The whist player can base the question of whether partner has the ace solely on mathematics. Let's first assume that trumps were set as spades without revealing a turn-up card. Each of the other three players is equally likely to hold the heart ace so the probability that your partner was dealt that ace is 1/3. Let us now suppose that trumps have been selected by turning over the dealer's last card. Clearly that card was not the heart ace, as hearts would have been trumps rather than spades. In this case the dealer has only twelve cards that are not known to the opening leader. Therefore, the ace is either one of the twelve other cards dealt to the dealer or thirteen cards dealt to the dealer's partner or thirteen cards dealt to your partner. Since there are 38 (12+13+13) equally likely places where the ace can be located, the probability that partner was dealt the ace is now 13/38. Slightly more than the value obtained in the prior case.

If we replace the whist table with the bridge table, this calculation is no longer appropriate. Suppose your hand consists of 7 HCP and the opponents think enough of their cards to bid a small slam. Clearly, there is an extremely small chance that your partner has any ace, let alone the heart ace. You would have to be an incredible optimist to lead the king. Suppose the opponents stopped at the two-level and you again have 7 points. Now your partner rates to have some nice cards and leading the king is not ridiculous but still a big gamble. If your partner has bid hearts, the opening lead is totally justified.

This example demonstrates that since the bidding in bridge provides so much information to the opening leader, any mathematics based on equally likely possibilities loses its value. At whist, the lack of information for the first few tricks results in probability being of great importance for decision-making. As the whist hand progresses with cards revealed and signals thrown about, information trumps probability.

In the prior example, the location of the queen of hearts becomes very important if partner lacks the ace. Partner's queen may save you from looking foolish and may result in your lead of the king still being brilliant. Therefore, whist players were often concerned with the probability that partner has at least one of two possible cards. The obvious intuitive answer of just adding the probability of partner having the ace to the probability that partner has the queen is wrong, wrong, wrong! It is not that simple. These events are not mutually exclusive since partner can hold both the ace and queen. With approximation,

P(ace or queen) = 1/3 + (2/3 × 1/3) = 5/9

Future Probability in Bridge

In the future, some aspects of bridge probability will change but most will remain the same. Let's first consider what will remain the same and then go into what may change.

Probability, statistics and combinatorics have been used in this book. Several centuries ago, these subjects were sufficiently developed to answer any modern bridge questions. Of course, since bridge did not exist till around 1890, these mathematical tools were not applied to the game. Since whist is a very similar but a much older game, many bridge card-play problems were solved in the days of whist. No new mathematical techniques need to be developed to solve any possible bridge problem. I don't want to leave readers with the false impression that these mathematical subjects are totally developed. Researchers are continually expanding the knowledge of these subjects. I am just stating that the mathematics needed to study bridge is fully developed.

Several decades ago, computation became much easier with the advent of calculators and computers. In the future no new computing tools need to be developed to solve bridge problems. As we saw, one can find a calculator on the internet for easily evaluating combinations and the binomial distribution. The arithmetic only requires plugging in a few numbers.

If the rules of bridge, particularly scoring rules, were to change then new problems would need to be solved. Our game was in great flux between 1890 and 1935. Since then there have been only a few changes in scoring. But scoring changes will alter strategy. Any computation using expected value, as in Chapter 17, would have to be redone. Decisions such as when to go to game and when not to are based on risk-benefit analysis. If the bridge scoring method is changed, the decisions will have to be reanalyzed.

Even though the game rules have hardly changed since 1935, the conventions players use are continually evolving. In the 1960s, when I played bridge with my father, at the start of every session we would rewrite our convention card. It seems wasteful but the card was so simple it took only one minute. A copy of my convention card appears below.

Actually, this is my father's handwriting: this is his card. My handwriting is too immature. Notice that Fishbein is the only convention name we had to write in. Beginning duplicate players would find this card much less intimidating than our modern cards.

There is no reason to believe that conventions and bidding systems will not continue to evolve. As new conventions enter our game, one may wish to calculate their frequency at the bridge table. Likewise, in future bidding systems, one may care about the frequency of specific bids.

When the experts start playing and endorsing a new convention, much of the bridge world follows. I should say, 'The bridge world follows suit'. Bridge conventions come into fashion and fall out of fashion. It is not unlike clothing fashion. With an outfit, what looks great on a fashion model may not look great on the average person. Similarly, a convention that is effective for an expert regular partnership may not perform well for the average player.

The main way that the future of bridge probability may change is in the area of statistics. In Chapter 18, we considered the type of questions that may be answered. One can either study an individual player's bridge performance or study the combined performance of players at a specified skill level. Generating reliable statistical conclusions for an individual player's performance can be difficult since there may not be an adequate amount of data. But it may prove a useful tool to study our faults. Do we want to know them?

In general, one of the main challenges in trying to draw conclusions from statistics is the process of collecting and organizing data. In some ways it is harder now than it was sixty years ago. At that time, phone surveys were common. Even though that would exclude people who did not own a phone, it was a rather successful method. Nowadays, everyone has several phone numbers, but usually will not answer any of them. We live in a world with annoying robocalls and a fear of fraud. We are too concerned about privacy issues to want to complete a survey.

The computer at your local club records your successes and failures on every hand. If that is not bad enough, it lets the whole world observe your bridge faults. Computers lack any discretion.

Afterword

In Chapter 11, The Principle of Restricted Choice, I described the history of the concept, but stated that I would make additional comments in this Afterword. I am returning to Restricted Choice since it so nicely represents the relationship between probability and bridge. At the very start of this book, I mentioned that bridge players have all gained a working knowledge of bridge probability through their playing experience. Alan Truscott observed Restricted Choice at the bridge table and in 1954 wrote important articles on hands that demonstrated its use. He did not use the name Restricted Choice, nor did he describe the mathematics to justify the principle's correctness. In examples, he noted that a defender holding QJ is equally likely to play either. I would assume other expert bridge players also observed the principle. Borel and Chéron provided a mathematical basis in the second edition (1955) of their book. Terence Reese's popular books educated the bridge world on the Principle of Restricted Choice, and established its name. So, all deserve credit for their important roles. Don't forget Thomas Bayes, who lived almost two centuries too early to be a bridge player, but still managed to contribute to the game. The joint work of mathematicians and bridge experts resembles the mutually beneficial relationship of gamblers and mathematicians that started in the late 1600s.

We are approaching the end. Don't forget to scan through the Bibliography and Appendices. We are down to our last Common Question Alert. Since this question is really two questions, I should say, down to the last two.

Over the past two years, players who are familiar with the fact that I have written several bridge books occasionally asked me, 'Are you writing any new books?' After I happily respond in the positive and eagerly provide them with the title of this book, they would ask, 'USEFUL is in the title. Do you really think probability is useful?' I can clearly hear some doubt in their voice. I feel a need to defend my book. In many ways this question is in the same spirit as the comment at the very start of Chapter 1. The short answer is YES. A longer answer follows.

Bridge players make decisions by relying on maxims, established card-play principles and personal estimates of probability based on relative frequency. Extensive experience at the bridge table will furnish reasonably good estimates of card-play probabilities. The goal of this book was to provide a solid mathematical basis for the reader's preexisting intuition concerning bridge probability, and thereby extend its usefulness.

Let me quickly review the usefulness of the three parts of this book.

Part I provided a talky introduction to probability. It demonstrated that probability questions are often not properly posed. The goal of these three chapters was to develop some general probability intuition.

Part II contained values and tables for almost all probability-related bridge issues, both for card play and bidding. The stated values and table entries were justified, but the full mathematics for obtaining the values was not demonstrated.

Part III introduced combinatorics, which enabled me to demonstrate how virtually all table entries and other values can be computed. The reader could then comfortably apply the technique for solving any bridge probability problem.

A deep understanding of probability will not make you into a great player but it will I hope help you appreciate the mathematical aspects of the game. But don't become your club's Sir Calculation. The next time a bridge player states, 'I wonder how likely ...', you now will have a choice of answers. You can either solve the problem or better yet — recommend this book. I prefer the latter.

Let me leave you with one last thought on usefulness. Athletes in different sports enjoy winning because it generates pride and a sense of accomplishment. Bridge players similarly enjoy winning because it generates pride and a sense of mental accomplishment. Isn't the sense of mental accomplishment greater when a player doesn't merely follow someone else's principles but can clearly appreciate why those principles are mathematically correct? Increased understanding should increase enjoyment. If this book improves your bridge enjoyment by generating a greater sense of mental accomplishment, it is certainly a very useful book. My proof is complete — so I guess the book is complete.

Hope you enjoyed your reading experience!

The world has an idea that bridge is a mathematical game, and that you need a computer-type mind to enjoy it and play it well. The world is wrong.*

Zia Mahmood

*Author note: I hid this quote until now in order to increase the probability that you would read the entire book.

APPENDICES

More Accurate Tables for Suit Splits

On page 38, I displayed six tables of suit splits. At that time, I used cruder but more relatable values since I was encouraging the reader to memorize some of the entries. In the tables in this Appendix, I am approximating with four decimal places. I am being somewhat repetitive but the tables are so useful in different bridge contexts, they deserve it.

Two cards held by the defense		Three cards held by the defense	
1-1	0.52	2-1	0.78
2-0	0.48	3-0	0.22

Four cards held by the defense		Five cards held by the defense	
2-2	0.4070	3-2	0.6783
3-1	0.4974	4-1	0.2826
4-0	0.0957	5-0	0.0391

Six cards held by the defense		Seven cards held by the defense	
3-3	0.3553	4-3	0.6217
4-2	0.4845	5-2	0.3052
5-1	0.1453	6-1	0.0678
6-0	0.0149	7-0	0.0052

Eight cards held by the defense		Nine cards held by the defense	
4-4	0.3272	5-4	0.5890
5-3	0.4712	6-3	0.3141
6-2	0.1714	7-2	0.0857
7-1	0.0286	8-1	0.0107
8-0	0.0016	9-0	0.0005

The two tables corresponding to two or three cards held by the defense have not changed since the entries are not approximations but exact values. I included two additional tables for eight and nine cards held by the defense.

On page 64, we looked at all possibilities when the defense held the Q, 4, 3 and 2. For all sixteen, we used the approximate probability values of 1/16 by pretending they were equally likely. We compared 1/16 to the more accurate values provided in this appendix. Each of the six cases where the suit splits 2-2 has a probability of 0.4070/6 = 0.0678. Each of the eight cases where the suit splits 3-1 has a probability 0.4974/8 = 0.0622. Each of the two cases where the suit splits 4-0 has a probability 0.0957/2 = 0.0479.

Appendix 2
The Formula for Bayes' Theorem

We have seen applications of Bayes' Theorem in Chapters 11 and 17. I have not provided any version of the general formula. I will do that in this appendix. The formula handles problems where there are many potential sources and some result. It is a technique for obtaining the probability of any potential source producing the result.

$$P(S_i \text{ given } R) =$$

$$\frac{P(S_i)P(R \text{ given } S_i)}{P(S_1)P(R \text{ given } S_1) + P(S_2)P(R \text{ given } S_2) + \ldots + P(S_n)P(R \text{ given } S_n)}$$

where the n possible sources are S_i and the result is R.

A rereading of the example on page 182 will make this formula more meaningful.

Appendix 3
A Priori and *A Posteriori*

Most bridge books on probability use the terms *a priori* and *a posteriori*. Even though I have avoided using this terminology, the importance of what the terms represent has surfaced throughout this book.

A priori probabilities are values obtained with the initial information. An example would be the values provided in the tables for suit splits.

A posteriori probabilities are modified values obtained with the ever-changing information that is available as the hand is played. It may result from the bidding, the division of other suits, the cards played and the lead. For example, when an honor appears, Restricted Choice may tell you that finessing is the correct action. The 2-2 split has become less likely.

The amount of information available depends on the player's level of ability and his capacity to draw inferences (both positive and negative) at the bridge table. The tables in Appendix 1 of *a priori* probabilities have taken substantial abuse from bridge probability writers who feared that they would be used blindly. It can be argued that *a priori* probabilities are more useful for weaker players than stronger players since they are less likely to observe and use bridge information.

Appendix 4
Playing Random Cards

We saw that there are times when a defender should select a card at random when following suit, such as when holding small spot cards or when holding honors of equal value. A defender should not want to be predictable. Of course, one would not want to select a card at random when the random choice involves cards that are not of equal value.

On page 54, we looked at the following enlightening example. I am repeating it here so that you do not have to turn back to the page of the book where it appeared. Suppose a fine declarer is certain that West was originally dealt three spades and East two. The five cards held by the defense consist of the queen and four low spot cards. Based on these certain facts and no other information, P(West holds the queen) = 3/5 and P(East holds the queen) = 2/5. So, obviously the odds that West holds the queen are 3 to 2.

Now declarer plays the ace, and both defenders follow with low spot cards. This leaves West with two cards in the suit, and East with only one card. Has the probability that West holds the queen increased to 2/3? No, no, no! Declarer has not obtained any information from the defenders following suit with small spot cards. This was totally predicable. Each defender was known to hold at least one spot card and each would naturally choose to play a spot card rather than the queen. The probability that West holds the queen has not changed: it is still 3/5. If a defender was having a real off-day, and decided simply to choose a card randomly when following suit, that would be a different situation. Avoid such a partner!

We will now look at always playing random cards; even though it is not useful when playing bridge, it is useful for understanding the underlying probability. Suppose when the ace was played, East took his two cards in the suit, discreetly shuffled them, and then picked the card on top to play. Similarly, West took his three cards in the suit, shuffled them, and then played the card on the top. These two players deserve each other! On that trick, the queen would appear 40% of the time. Notice that if East had been dealt the queen, the queen would have been played 50% of the time from his hand, but If West had held the queen, it would have been played only 33% of the time.

P(East dealt queen and not randomly played) = 2/5 x 1/2 = 1/5

P(West dealt queen and not randomly played) = 3/5 x 2/3 = 2/5

We see that if two spot cards are played on the ace, West becomes twice as likely as East to hold the queen.

Remember that this analysis has no bearing on how bridge players play cards because nobody would choose a random card in the above example. I must confess that on bad days, I have felt that my results would have been better if I had played cards totally at random.

The probability principle is important. There are two related non-bridge examples that appeared in Chapter 6, the Monty Hall Problem and the two piles of coins problem described by Reese.

Appendix 5
The Birthday Problem

In Chapter 3, the famous Birthday Problem was described. The results are a surprise to most. Since I recommended trying it out at clubs, I feel a need to justify the results mathematically, particularly since you may try it at your club and look foolish.

Let's first consider the probability that three people are born on different days. The first person can be born on any day. The second person can be born on any date except for the birthday of the first person (364 possibilities), and the third person can be born on any day other than the birthday of either the first or second person (363 possibilities). Notice that we ignored Feb. 29th.

P(three people born on different days) =
365/365 x 364/365 x 363/365 = 0.9918

Very likely. No surprise! The first term is unnecessary since the first person could have been born on any of the 365 days, no restriction. I merely included it for completeness and clarity.

Let's repeat this example for five people:

P(five people born on different days) = 0.9729

Not surprisingly, this value is a little smaller than with three people. The more people, the less likely that they will be born on different days. Mathematically it is clear since for each additional person the prior result is multiplied by a value smaller than 1.

P(two or more people born same day) = 1 − P(all born different days)

This reduces the problem to seeing how many people are needed for the probability that all are born on different days to fall below 1/2. At that point, the probability that two or more people are born on the same day will rise above 1/2. The answer, as stated in Chapter 3, was a surprising 23 people! With 23 people, the probability that they all have different birthdays is 0.493, so the probability that at least two share the same birthday is 0.507. I hope it works for you at your club.

Appendix 6
Summary of Mathematical Pretending

Throughout this book, I have often violated the laws of probability, always with good intentions. It was done with the goal of increasing the readers' understanding and intuition. I usually pointed out my crime at the time I was committing these sins. In this Appendix, I will list the mathematical rules I disobey and refer to a sample example of each.

1) Sometimes the outcomes are not equally likely but I pretended that they were. For example, we listed the sixteen suit splits when the defense held Q432 and pretended that they each had a probability of 1/16.

2) I obtained the probability of either of two events occurring by adding their individual probabilities. This addition is only appropriate for mutually exclusive events. But when they are unlikely to occur simultaneously, I pretended that they were mutually exclusive. For example, the probability of being dealt a hand with either a six-card spade suit or a five-card heart suit is the sum of the individual probabilities minus the probability of both occurring. But both occurring is so unlikely, forget about it.

3) I obtained the probability of two events both occurring by multiplying their individual probabilities. This multiplication is only appropriate for independent events. But when the occurrence of one event only slightly alters the likelihood of the other event, I pretended that they were independent events. Throughout the last several chapters of Part II, I obtained the probability of a hand being appropriate for a certain bid by first computing the probability of the appropriate HCP and the probability of the appropriate shape. Then I would multiply those values even though HCP and shape are not independent.

4) I took the liberty of crudely approximating results. This fourth wrong makes the first three items above acceptable. Some say two wrongs don't make a right. But we see that a fourth wrong can make three rights.

Selected Bibliography

ACBL Encyclopedia of Bridge. 7th edition. Ed. Brent Manley; co-eds., Mark Horton, Tracey Greenberg-Yarbro, Barry Rigal. Horn Lake MS, 2011.

Borel, Émile and André Chéron. *The Mathematical Theory of Bridge*. Trans. Alec Traub. Rev.ed. and corr. Giles Laurén. Toronto: Master Point Press, 2017.

Borel, Émile and André Chéron. 1940. *Théorie mathématique du bridge à la portée de tous*. Deuxième éd. revue et corrigée. Paris: Éditions Jacques Gabay, 1955.

Frost, Fredrick H. *Bridge Odds Complete. Probabilities in Contract Bridge. A Contract Bridge Series*. 3rd ed. Laguna Hills, CA: Aegean Park Press, 1976.

Gitelman, Fred and Jeff Rubens. *Playing Suit Combinations*. New York: Bridge World Books 2017.

Kantar, Eddie. *Take All Your Chances at Bridge*. Toronto: Master Point Press, 2009.

Kelsey, Hugh and Michael Glauer. 1980. *Bridge Odds for Practical Players. Master Bridge Series*. Reprint. London: Orion Books, 2013.

MacKinnon, Robert F. *Bridge, Probability & Information*. Toronto: Master Point Press, 2010.

———. *Never a Dull Deal: Faith, Hope and Probability in Bridge.* Toronto: Master Point Press, 2017.

McKinnon, Ian. *Duplicate Bridge Schedules, History and Mathematics.* Ed. Ron Klinger; Foreword Dr. Ross Moore. Toronto: Master Point Press, 2012. (no probability – mathematics of duplicate movements)

Northrop, Eugene and Arthur Stein. *Mathematical Odds in Contract.* London: Williams & Norgate, Ltd., 1934.

Reese, Terence and Roger Trézel. *Master the Odds in Bridge. Master Bridge Series* (General ed., Hugh Kelsey). London: Victor Gollancz Ltd., in assoc. with Peter Crawley, 1979.

Rubens, Jeff. *Expert Bridge Simplified: Arithmetic Shortcuts for Declarer.* New York: Bridge World Books, 2009.

Vivaldi, Antonio and Gianni Barracho. *Probabilities and Alternatives in Bridge.* Trans. and ed. Phil King. London: B.T. Batsford, 2001.